Outreach Strategies and Innovative Teaching Approaches for German Programs

Outreach Strategies and Innovative Teaching Approaches for German Programs explores recruitment, curricular design and student retention in modern language instruction by sharing best practices and a wide variety of pragmatic initiatives from teacher-scholars who have been involved in the successful building of German programs.

With German programs facing dwindling grant monies as students across the country shift from the liberal arts into career-oriented fields, it is paramount to promote German programs vigorously, to offer courses that reflect and compel students' interest, to keep students engaged in extracurricular activities and to establish a community of like-minded language learners.

The combination of curriculum-based strategies coupled with innovative projects and extracurricular and outreach activities is intended to serve as a guideline for teachers and scholars alike who are in need of best practices they can use to boost enrollment and attract and retain more students.

Melissa Etzler is a Lecturer of German and First Year Seminar at Butler University in Indianapolis. She has published book chapters related to her research on author W. G. Sebald and has recently shifted her focus to eco-critical readings of Gothic German texts and films, her most recent article appearing in *German Quarterly*. In addition to her regular coursework, she teaches in honors and co-leads the annual short-term study abroad program Bulldogs in Berlin. She is the recipient of the AATG Indiana Post-Secondary Teacher of the Year Award (2018), the College of Liberal Arts and Sciences Outstanding Faculty Award for Excellence in Teaching (2018) and an Outstanding Professor of the Year Award for Teaching (2018–19).

Gabriele Maier is Associate Teaching Professor of German Studies and Director of the M.A. program in Global Communication and Applied Translation at Carnegie Mellon University (CMU) in Pittsburgh. Her research includes literature of the 20th and 21st century and focuses primarily on travel writing, questions of home and identity, transcultural writers and graphic novels. She has published on Christian Kracht, Hans-Ulrich Treichel and Christoph Ransmayr, among others; co-edited an anthology on *Heimat*;

and her textbook *Deutschland im Zeitalter der Globalisierung* came out in 2015. Lately, she has contributed an article to the MLA Handbook *Strategies and Perspectives on Social Justice Work*. She is a fellow of the "How Well?" project funded by the Center for the Arts in Society at CMU, where she works with various student groups to educate the public about food insecurity and how to improve well-being on the CMU campus.

Outreach Strategies and Innovative Teaching Approaches for German Programs

Edited by
Melissa Etzler and Gabriele Maier

LONDON AND NEW YORK

First published 2021
by Routledge
2 Park Square, Milton Park, Abingdon, Oxon OX14 4RN

and by Routledge
52 Vanderbilt Avenue, New York, NY 10017

Routledge is an imprint of the Taylor & Francis Group, an informa business

© 2021 selection and editorial matter, Melissa Etzler and Gabriele Maier; individual chapters, the contributors

The right of Melissa Etzler and Gabriele Maier to be identified as the authors of the editorial material, and of the authors for their individual chapters, has been asserted in accordance with sections 77 and 78 of the Copyright, Designs and Patents Act 1988.

All rights reserved. No part of this book may be reprinted or reproduced or utilised in any form or by any electronic, mechanical, or other means, now known or hereafter invented, including photocopying and recording, or in any information storage or retrieval system, without permission in writing from the publishers.

Trademark notice: Product or corporate names may be trademarks or registered trademarks, and are used only for identification and explanation without intent to infringe.

British Library Cataloguing in Publication Data
A catalogue record for this book is available from the British Library

Library of Congress Cataloging-in-Publication Data
Names: Etzler, Melissa, editor. | Maier, Gabriele, editor.
Title: Outreach strategies and innovative teaching approaches for German programs / Melissa Etzler, Gabriele Maier.
Description: London ; New York : Routledge, 2020. | Includes bibliographical references and index.
Identifiers: LCCN 2020031255 (print) | LCCN 2020031256 (ebook) | ISBN 9780367343651 (hardback) | ISBN 9780367343668 (paperback) | ISBN 9780429325298 (ebook)
Subjects: LCSH: German language–Study and teaching (Higher)–United States.
Classification: LCC PF3068.U6 O98 2020 (print) | LCC PF3068.U6 (ebook) | DDC 438.0071/1–dc23
LC record available at https://lccn.loc.gov/2020031255
LC ebook record available at https://lccn.loc.gov/2020031256

ISBN: 978-0-367-34365-1 (hbk)
ISBN: 978-0-367-34366-8 (pbk)
ISBN: 978-0-429-32529-8 (ebk)

Typeset in Times New Roman
by Taylor & Francis Books

Contents

List of contributors vii

Introduction: When global citizenry does not include language learning: The challenges of foreign languages departments in the 21st century 1
MELISSA ETZLER AND GABRIELE MAIER

1 Reinvigorating a small undergraduate German program through an integrated, literacies-based curriculum 11
JENNIFER REDMANN

2 Bringing global and local together: Program building through ACTFL's "Community C" 23
WENDY WESTPHAL

3 Learning German in and for the 21st century 45
BIRGIT A. JENSEN, SUSANNE LENNÉ JONES, DAVID L. SMITH AND JILL E. TWARK

4 Diversity programming, student outreach and the politics of visible inclusivity for small German programs 64
ERVIN MALAKAJ

5 Southern Illinois University Carbondale: One public university's experience with international studies in the Midwest 75
MARY A. BRICKER

6 Designing a language lab that encompasses cultural and interdisciplinary experiences 88
MARTINA WELLS

7 The courage to construct and experiment: Initiatives in updating the German minor program at Concordia University 102
STEFAN BRONNER AND REGINA RANGE

8 Strategies for teaching 18th-century German texts in the context of program building 118
JEFFREY L. HIGH, ELENA PNEVMONIDOU AND FRIEDERIKE VON SCHWERIN-HIGH

9 Technology-enhanced learning approaches to curriculum development: Architecture meets the humanities 135
GABRIELE MAIER

10 *Freundschaft*, *Motivationstraining* und *Märchen*: Learning by living life in the GDR 156
ANDREA MEYERTHOLEN

11 Branching out with STEM in the German classroom 172
MELISSA ETZLER AND MICHELLE STIGTER-HAYDEN

12 The *Deutsche Sommerschule am Pazifik*: A model and asset to small German programs 189
CARRIE COLLENBERG-GONZÁLEZ

Conclusion: The future is now: Saving German studies in a brave new world 204
MIRKO M. HALL

Index 211

Contributors

Mary A. Bricker earned her doctorate from the University of Illinois, Urbana-Champaign. She is Associate Professor of German at Southern Illinois University, Carbondale. Her research spans 18th-, 19th- and 20th-century German literature. Her scholarship has appeared in *Neophilologus, PsyArt*, the *Yearbook of German-American Studies* and *Bakhtiniana*. Her chapter "Teaching Genre: Fairy Tales and Their Retellings in Young Adult Literature" was published 2020 in the MLA Series: *Options for Teaching Young Adult Literature*, edited by Karen Coats et al. In 2018 she co-edited the special section "Lessing's Laughter" in the *Lessing Yearbook/Jahrbuch*. She is also a member of the *Bakhtiniana* editorial board.

Stefan Bronner is Assistant Professor in Residence in German Studies and Director of the graduate program at the University of Connecticut. He earned an M.A. in German Studies from the University of Pittsburgh in 2007 and a doctorate from the Otto-Friedrich-Universität Bamberg. His dissertation on Swiss author Christian Kracht was published in 2012 with Narr Francke Attempto Verlag in Tübingen. He is the founder of the Literaturhaus Augsburg, which organizes literary events together with a team of volunteers. In 2018, together with Dr. Marcel Schmid, he founded the Passionate Humanities Movement as a reaction to the crises facing the humanities today. His current research interests focus on contemporary German metaphysical identity narratives.

Carrie Collenberg-González is Assistant Professor of German Studies at Portland State University, the Director of the *Deutsche Sommerschule am Pazifik* and Testing Chair for the Oregon Association of Teachers of German. She is the coauthor of the second-year German textbook *Cineplex: German Culture and Language Through Film* (2014), co-editor of *Affected Frames: Photographs and German Cinema* (forthcoming 2021) and *Heinrich von Kleist's Artistic and Philosophical Legacies* (forthcoming 2021). She has published articles on the aesthetic representation of terrorism, the reception of Heinrich von Kleist, German film and Goethe's *Faust* in journals such as *Feminist German Studies* and the *Goethe Yearbook*.

Melissa Etzler is a Lecturer of German and First Year Seminar at Butler University in Indianapolis. She has published book chapters related to her research on author W. G. Sebald and has recently shifted her focus to eco-critical readings of Gothic German texts and films, her most recent article appearing in *German Quarterly*. In addition to her regular coursework, she teaches in honors and co-leads the annual short-term study abroad program Bulldogs in Berlin. She is the recipient of the AATG Indiana Post-Secondary Teacher of the Year Award (2018), the College of Liberal Arts and Sciences Outstanding Faculty Award for Excellence in Teaching (2018) and an Outstanding Professor of the Year Award for Teaching (2018–19).

Mirko M. Hall is Professor of German Studies and Chair of Languages, Cultures and Literatures at Converse College. As the first full-time Germanist to be hired in over 60 years, he has developed a small, but dynamic German Studies program since his arrival at the college in 2007. Among other accolades, he is the recipient of a South Carolina Independent Colleges and Universities Excellence in Teaching Award. In 2011 and 2018, the college's senior class presented him with the Joe Ann Lever Award of Excellence. Trained as an intellectual historian at the University of Minnesota, he is the author of *Musical Revolutions in German Culture: Musicking against the Grain, 1800–1980* (Palgrave Macmillan, 2014) and co-editor of *Beyond No Future: Cultures of German Punk* (Bloomsbury, 2016).

Jeffrey L. High is Professor and Section Chair of German Studies at California State University, Long Beach (CSULB), as well as Guest Professor at Portland State University's *Deutsche Sommerschule am Pazifik*. He is the author and editor or coeditor of five books on Schiller, Kleist and the Late Enlightenment, with two co-edited volumes on Kleist and one on Napoleon Bonaparte forthcoming. He is a 2018 recipient of the CSULB "President's Award for Outstanding Faculty Achievement in Scholarship and Mentoring," the CSULB Honor Program's 2019 "Most Valuable Professor" and the 2020 recipient of the CSULB Faculty Senate's awards for both scholarly mentoring and advising.

Birgit A. Jensen is Associate Professor of German at East Carolina University. She is the author of *Auf der morschen Gartenschaukel: Kindheit als Problem bei Theodor Fontane* (Rodopi, 1998). Her literary research on marginalized groups and communities frequently illuminates the life-writings of German working-class authors of the late 19th century and appeared in *German Life and Letters, Critique, Amsterdamer Beiträge, a/b: Autobiography Studies* and *Biography*. More recently, her pedagogical research focuses on the efficacy of flipped learning in the L2 classroom, curricular design for cross-cultural critical thinking and student perceptions of flipped learning. She has published in *Unterrichtspraxis* and

Journal on Excellence in College Teaching and co-authored *Impuls Deutsch II*, a Beginning German textbook for flipped instruction.

Susanne Lenné Jones is Associate Professor of German Studies at East Carolina University (ECU). She enjoys teaching a wide spectrum of courses, ranging from language to literature and film. She regularly teaches a course on the Holocaust, both at ECU and in a summer study abroad program she directs in Berlin. In her research she has examined the role of photographs in contemporary German memory texts as well as the relationships between memory and city space. She has also published on Jewish humor in German film as well as on German program building. More recently, she has become interested in cultural productions zooming in on the immediate postwar years, during which perpetrators and victims needed to renegotiate their new positions in this young German democracy.

Gabriele Maier is Associate Teaching Professor of German Studies and Director of the M.A. program in Global Communication and Applied Translation at Carnegie Mellon University (CMU) in Pittsburgh. Her research includes literature of the 20th and 21st century and focuses primarily on travel writing, questions of home and identity, transcultural writers and graphic novels. She has published on Christian Kracht, Hans-Ulrich Treichel and Christoph Ransmayr, among others; co-edited an anthology on *Heimat*; and her textbook *Deutschland im Zeitalter der Globalisierung* came out in 2015. Lately, she has contributed an article to the MLA Handbook *Strategies and Perspectives on Social Justice Work*. She is a fellow of the "How Well?" project funded by the Center for the Arts in Society at CMU, where she works with various student groups to educate the public about food insecurity and how to improve well-being on the CMU campus.

Ervin Malakaj is Assistant Professor of German Studies and affiliate faculty in the Institute for European Studies at the University of British Columbia. He has coedited two volumes: *Market Strategies and German Literature in the Long Nineteenth Century* (de Gruyter, 2020) and *Diversity and Decolonization in German Studies* (Palgrave, 2020). Together, with Regine Criser, he cofounded the scholarly collective Diversity, Decolonization, and the German Curriculum in 2016. His research interests are German media studies, 19th-century literary cultures, film studies and queer theory.

Andrea Meyertholen is Assistant Professor of German at the University of Kansas. Her interests connect post-1750 German literature and culture with art history and museum studies to focus on intermedial encounters of literature with painting and tourist spaces. Bringing this fascination into the classroom, she engages art, film and other visual media to energize and enhance language learning. She has taught language and literature courses at all undergraduate levels, including overseas programs in both Germany and Austria. She has published on Heinrich von Kleist, Caspar David Friedrich and Johann Wolfgang Goethe's cloud poetry, and presented on German fairy tales, the intersection of the modern zoo with Expressionist painting and poetry and pedagogical strategies for introducing classic texts to contemporary students.

Elena Pnevmonidou is Associate Professor in the Department of Germanic and Slavic Studies and Director of the European Studies Program at the University of Victoria. Her research revolves around aesthetic theory and gender in the Age of Goethe, poetics, critical theory and drama pedagogy. She has published on Novalis, Dorthea Schlegel, Ottilie von Goethe, Bertolt Brecht and Franz Kafka, appearing in *German Quarterly, German Life and Letters, Brecht Yearbook,* etc. Her interest in drama pedagogy was originally motivated by the desire to bridge the gap between language and literature/culture teaching, but she recently broadened her research to explore the extent to which drama pedagogy can support social-justice-minded teaching and learning, which will appear in a forthcoming article in a volume on social justice pedagogy.

Regina Range is Assistant Professor of German and Language Program Director for elementary- and intermediate-level German language instruction at the University of Alabama. She earned a teaching degree from the Technische Universität Dortmund in 2006 and a Ph.D. in German from the University of Iowa in 2012. Her main research focuses on German-speaking émigré writers and film professionals, autobiographical writing, exile literature, film and scriptwriting. Her secondary research agenda concentrates on language pedagogy, teacher professionalization and program building.

Jennifer Redmann (Ph.D., University of Wisconsin-Madison) is Professor of German at Franklin & Marshall College in Lancaster, PA. Over the course of her career, Redmann has published in the areas of both German literary studies and foreign language curricula and pedagogy. She is the author (with Pennylyn Dykstra-Pruim) of *Schreiben lernen: A Writing Guide for Learners of German* (Yale University Press, 2012), which will appear in a second edition in 2021. After completing successful curricular revisions at three small liberal arts colleges, she has given numerous workshops and seminars across the U.S. on strategies for strengthening small German programs.

Friederike von Schwerin-High is Professor of German and Chair of the German and Russian Department at Pomona College. She is the author of *Shakespeare: Germany and Japan: Reception and Translation* (Continuum Press, 2005) and has published research on Lessing, Goethe, A. W. Schlegel, Kleist, Thomas Mann, Doris Dörrie and Jenny Erpenbeck, among other writers. She served as coeditor of *Pacific Coast Philology* from 2011–16. Her most recent articles appeared in *Jahrbuch der internationalen Achim von*

Arnim Gesellschaft and *Gegenwartsliteratur*. In 2018–19 she was a Humanities Studio Fellow at Pomona College. Her research interests include fictional biography, theories of friendship and otherness, and the use of blank verse in 18th-century German dramas.

David L. Smith is Associate Professor of German at East Carolina University. Fascinated by intersections of belief and cultural identity, he is currently conducting research for a manuscript on representations of the Holy Family in German-language literature after 9/11. His past publications include articles on Christoph Ransmayr, Wilhelm Hauff, J. C. Gottsched and J. M. R. Lenz, as well as on baroque language theorists J. G. Schottelius and Johann Klaj.

Michelle Stigter-Hayden is the Modern Language Center Director and a German Lecturer at Butler University. In addition to supporting learning and teaching across the language programs, she teaches German and core curriculum courses. She has developed several innovative courses including Germany: Land of Science and Innovation; Language Major Senior Keystone, a course for language majors to help them professionally articulate their skills; and So, Where are you From? a service-learning course on community and identity. Her research agenda includes flipped language classroom approaches, intercultural competence and service-learning. She is the past president of the Indiana chapter of the American Association of Teachers of German and 2020 recipient of the Judith Eaton Award from the Indiana Association of Students of German.

Jill E. Twark is Associate Professor of German at East Carolina University. Her research interests include late 20th- and early 21st-century German literature and culture. She has published the monograph *Humor, Satire, and Identity: Eastern German Literature in the 1990s* and the edited volumes *Strategies of Humor in Post-Unification German Literature, Film, and Other Media* and *Envisioning Social Justice in Contemporary German Culture*. She collaborated with two undergraduate apprentice teachers on the article "The Benefits of Apprentice Teaching with Undergraduates in German Language Classes" for *Die Unterrichtspraxis* and is currently editing the book *Invested Narratives: German Responses to Economic Crisis and Ordnung* and working on a monograph on the history of humor in the U.S. and Europe in the 20th and 21st centuries.

Martina Wells is the Coordinator of Modern Languages at Chatham University. She oversees the foreign language program and teaches German and French. In addition to being responsible for curriculum development and implementation for all language courses, she manages and supervises the language teaching staff. Her research interests include post-WWII and contemporary German literature and film and German-Jewish literature and culture with a focus on 20th- and 21st-century texts. Originally from

Germany and Switzerland, she obtained her M.A. and Ph.D. in German Studies from the University of Pittsburgh.

Wendy Westphal is Associate Professor of German and Director of Study Abroad at Marian University. She serves as the university's Fulbright and Gilman Program Advisor. She received her *Magister* in English and German from the Universität Konstanz and her Ph.D. from the Department of Germanic Studies at Indiana University in 2010. Her research focuses on the portrayal of the GDR in contemporary literature, film and museums. She was the 2010 winner of the German Studies Association Graduate Student Paper Prize and has also published articles on the films *Good Bye, Lenin!* and *Das Leben der Anderen*. In 2016, she was selected as Indiana's Foreign Language Teacher of the Year and represented Indiana at the 2018 Central States Conference on the Teaching of Foreign Languages.

Introduction
When global citizenry does not include language learning: The challenges of foreign languages departments in the 21st century

Melissa Etzler and Gabriele Maier

The decision to study a foreign language can be a life-changing one. Not only is immersing oneself in a different language and culture a wonderfully enriching experience, but traveling to the country where that language is spoken and communicating with the local population "teaches students to appreciate difference and diversity first hand" and helps navigate our "interconnected global world" (Goodman and Berdan 2014). Yet, despite the many benefits that studying a foreign tongue can provide, foreign language programs across the nation have been facing steep challenges for years. As more and more students across the country shift from the liberal arts into career-oriented fields, enrollment in foreign language programs has plummeted, and an upward trend is not in sight. In fact, as a 2016 Modern Language Association report predicts, the numbers might decline even more over the next years, despite concerted efforts to restructure and revitalize departments (Looney and Lusin 2019). Therefore, it is paramount in this day and age to promote foreign language programs vigorously, offer courses that reflect and compel students' interests, keep students engaged in extracurricular activities and establish a community of like-minded language learners.

As Kathleen Stein-Smith points out in her article "Foreign Language Classes are Becoming More Scarce," one major problem that pertains to the decline in foreign language learning is the low interest that can be detected among middle and high school students. This indifference towards foreign languages is, to a large extent, due to the significant lack of available programs in the American school system (only 58% of all middle schools offer a foreign language), which makes it impossible for students to become acquainted with a foreign tongue even if they wanted to. Nationwide only 20% of all K-12 students take a foreign language, and at the college and university level the situation is even grimmer, with an overall percentage of only 7.5% of students involved in foreign language studies. Yet, here, too, schools are to blame: despite the fact that at many universities "demonstrated proficiency in a second language will improve your chances of being admitted" (Grove 2019), according to an ACTA (American Council of Trustees and Alumni) study that examined the core curricula at 1,100 U.S. colleges and universities in 2018–19, "only 12% require intermediate-level foreign language study" (Urban 2018). Considering the low number of universities and colleges that uphold a language requirement, it becomes all the more important for language instructors to retain those students beyond the completion of the requirement in order to ensure that they truly gain the competencies which most institutions of higher education claim to value. In what ways can instructors assist their students in becoming global citizens with intercultural competencies?

Over the years, with declining student enrollments and the elimination of countless foreign language programs, foreign language instructors have felt a pronounced urgency to find ways to remedy the dire situation in which they find themselves. Boosting student numbers by strengthening a small language program is a goal many of us have been trying to pursue but, as many contributors of this anthology point out in their respective chapters, bringing this admirable goal to fruition requires a Herculean effort. Not only do many foreign language instructors – and in particular instructors in programs with less popular languages, such as Italian, Russian or German – constitute the only point-person in their field and consequently run an entire language program on their own, but they additionally face challenging teaching loads, research requirements and the need to overhaul outdated curricula to make courses more attractive to students. Class preparation, classroom instruction, grading, advising minors and majors as well as study abroad applicants, organizing extracurricular activities such as karaoke nights or film screenings and so on often rest on the shoulders of only one or two people, which makes it extremely challenging for instructors to stay motivated. In addition, many faculty positions do not grant job security but rather offer only temporary contracts with limited renewal options. Contingent faculty members are forced to change positions every few years, which can be disruptive for a program when different visions and ideas are introduced on a regular basis. Hence, with all those odds stacked against language programs – especially small German Studies programs – the question arises: how does one not only guarantee the survival of those existing language departments but also create a flourishing language program that encompasses healthy student numbers, innovative language instruction and practical advice for students going on the job market?

Since program building is a recurrent topic among college-level German instructors, conference panels, roundtables and interest groups on small German program building have been and still are organized on a regular basis. As early as 1998, more than two decades ago, the American Council on the Teaching of Foreign Languages (ACTFL) established a Special Interest Group (SIG) to promote discussions on German program building, to organize webinars, share teaching materials and promote conference panels on innovative pedagogical methodologies. These discussions have been part and parcel of a number of conferences and seminars such as "College Faculty Seminar on Strategies for Strengthening Small German Programs" offered by the Goethe-Zentrum in 2015, "Strategies for Strengthening Small German

Programs" by the German Studies Association in 2017, the round-table "Outreach Strategies and Innovative Teaching in Small German Program Building" as part of the Northeast Modern Languages Association in 2018 and the "AATG Seminar for College Faculty: Program Building through Curricular Reform, Co-Curricular Enhancement, and Inclusion" in 2019 at Valparaiso University, just to mention a few. Last but not least, in 2018 the German Studies Association added "Teaching" to their list of interdisciplinary networks, thereby highlighting the heightened need to focus on pedagogical questions and classroom instructions in an age when language programs are increasingly subject to radical elimination.

However, despite an obvious interest in strengthening small language programs over the last few years, the number of publications that directly address the issues at hand has remained rather small. In the fall of 2009, *Die Unterrichtspraxis* published a series of articles in response to the crisis in German Studies as outlined by the MLA Task Force on foreign languages in 2007. The articles stress language development and integrating specific literary texts to bridge the gap in the third year to "engage students in meaningful and productive ways and to challenge programs to rethink their course content and pedagogy used" (editorial vii). While this orientation is understandable, it does not go far enough at a time when students' desire to learn material relevant to their long-term career goals and literary-based upper level German courses are no longer the crux of the curriculum – and have not been for a while.

To be sure, the study of German has experienced difficulties for decades. Indeed, in 1976, we find one of the first anthologies – *German Studies in the United States: Assessment and Outlook* (1976) by Walter F. W. Lohnes and Valters Nollendorfs – addressing "strategies of survival and suggestions for self-improvement" (4) regarding the instruction of German in the U.S. Other volumes such as *Teaching German in America: Prolegomena to a History* (1988) by David P. Benseler et al. followed, often with a focus on the historical trajectory of *Germanistik* in the U.S. context, its ups and downs over the years and its ultimate transition to German Studies, which entailed a shift away from literary studies to include aspects of culture, history and politics. In the new millennium with *Teaching German in the Twentieth-Century America* (2001), *Globalization and the Future of German* (2004) and *The Meaning of Culture: German Studies in the 21st Century* (2009), to name a few, a strong emphasis on innovative classroom instruction, the significance of culture in language teaching as well as contributions from the field of second language acquisition can be detected. Practical suggestions on how to revitalize and reinvent the field with regard to its pedagogical underpinnings have taken center stage and mirror a number of articles such as Len Cagle's "Community Building: Study Abroad and the Small German Program," Ervin Malakaj's "Building a Small German Program from the Ground Up," Nicole Grewling and Erika Hille Rinker's "Going Global in Small German Programs" as well as Rachel J. Halverson and Carol-Anne Costabile-Heming's anthology *Taking Stock of German Studies in the United States*

(2015), which do precisely that: share best practices from teacher-scholars across the nation who have been involved in the successful building of small German programs.

The scholarly works mentioned above function as crucial stepping-stones for our anthology *Outreach Strategies and Innovative Teaching Approaches for German Programs*, in that they are important contributions – directly or indirectly – in the debates regarding the importance of program building. *Outreach Strategies and InnovativeTeaching* has to be seen as a sequel in particular to *Taking Stock of German Studies in the United States*, since it continues to find answers to questions regarding student recruitment, curricular design, extracurricular activities, innovative interdisciplinary partnerships and student retention – themes that are on-going and call for periodic reevaluations. *Outreach Strategies and Innovative Teaching for German Programs* is intended to serve as a practical guide for: 1) college and university instructors of German, who need concrete tools to boost student numbers; 2) graduate students of German, who need to learn about program building as part of their pedagogy training and 3) high school teachers, who need strategies to deepen student interest in the German language and culture to improve enrollments in advanced courses. Since most foreign languages departments struggle with low enrollments – even languages that used to be blessed with high numbers such as Chinese, Japanese and Spanish are now affected by the downward trend – the advice found in this book is transferable to other languages since they, equally, lack a comprehensive book that could serve as a resource to modern languages departments and instructors.

Outreach Strategies and Innovative Teaching addresses the question of program building in two ways. On the one hand, it focuses on curricular designs that target class content and pedagogical methods to enhance student learning and boost retention and enrollment. Chapters with this emphasis feature integrated, multiliteracies-based curricula that place texts at the center of every class at every level; socio-interactive learning and communication through a language lab; the promotion of German via International Studies; and diversity programming and outreach, just to name a few. On the other hand, the volume delineates innovative strategies that pique students' interest and encourage deeper, more reflective engagement with the course material. In their essays, our contributors suggest a number of pedagogical methods on how to involve students in projects that encourage intercultural understanding, experiential learning and participation in German-language based projects beyond the boundaries of the classroom. Their essays discuss German Clubs that offer a rotating schedule of cultural discussions, political debates, game days and *Stammtische*; interdisciplinary teaching models that combine different academic fields, such as German Studies and Architecture; and immersion schools that help sustain small German programs. The remainder of this introduction will outline the content of the respective chapters in more detail.

As Jennifer Redmann posits in Chapter One, "Reinvigorating a small undergraduate German program through an integrated, literacies-based curriculum," a means of retaining and inspiring students from day one is through a multiliteracies-based German curriculum. Redmann outlines the successful curricular revision process at Franklin & Marshall College which involved creating a series of theme-based courses that foreground texts and films at every level of German-language learning. In doing so, Redmann's department was able to overcome the bifurcation seen at so many institutions that offer "language" at their lower levels and "culture" courses as of the third year. The strategies employed at Franklin & Marshall College can be utilized in any language program seeking to develop students' linguistic and cultural proficiency from the first semester onwards.

In Chapter Two, the focus shifts from in-class strategies to inspire students to get involved in the larger community. Wendy Westphal's "Bringing global and local together: program building through ACTFL's 'Community C'," explains how she improved student enrollment at Marian University by utilizing what has often been referred to as the "Lost C." As outlined by the National Standards Collaborative Board, finding ways to educate students to "use the language both within and beyond the classroom to interact and collaborate in their community and the globalized world" can be a daunting task (1). Westphal outlines several activities that assisted her in expanding her German program from zero minors to an average of 15 to 20 per year. Examples of Westphal's outreach strategies include: Skyping with students studying abroad, hosting native German speakers as class guests, organizing German class trips to various German cultural centers and establishing a shadowing internship at a German hospital.

Westphal's strategies that focus on student interactions with their (g)local communities, are also touched upon in Chapter Three, entitled "Learning German in and for the 21st century." The authors Birgit A. Jensen, Susanne Lenné Jones, David L. Smith and Jill E. Twark stress the ways faculty can best prepare students to ready themselves for their future careers in a rapidly changing world by developing transferable skills such as creative and innovative thinking. Furthermore, the authors highlight the importance of moving beyond the personal skills of the individual to cultivate students' abilities to interact within their communities. A sense of communal cooperation, social responsibility and civic accountability are necessary in order for students to ultimately effect social change. A few of the specific instructional practices shared by the authors include: involving students in a collaborative effort via film production; incorporating professional preparation and service learning into the German curriculum; encouraging Flipped Learning 3.0 and engaging in various forms of outreach which extend from on-campus, to regional and international.

In Chapter Four, "Diversity programming, student outreach and the politics of visible inclusivity for small German programs," Ervin Malakaj presents various initiatives for ensuring that undergraduate German classrooms are safe, inclusive intellectual homes and diverse spaces. In considering how to serve the needs of structurally disadvantaged and minoritized learners,

Malakaj advocates the creation of access points for learners traditionally underrepresented in German classrooms. He also depicts a number of outreach activities that attract students to the program while simultaneously generating a high level of visibility across campus and within the regional community. Such outreach initiatives expand upon the traditional German space, in which events such as film nights and coffee hours occur, to secure a place in which students can articulate how they position themselves vis-à-vis social problems and social justice issues. Through the types of outreach outlined in his chapter, instructors become allies, role models and supporters of student success.

Like Malakaj, Mary A. Bricker stresses the importance of exposing as many students as possible to the value of learning about other cultures and foreign languages. As Rosemary Feal, Executive Director Emerita of the Modern Language Association, highlights, learning languages is crucial to cultivate empathy and combat national isolationism (Flaherty 2017). In Chapter Five, "Southern Illinois University Carbondale: one public university's experience with international studies in the Midwest," Bricker describes the initiatives taken at her institution to save the language program. Bricker's method of outreach included offering an international studies introductory course that both attracted non-language majors and endowed students with a sense of community in the program. The chapter describes the specifics of the course, including student presentations, invited guest speakers and international initiatives within the Carbondale community. The course honed students' oral communication and leadership skills while preparing them for future study abroad programs and potential careers in the international workplace.

In Chapter Six, "Designing a language lab that encompasses cultural and interdisciplinary experiences," Martina Wells explains how her 1-credit lab course focusing on German culture in context created a space for sociointeractive learning and communication that complemented in-class learning. Spurred on by the objective tasked in the MLA report from 2007 to systematically incorporate cultural inquiry at all levels, Wells used this lab course to immerse her students into the culture of German-speaking countries. She discusses lab projects that include a German Election Workshop, Conversation Partner Program, Chatham-in-Germany-Brochure and International Karaoke, and showcases how they inform the lab as a formal platform for integrating the German program into academic culture and resources at Chatham University and beyond.

In Chapter Seven, "The courage to construct and experiment: initiatives in updating the German minor program at Concordia University," Stefan Bronner und Regina Range illustrate how their collaborative efforts enabled them to invigorate a wilting German program at Concordia University in spite of the challenges they faced due to their three-year Limited Term Appointments (LTA). In an effort to establish a viable five- to ten-year plan, the authors focused on revamping the curriculum by updating their language-learning textbooks, by creating innovative interdisciplinary courses offered in English and by introducing a pedagogical device that Bronner called Rhizomatic Response Projects (RRPs). In addition, the authors enhanced local and international program visibility through their outreach efforts which included the planning and organizing of major events as well as hosting high-profile guest speakers from German-speaking countries. Overall, Bronner and Range demonstrate the types of long-term success a department can acquire when fueled by the passionate engagement of the instructors.

In Chapter Eight, "Strategies for teaching 18th-century German texts in the context of program building," authors Jeffrey L. High, Elena Pnevmonidou and Friederike von Schwerin-High explain how they have inspired students by actualizing classical German texts and making them relevant within the 21st-century context. In Elena Pnevomidou's contribution to the chapter, "The potential of drama pedagogy and peer-assisted learning for teaching 18th-century German literature in the L2 classroom," she uses Lessing's *Nathan der Weise* as the quintessential example to demonstrate how performative explorations lead to experiential and community learning. By way of emotive and kinesthetic learning, peer teaching and collaborative directing, students overcome the typical hurdles so prevalent when first encountering 18th-century texts and ultimately become enthusiastic participants in class. Friederike von Schwerin-High's section "18th-century plays in the German drama survey course," explains, how close, lexically driven readings can guide students into an understanding of the more profound layers of a text such as the intertwinement of power-relations, aesthetics, class and gender representations. Though related to in-class discussions, Jeffrey L. High's "On the importance of 18th-century literature: recruitment, opportunity, retention and the pursuit of happiness," branches out of the classroom to clarify the critical role of 18th-century texts in program building. Age-of-Schiller authors' complex and nuanced humanistic arguments foster a lively scholarly community and serve as a springboard to student engagement in academic conferences, summer immersion experiences and a wide variety of high-profile on-campus events.

In Chapter Nine, "Technology-enhanced learning approaches to curriculum development: architecture meets the humanities," Gabriele Maier highlights her encounter with interdisciplinary team-teaching as a possible way of boosting student enrollments. By offering a collaborative course with her colleague Francesca Torello from the School of Architecture, Maier outlines how the rather traditional course, Vienna 1900, a staple in many German Studies departments, was transformed into a project-based learning experience with a digital component in the form of an interactive map that students helped build. This technology-enhanced learning approach entailed the creation of 3D models, collections of artifacts as well as networks of people who used to frequent the spaces reconstructed by the students. What Maier contemplates in her contribution is whether interdisciplinary teaching together with a project-based learning approach ultimately leads to more student satisfaction and an increased interest in becoming a minor or major of German Studies in the

8 *Introduction*

Department of Modern Languages at Carnegie Mellon University in Pittsburgh.

In a similar vein to the discussions of the benefits of drama pedagogy offered in Chapter Eight, Andrea Meyertholen's *"Freundschaft, Motivationstraining* und *Märchen*: Learning by living life in the GDR," (Chapter Ten) illustrates strategies that develop critical thinking skills and guide students towards a nuanced understanding of cultural phenomena while simultaneously targeting foreign-language skills. Using drama pedagogy, students engage in a self-reflective exploration of the former East Germany with the help of textual materials such as popular films which launch students into the reality of a historical time radically different from their own. While maintaining a focus on linguistic proficiency, drama pedagogy triggers students' empathy in profound ways and contributes to cultural competency, media literacy and an expansion of the students' worldview.

Considering the interdisciplinary interests of many current students of German, in Chapter Eleven, "Branching out with STEM in the German Language Classroom," Melissa Etzler and Michelle Stigter-Hayden discuss the ways in which they have incorporated elements of STEM fields within their curriculum at Butler University. Since roughly 25% of students major in STEM fields, and instructors are thus encouraged to provide their students pragmatic knowledge that will assist them in their future careers, the authors eagerly participated in the AATG *MINT-Fortbildungsseminar* in 2017 and 2018 to gather strategies on how to effectively include STEM-based lesson plans within various courses. The materials collected during those *MINT-Fortbildungsseminare* continue to be of great help in upper-division German courses, and the first half of this chapter provides an overview of exemplary textbooks that are conducive to in-class use with more advanced learners. The second half of the chapter details the specifics of Stigter-Hayden's newly created Land of Science and Innovation course, explains the conducted in-class experiments and depicts how experiential learning contributes to intrinsic motivation.

Last but not least, Carrie Collenberg-González discusses the *Deutsche Sommerschule am Pazifik* in Chapter Twelve – a German immersion school located in Portland, Oregon that offers intermediate students an intensive five-week language program as well as one-week teacher trainings. As one of the few immersion schools left in the country to survive the most recent budget cuts to small language programs, Collenberg-González's contribution addresses the organization of the school, its key features and the benefits to students who have attended it in the past. It also delineates various debates regarding the cultural and financial implications for students in U.S. immersion schools versus study abroad, as well as student credit hours and progress toward degrees.

It is the hope of the editors that this combination of curriculum-based strategies coupled with innovative projects, extracurricular and outreach activities will inspire our readers with pragmatic initiatives that they can experiment with at their respective institutions. Considering the current state in which foreign language departments find themselves – struggling with increasing budget cuts, departmental closures and contingent faculty positions replacing tenure lines – it is crucial that language instructors remain motivated, devoted to the success of their students and their programs and educate themselves regarding best practices. We end our volume on a positive note with the concluding thoughts offered by Mirko M. Hall in "The future is now: saving German studies in a Brave New World," who reminds us that we must use our pedagogical expertise and acumen to cultivate our students' skills both in terms of linguistic ability but also in terms of intercultural awareness, sensitivity and empathy. Hall, furthermore, emphasizes the essential nature of collaboration, which is exactly what we hope this collective volume will inspire. The world of German Studies requires more sharing of pedagogical strategies and ideas for curricular reform and outreach, more interdisciplinary efforts and a continued enthusiasm for this subject and profession which we feel so passionately about.

Bibliography

Benseler, David P., et al., editors. *Teaching German in America: Prolegomena to a History*. U of Wisconsin Press, 1988.

Benseler, David P., et al., editors. *Teaching German in the Twentieth Century*. U of Wisconsin Press, 2001.

Cagle, Len. "Community Building: Study Abroad and the Small German Program." *Die Unterrichtspraxis*, vol. 44, no. 1, 2011, pp. 12–19. Editorial. *Die Unterrichtspraxis*, vol. 42, no. 2, 2009, p. vii.

Flaherty, Colleen. "Language Study as a National Imperative." *Inside Higher Ed*. 28 February 2017, www.insidehighered.com/news/2017/02/28/academy-arts-and-sciences-makes-case-increasing-foreign-language-learning-capacity. Accessed 23 June 2020.

Gardt, Andreas, and Bernd Hüppauf, editors. *Globalization and the Future of German*. Mouton de Gruyter, 2004.

Goodman, Allen E., and Stacie Nevadomski Berdan. "Every Student Should Study Abroad." *The New York Times*, 12 May 2014, www.nytimes.com/roomfordebate/2013/10/17/should-more-americans-study-abroad/every-student-should-study-abroad. Accessed 22 June 2020.

Grewling, Nicole, and Erika Hille Rinker. "Going Global in Small German Programs." *Die Unterrichtspraxis*, vol. 52, no. 2, 2019, pp. 230–236.

Grove, Allen. "Foreign Language Requirement for College Admissions." *ThoughtCo*. 20 June 2019, www.thoughtco.com/foreign-language-requirement-college-admissions-788842. Accessed 22 June 2020.

Halverson, Rachel J., and Carol Anne Constabile-Heming, editors. *Taking Stock of German Studies in the United States*. Camden House, 2015.

Kagel, Martin, and Laura Tate Kagel, editors. *The Meaning of Culture: German Studies in the 21st Century*. Wehrhahn, 2009.

Lohnes, Walter F.W., and Valters Nollendorffs, editors. *German Studies in the United States: Assessment and Outlook*. University of Wisconsin Press, 1976.

Looney, Dennis, and Natalia Lusin. "Enrollments in Languages Other Than English in United States Institutions of Higher Education, Summer 2016 and Fall 2016: Final Report." MLA, 2019, www.mla.org/content/download/110154/2406932/2016-Enrollments-Final-Report.pdf. Accessed 26 June 2020.

Malakaj, Ervin. "Building a Small German Program from the Ground Up." ervinmalakaj.weebly.com/blog/building-a-small-german-program-from-the-ground-up. Accessed 26 June 2020.

The National Standards Collaborative Board. *World-Readiness Standards for Learning Languages*. 4th ed., American Council on the Teaching of Foreign Languages, 2014.

Stein-Smith, Kathleen. "Foreign Language Classes are Becoming More Scarce." *The Conversation*, 6 Feb. 2019, theconversation.com/foreign-language-classes-becoming-more-scarce-102235. Accessed 24 June 2020.

Urban, Nathaniel. "The Defense of Foreign Language Requirements." American Council of Trustees and Alumni (ACTA). 31 October 2018, www.goacta.org/2018/10/the-defense-of-foreign-language-requirements/. Accessed 22 June 2020.

1 Reinvigorating a small undergraduate German program through an integrated, literacies-based curriculum

Jennifer Redmann

Every undergraduate German program in the United States today must grapple with issues of viability and vitality. College-level German enrollments decreased by 16% between 2009 and 2016, the MLA reported in 2019, and the total number of institutions offering German declined by 11%, more than any other language (Looney and Lusin 2019). Data on U.S. high school German enrollments is hard to come by, but *The National K-16 Foreign Language Enrollment Survey Report* released by the American Councils for International Education in 2017 indicates that only three percent of students enrolled in high-school language courses were studying German. As ever fewer students arrive at college with a background in German, faculty in German programs must find ways both to attract students at their institutions to the study of the language and to inspire them to continue with German courses beyond completion of a language requirement. The difficulty of this task is magnified by a pervasive shift in post-secondary enrollments away from the humanities toward STEM fields and professional programs. Even as a drive toward "internationalization" and the need to educate "global citizens" have found a central place in the discourse of higher education over the last decades, German programs across the country continue to face the threat of elimination. Those outside the field question the value of German programs when relatively few students choose to continue their study of the language beyond the elementary level, much less pursue a major.

Professionals in the field, of course, have been grappling with these issues for years. In 2007, the Modern Language Association's Ad Hoc Committee on Foreign Languages released its widely read report, "Foreign Languages and Higher Education: New Structures for a Changed World," in which the committee called on language departments to reassert the importance of languages and cultures in American education through a new focus on "translingual and transcultural competence" (237). If such a goal is to be achieved, the committee argued, language departments must develop new programs and approaches. In place of the "narrow model" of most post-secondary foreign language curricula (a two- or three-year language sequence, followed by a set of advanced courses focused on literary and cultural topics), post-secondary language programs should offer integrated courses of study that combine functional language learning with cultural and literary content at every level of the curriculum.

Despite the widespread dissemination of the MLA report, its recommendations have not been enacted on a wide scale. A survey of post-secondary language faculty conducted in 2016 revealed that, although 57% of respondents had read the MLA report and, on the whole, had a positive view of curricular integration, 45% of those surveyed had not made any curricular changes as a result (Lomicka and Lord 2018, 118). Thus it is clear that the "additive model" of the language curriculum, defined by Heidi Byrnes in her summary report from 1996 on the "Future of German in American Education" as "first mastery of the formal inventory of German, then content knowledge, then culture, then literature" (256), still holds sway in American foreign language programs.

In the pages that follow, I offer a case study in how curricular integration through a literacy-based approach can serve to reinvigorate German programs. As I outline below, the fully integrated, literacies-based German curriculum at Franklin & Marshall College, which has been fully in place since 2014, situates texts, along with level-appropriate tasks, at the center of every course at every level. By engaging with texts (even in the first year of German instruction), students sharpen their interpretive skills, become literate members of a German-speaking community on campus and beyond, and acquire a critical understanding of issues that have shaped German society of the past and present.

Curricular integration through a literacies-based approach

A literacies-based foreign language pedagogy offers an alternative to (or enhancement of) the communicative approach that has long dominated collegiate foreign language instruction in the United States. In a literacy-oriented curriculum, instructors focus not (only) on the development of students' oral skills in functional contexts (such as ordering a meal in a restaurant or buying a train ticket) but, from the beginning of the curriculum, on students' ability to make meaning in the target language "through the acts of interpreting and creating written, oral, visual, audiovisual, and digital texts" (Paesani et al. 2016, 23).

An appeal to the importance of texts begs the question of what we are trying to achieve in our undergraduate German curriculum. What knowledge, skills, and attitudes should graduating German minors and majors be able to demonstrate? For what purpose? These are challenging questions that faculty in every German program can and will answer differently. But in addition to defining the end point, we must also consider how those goals will be realized *at each stage* of the German curriculum. As Richard Kern explains, "curriculum can be thought of as a conceptual map of what students and teachers do over time, and the relationships among the various things they do. This conceptual map encodes decisions about *what* to teach (i.e. content), *how* to teach it (i.e. method and sequencing) and *why* (i.e. goals)" (2004, "Literacy and Advanced Foreign Language Learning," 6). How will students become proficient in German? What should they know about the German-speaking world? How should they view themselves in relation to that world? And most importantly: How will our curriculum facilitate the achievement of these goals over time?

As one approach to answering these questions, I offer the concept of foreign language literacy as developed by Heidi Byrnes, Richard Kern, Janet Swaffar, Katherine Arens and others. In its focus on texts, foreign language literacy offers a means of unifying the curriculum while maintaining the centrality of the language itself.[1] A literacy-based foreign language curriculum does not distinguish between "skills" and "content" courses. Instead, working with texts becomes the central enterprise at every level, through pedagogical practices that extend far beyond basic reading and writing skills.

Literacy involves not only cognitive skills, which we associate with teaching students how to decode and encode words on the page, but also social and cultural practices and exchanges. As Richard Kern explains, literacy is about "relationships between readers, writers, texts, culture, and language learning. It is about the variable cognitive and social practices of taking and making textual meaning that provide students access to new communities outside the classroom, across geographical and historical boundaries" (2004, "Literacy and Advanced Foreign Language Learning," 3). Understanding a text requires knowledge of genre conventions and the social, historical and cultural contexts from which it arose, and it is also subject to the individual interpretive position and creative power of the reader. Because literacy is not absolute but relative to contexts and communities, it is therefore helpful to think in terms of plural *literacies* (Kern and Schultz 2005, 383). Literacies are also closely linked to social identities, for in borrowing, adapting and using the target language, learners come to develop their own voices.

The initial application of this literacies-based theoretical framework to the American post-secondary German curriculum began at Georgetown University in the late 1990s. The faculty there set out to design an "integrated, task-based, content-oriented" German curriculum with the goal of fostering students' "multiple literacies." For those seeking to learn more about this work, the Georgetown University German Department website contains a wealth of background information, descriptions of the topics and goals of the various levels of the curriculum, and much more. What it doesn't include, however, are the actual tasks and assignments that show us how Georgetown students of German engage with the assigned texts, although examples can be found in publications by current and former faculty members (see Byrnes and Kord 2002; Eigler 2001; Maxim 2005, "Articulating Foreign Language Writing"). This gap between the curricular framework and its classroom realization presents a challenge for faculty members who want to develop a literacies-based curriculum but are uncertain of how to design materials that will meet the needs of beginning and intermediate learners. In response to this lack of information, I will describe in the pages that follow how we have enacted a literacies-based curriculum at Franklin & Marshall College through our approaches to reading, writing and speaking about texts.[2]

Designing materials for an integrated, literacies-based German curriculum

In the German curriculum at Franklin & Marshall College, authentic texts – print, visual and audiovisual – take center stage in every course at every level. In choosing texts for first- and second-year German courses, we rely heavily on children's and youth literature. Youth literature provides an opportunity for extended reading practice at a linguistic level appropriate for beginning and intermediate learners and, if chosen well, lays an excellent foundation for later engagement with literary and other types of sophisticated texts. Not only do students acquire reading strategies, but they can also draw on their native language cognitive abilities to begin to develop critical thinking skills in German through interpretation and analysis. Depending on the work at hand, youth novels can be rich sources of authentic historical, geographic and cultural information about the German-speaking world.[3]

The communicative textbooks used in most beginning German courses are designed to give students the tools to talk about themselves in German. In so doing, students often struggle to translate the terminology of their lives on American campuses *("Wie sagt man 'sorority sister' auf Deutsch?")*, and because their discourse partners are other American students, it is hardly surprising that students often resist communicating in German, since English is admittedly more accurate and efficient. On the other hand, when language teachers place texts at the center of their curricula, they can transform classrooms from places where students mimic the contexts of authentic language use to places where students speak about the text before them, and together try to arrive at its various German-language meanings. In this way, a group of students becomes a discourse community, different from the one that the author of a literary work had in mind, but just as authentic. I would argue that the difficulties that students experience as "non-intended" readers of the text provide opportunities for cultural exploration that are far more meaningful than the "culture capsules" found in most textbooks.[4]

In the Franklin & Marshall College German curriculum, students read most of a 100-page youth novel at the end of the first year of instruction. In third- and fourth-semester German, they read two novels each semester that range in length from 50 to 175 pages. Although students in the second year do read some shorter texts in other genres, the emphasis placed on relatively simple, straightforward fictional narrative texts corresponds to learners' limited, albeit expanding, linguistic and cultural knowledge of German. As members of the German faculty at Emory University explain in a discussion of a curricular restructuring project in their department, research into connections between text genres and language development supports a genre-based curricular sequence that moves from narration (at the beginning and intermediate levels) to explanation (at the upper-intermediate to advanced levels) to argumentation (at advanced levels) (Maxim et al. 2013, 6). Because the linguistic and thematic complexity of youth literature corresponds to the age of its target-culture intended readership, we can sequence works within the genre by choosing shorter books aimed at younger readers (8–11 years) for beginning German courses, while gradually moving to longer books for older readers (12–16 years) in the second year.

At Franklin & Marshall College, we have worked toward a vertically integrated German curriculum by choosing themes and texts for all levels. Yet, even more importantly, we have institutionalized a set of approaches to reading, writing and speaking that are designed to guide students step-by-step toward advanced proficiency. In terms of reading, this means that students work with a carefully designed reading journal in conjunction with every text at every level; in terms of writing, students complete model- and genre-based writing assignments for every level through the fourth year, where the focus is primarily on academic writing; and in terms of speaking, students acquire the linguistic tools to converse about texts in the classroom and to deliver formal oral presentations of increasing length and thematic complexity in every course at every level.

In the sections that follow, I will briefly describe these vertically articulated approaches to reading, writing and speaking. I should note that in designing these materials, Richard Kern's book *Literacy and Language Teaching* (2000) has been a particularly valuable resource.[5] Kern describes four curricular components outlined by the New London Group (1996) as a means of addressing students' literacy needs. They are: 1) "situated practice," which involves meaningful immersion in language use; 2) "overt instruction," which helps students develop a meta-language for understanding the complexities of reading and writing foreign language texts; 3) "critical framing," through which students learn to analyze and evaluate what they read and 4) "transformed practice," which takes place when students learn to transform meaning into new representations (133). By attending to these four foundational principles in creating activities and materials for every German course in the curriculum, we can ensure that students move through an internally coherent curriculum toward advanced linguistic and cultural proficiency.

Approaches to reading

I first developed the format for a reading journal workbook, or *Lesejournal*, two decades ago when I was teaching my first literature classes and discovering that, even when students claimed to have read an assigned text, they were often unable to say anything about it. As we know, reading involves more than moving one's eyes over the page, and many of the things we are able to do as a matter of course in our native language, like summarize orally the contents of what we read, must be consciously and repeatedly practiced when we are reading in a foreign language. The reading journal format presented here requires that while reading, students engage deeply with a text *through writing*. The various sections of the journal ask students: 1) to preview what they will read; 2) to summarize their reading; 3) to reflect on the reading process; 4) to compile key vocabulary items; 5) to ask and answer questions about the text and 6) to give a personal response to it.[6]

Within the context of *situated practice,* Kern explains the importance of making students aware of their mental activity while they read. For that reason, one section of the journal asks students to think about how difficult or easy the reading was for them, and how long it took them to finish the assignment. This raises their metalinguistic awareness of the reading process, a key aspect of overt instruction. Overt instruction also involves calling students' attention to how word choice shapes meaning. Because students often cite a lack of vocabulary knowledge as a reason why they have trouble reading, another section of the reading journal provides a space for students to note down vocabulary words that are *important* for understanding the text (not simply words they didn't know). In class, we frequently compile a common list of key words from students' individual lists. This allows us as a group to recall the contexts in which the words occurred and to reflect on the connotations of a particular word and why it might have been used in the text instead of another.[7] By focusing on individual words in context and their meanings, students move beyond simply looking up words to a form of discourse analysis.

Central to literacy development is the ability to analyze and interpret textual content and form. Students accomplish this through the process of *critical framing*, which "involves distancing oneself from a text as well as from one's response to the text to examine the nature of the text-response relationship" (Kern, Literacy 156). The reading journal facilitates critical framing by asking students to formulate questions for class discussion. This requires that students learn what it means to write a "good question," that is, one for which there is no clear answer on a particular page of the text. During the class period, I often gather questions from every class member and let them guide our discussion. Students frequently speculate on the motivations of the characters, on the meaning of symbols in the text, or they ask their classmates to put themselves in a character's shoes. I am often surprised by the sophisticated topics students choose to address, as they often deal with aspects of the text I had never thought of. When the students respond to questions posed by their peers, the traditional pattern of teacher-student interaction in the classroom breaks down and a truly student-centered environment can emerge.

Another part of the reading journal, a written summary of the assigned reading (usually about 100 words), also functions as a first step toward interpretation, since it requires the identification of more-important and less-important elements within a work. We regularly compare summaries in class, noting differences between them, filling in gaps and pulling information together to arrive at a communal record of key elements in the story. Students find this daily work of summarizing very challenging at first, but over time they improve significantly. They learn how to make an effective opening statement that summarizes the main events of the text, and they become practiced at using temporal and causal markers to make connections between the parts of the text. In writing a summary, students also engage in *transformed practice* by reworking the text into something new which they have created.

Approaches to writing

As the reading journal makes clear, in a literacy-based curriculum, reading and writing are viewed not as separate skills but as intimately connected processes. In discussing approaches to writing in this section, however, I am shifting from the kind of writing that facilitates reading to the creation of a final, polished, written product. I developed this approach to writing with Pennylyn Dykstra-Pruim, my co-author of the textbook *Schreiben lernen: A Writing Guide for Learners of German* (2011), which will appear in a second edition in 2021. It is important to note that *Schreiben lernen* is not a text for a composition course but rather a supplementary writing guide intended for use at all levels of the German curriculum to assist students in developing their writing skills in increasingly complex and abstract genres.

Dykstra-Pruim and I came to our project out of frustration over the quality of our students' writing. Too often we found ourselves either struggling to decode incomprehensible compositions or simply despairing over uninspired, simplistic writing. None of the commercially available textbooks we reviewed in preparation for writing *Schreiben lernen* addressed writing in a thorough, systematic manner. In response, we created a whole-curriculum writing guide founded on a *Model-based, Process-oriented, Genre-focused* (MPG) approach. We believe that the MPG orientation, described below, should inform effective writing instruction at any level, independently of any textbook.

In providing students with culturally authentic *models* for the kinds of writing we would like them to produce, we are pointing the way toward literacy and membership in a community of German speakers. If we want students to learn to write a job application letter, for example, we need to introduce them to letter writing conventions, particularly greetings and closings. An interpersonal genre like the letter also requires us to attend to audience and the linguistic markers of formal and informal register. An appropriate German job application letter has a particular structure and often makes use of particular phrases. By providing students with model letters to read and analyze before they write their own, we raise their awareness of the complex web of choices a writer must make in conveying meaning. At the same time, we invite students to borrow words and phrases that are characteristic of a particular text genre and to consider the contexts of their use.[8]

A *process orientation* goes hand in hand with models, since it asks students to plan their writing and consider the various steps they need to take to produce a finished product. Faculty members understand the importance of process writing for major assignments such as research papers – we know that students will produce a better final paper if we ask them to submit in advance bibliographies, thesis statements, outlines and so on. The same is true for writing in German courses, where in-class activities can prepare students in stages for writing at home.

Bringing a *genre-focus* to writing instruction means thinking beyond a single unit or course to an entire curriculum. If we want students to be able to write a lengthy, sophisticated analysis of a work of German literature by the time they graduate, what steps do we need to take to get them there? And if our graduating students are proficient speakers and writers who are not only going to graduate school in German literature but will also use the language in various contexts, what kinds of texts should they be able to write? In creating a whole-curriculum writing guide, Dykstra-Pruim and I sought to address these questions by introducing eight different genres divided into three scaffolded sub-genres for the beginning, intermediate and advanced levels of the curriculum. For example, in the chapter *Briefe schreiben*, beginning students write a short postcard or e-mail, intermediate students write a thank-you letter and advanced students write a letter of application. In some cases, this means bringing genres to the lower levels that may not be entirely appropriate from a linguistic standpoint, but in such a case, the writing task is scaled down to fit the proficiency level of the learner. For example, in the chapter *Meinungen äußern*, students at the advanced level write a *Texterörterung*, an argumentative essay in which the writer takes a position on a controversial topic. Intermediate students are also asked to take a stand on a debatable question, but their response takes the form of a short online post (*Stellungnahme*) rather than a full essay. In its entirety, this writing curriculum supports literacy development by focusing students' attention on why and how we write, and how grammatical structures and word choices shape the nature and impact of all communication.

Approaches to interpersonal and presentational speaking

In the communicative classroom, great emphasis is placed on the development of oral skills as students learn to discuss topics in the target language such as their daily routines, their families, their favorite foods and their future plans. In a literacy-based classroom, students also talk about themselves and their lives, but these personal conversations serve as an entry point for the discussion of texts. In my third-semester German course, for example, we spend several weeks on *Almanya – Willkommen in Deutschland* (2011), a film about three generations of a Turkish-German family coming to terms with their cross-cultural identities. Before viewing the first scenes, a classroom conversation about students' extended families allows us to review family vocabulary and descriptive personal adjectives, but it also serves as a springboard for the discussion of the Yilmaz family relationships in *Almanya*. Similarly, the film's depiction of the history of the *Gastarbeiter* in Germany provides a context for learning about life in post-war Germany and encourages students to reflect on their own immigrant backgrounds. Students' interpersonal exchange of information about their immigrant forebears is later reinforced through brief (two-minute) presentations about their family backgrounds in front of the class.

The theme of third-semester German at Franklin & Marshall College, *Familie, Freundschaft und Heimat,* also lends itself well to the topic of German geography. We spend time on Germany's capital Berlin in conjunction with the film *Lola rennt* (1998), and students subsequently choose a German city to present to the class at a simulated tourism conference. In preparing the presentation, students follow a step-by-step process similar to that of their writing assignments. I offer linguistic support in the form of sample phrases that students must use to deliver their presentations in a culturally appropriate and well-structured form. In the appendix to their article "Developing Literacy and Literary Competence: Challenges for Foreign Language Departments" (2002) Byrnes and Kord offer a set of such phrases for presentations on texts in an advanced course on German comedy (65–67). Inspired by their work, I have created "phrase toolkits" for advanced student presentations on the life and work of an author, on an issue in contemporary Germany, on a poem and so on. These presentations are particularly important for students who plan to study in Germany, since the *Referat* is a central requirement for many courses at German universities. Because students must think carefully about what they want to say, practice extensively, memorize phrases and then work on speaking freely, the presentational mode helps students improve their interpersonal oral skills in ways that spontaneous speaking often cannot.

Reinvigorating the German program at Franklin & Marshall College

The literacies-based curricular reform in the German program at Franklin & Marshall College has served to revitalize the program by several measures, including our number of majors, retention rates from the third to fourth semester of the curriculum and assessment of student language proficiency. Since 2009, the total number of declared German majors at Franklin & Marshall College increased by nearly 400% and now averages between 15 and 18 students. In addition, over the past eight years, we have retained 59% of students enrolled in third-semester German (the last semester of the college's language requirement) to the fourth semester, and most of those students have chosen to major or minor in German. Assessment data also points to the success of the new German curriculum. From 2012–14, we administered a modified Goethe-Institut B1 exam in third-year German. Student language proficiency was borne out in the 100% passing rate on the exam in all three years.

In exit interviews, graduating seniors were asked to reflect on their experiences with the integrated curriculum at Franklin & Marshall College. Nearly every respondent described its positive impact on their learning and their decision to pursue German as a course of study. As one student in 2015 wrote: "I think it's the way to approach teaching the language – if the students only learn the grammar during the first years, they will have a weak connection to the culture and therefore will be less likely to continue with the language." A student writing in 2016 concurred: "I think this integration is an important part of the German curriculum. It keeps students interested in taking German past the completion of the language requirement."

A year after the release of the MLA report, the *Chronicle of Higher Education* published the following quote from MLA executive director Rosemary G. Feal: "Without changes in the structure of language departments and approaches to teaching foreign languages, the profession may see the language major disappear entirely within the next decade or two" (Wasley 2008). Ten years later, the profession as a whole is still faced with the urgent task of rethinking how we teach and learn in the foreign language classroom. It is simply not enough for students to acquire "language skills." They must develop the ability to interpret and critically evaluate, orally and in writing, texts of all kinds. Only then will they come to understand and appreciate not only the different beliefs and values, but the different ways of thinking that underlie the discourses of all of the world's languages.

Notes

1 This approach to curricular integration stands in contrast to those which seek to bring content to the lower levels of the curriculum through German Studies courses offered in English.
2 For more information about the German curriculum at Franklin & Marshall College, including an overview of curricular themes, goals for the major and a detailed curriculum map, visit the department's website.
3 Instructors can find high-quality works of German youth literature by reviewing the winners of the "Deutscher Jugendliteraturpreis" in the category of "Jugendbuch." The website archive of the *Jugendliteraturpreis* extends back to the year 2000, and the site includes short summaries of each book. One should note that many of the nominees are works in translation, but the name of the translator always appears with the author, making it easy to distinguish works in the German original from translations.
4 Kramsch and Nolden believe that the culturally determined gaps in students' knowledge – gaps that interfere with their understanding of a foreign language text – provide a valuable opportunity for "oppositional practice" in the classroom. When students enter into dialogue with the text and each other, thereby transforming the text from the position of outsider, they begin to develop what Kramsch and Nolden describe as "cross-cultural literacy." The authors apply this term not to the exchange of products or ideas across cultures, but to the "relational process of border crossing itself" (30). In this way, the very act of reading – the struggle to comprehend and respond to a foreign language text – allows students to travel into and participate in another culture while still maintaining a sense of otherness and difference.

5 Another invaluable resource for those seeking to develop a multiliteracies-based language curriculum is Paesani, Allen and Dupuy's book *A Multiliteracies Framework for Collegiate Foreign Language Teaching* (2016). Aimed at an audience of graduate assistants in methods courses, the book concisely outlines the theoretical underpinnings of literacies-based language instruction, as well as how those ideas can be practically enacted within the context of the four skills.
6 For more details on the reading journal and its format, see Redmann's article "An Interactive Reading Journal for all Levels for the Foreign Language Curriculum."
7 Swaffar and Arens make the point that learning isolated lists of words in beginning foreign language courses leaves students unprepared when they later encounter those words in context: "textbooks tend to isolate the furniture names instead of introducing them through authentic texts: FL movies, book excerpts, or magazine articles that illustrate various types of home or apartment interiors, all of which would help students see the contexts within which the vocabulary resides" (2005, 21).
8 Students and instructors alike often shy away from the idea of borrowing words and phrases because of the oft-cited prohibition against plagiarism and the notion that we should foster in students "creative" language use. The emphasis on creativity comes out of the communicative classroom, where we ask students to make meaning by applying grammar rules and choosing their own words from a vast array of possibilities. Maxim notes that this is an individualistic rather than social understanding of language, and although student utterances generated in this way might be linguistically accurate, they're only meaningful when situated in a social context and accepted by a discourse community (2009, "It's Made to Match," 183).

Bibliography

Almanya – Willkommen in Deutschland. Directed by Yasemin Samdereli, Concorde, 2011.
Byrnes, Heidi. "The Future of German in American Education: A Summary Report." *Die Unterrichtspraxis*, vol. 29, no. 2, 1996, pp. 253–261.
Byrnes, Heidi, and Susanne Kord. "Developing Literacy and Literary Competence: Challenges for Foreign Language Departments." *SLA and the Literature Classroom: Fostering Dialogues*, edited by Virginia M. Scott and Holly Tucker, Heinle, 2002, pp. 35–73.
Dykstra-Pruim, Pennylyn, and Jennifer Redmann. *Schreiben lernen: A Writing Guide for Learners of German*. Yale UP, 2011.
Eigler, Friederike. "Designing a Third-Year German Course for a Content-Oriented, Task-Based Curriculum." *Die Unterrichtspraxis*, vol. 34, no. 2, 2001, pp. 107–113.
Department of German Undergraduate Program Curriculum. Georgetown U, 2016, german.georgetown.edu/undergraduate/curriculum/. Accessed 8 Jun. 2020.
Kern, Richard. "Literacy and Advanced Foreign Language Learning: Rethinking the Curriculum." *Advanced Foreign Language Learning: A Challenge to College Programs*, edited by Heidi Byrnes and Hiram Maxim, Heinle, 2004, pp. 2–18.
Kern, Richard. *Literacy and Language Teaching*. Oxford UP, 2000.
Kern, Richard, and Jean Marie Schultz. "Beyond Orality: Investigating Literacy and the Literary in Second and Foreign Language Instruction." *Modern Language Journal*, vol. 89, no. 3, 2005, pp. 381–392.
Kramsch, Claire, and Thomas Nolden. "Redefining Literacy in a Foreign Language." *Die Unterrichtspraxis*, vol. 27, no. 1, 1994, pp. 28–35.
Lola rennt. Directed by Tom Tykwer, X-Film Creative Pool, 1998.

Lomicka, Lara, and Gillian Lord. "Ten Years after the MLA Report: What has Changed in Foreign Language Departments?" *ADFL Bulletin*, vol. 44, no. 2, 2018, pp. 116–120.

Looney, Dennis, and Natalie Lusin. *Enrollments in Languages Other Than English in United States Institutions of Higher Education, Summer 2016 and Fall 2016: Final Report*. MLA, 2019, www.mla.org/content/download/110154/2406932/2016-Enrollments-Final-Report.pdf. Accessed 2 April 2020.

Maxim, Hiram H. "'It's Made to Match!' Linking L2 Reading and Writing through Textual Borrowing." *Crossing Languages and Research Methods: Analyses of Adult Foreign Language Reading*, edited by Cindy Brantmeier, Information Age Publishing, 2009, pp. 97–122.

Maxim, Hiram H. "Articulating Foreign Language Writing Development at the Collegiate Level: A Curriculum-Based Approach." *Language Program Articulation: Developing a Theoretical Foundation*, edited by Catherine M. Barrette and Kate Paesani, Heinle, 2005, pp. 78–93.

Maxim, Hiram H., et al. "Overcoming Curricular Bifurcation: A Departmental Approach to Curriculum Reform." *Die Unterrichtspraxis*, vol. 46, no. 1, 2013, pp. 1–26.

MLA Ad Hoc Committee on Foreign Languages. "Foreign Languages and Higher Education: New Structures for a Changed World." *Profession*, 2007, pp. 234–245.

"*The National K-16 Foreign Language Enrollment Survey Report*." American Councils for International Education, 2017.

Paesani, Kate, et al. *A Multiliteracies Framework for Collegiate Foreign Language Teaching*. Prentice-Hall, 2016.

Redmann, Jennifer. "An Interactive Reading Journal for all Levels of the Foreign Language Curriculum." *Foreign Language Annals*, vol. 38, no. 4, 2005, pp. 484–493.

Swaffar, Janet, and Katherine Arens. *Remapping the Foreign Language Curriculum: An Approach through Multiple Literacies*. MLA, 2005.

Wasley, Paula. "MLA Report on Foreign-Language Education Continues to Provoke Debate." *The Chronicle of Higher Education*, 14 March 2008, A12.

2 Bringing global and local together
Program building through ACTFL's "Community C"

Wendy Westphal

In its *World-Readiness Standards for Learning Languages*, ACTFL identifies five goal areas for the language-learning classroom: Communication, Cultures, Connections, Comparisons, and Communities. The "Community C" is defined as providing students with the skills to "communicate and interact with cultural competence in order to participate in multilingual communities at home and around the world" and calls for "learners [to] use the language both within and beyond the classroom to interact and collaborate in their community and the globalized world" (1). ACTFL's 2011 survey of 2,134 language instructors regarding their implementation of the World-Readiness Standards, "A Decade of Foreign Language Standards: Influence, Impact and Future Directions" reveals that the "Community C" ranks last in the percent of classroom time (8%) dedicated to teaching each "C" and for this reason is dubbed the "Lost C" in the report (47). By contrast, the most emphasis in classroom instruction was reported as going to Communication (70%) and Cultures (22%) (26). Teachers stated that the "Community C," along with the "Connections C" were the "most difficult to teach" and found the goal area "nebulous, out of their control, and not assessable" (26). In addition, teachers interpreted the goal as requiring them to take students into the local community or abroad. Thus, despite the importance of the "Community C" as the motor for language instruction in its ability to bring people together, language teachers are not incorporating it into their courses.

One of my strategies in building the German program at Marian University has been to focus on the "Community C" by intentionally creating a sense of community with the language learners on campus and then connecting my students with German activities and resources in the local community and region. For example, these activities include Skyping with students studying abroad in Austria, hosting native German speakers as class guests, organizing German class trips to Chicago to visit the German American Chamber of Commerce and the Goethe-Institut and also establishing a shadowing internship at a German hospital. Through this engagement, the German program has grown significantly and is now averaging fifteen to twenty minors where there were no minors previously.

Institutional and departmental profile

Marian University is a small, private Catholic university, located in Indiana's state capitol, Indianapolis. Marian University serves more than 2,400 undergraduate students, the large majority of whom (2,200) are traditional students from the Midwest. In addition, between the College of Osteopathic Medicine and other graduate programs, Marian University also serves 1,160 graduate students ("This is What We're Made Of"). While this makes it a comprehensive university, its mission is informed by the Franciscan and the liberal arts traditions, since the university was founded as a Franciscan college in 1937 by the Sisters of St. Francis of Oldenburg, Indiana. What is especially unique about Marian's history is that the college (which became a university in 2009) grew out of a school in Oldenburg, Indiana specifically established to serve German-speaking children. The school was founded in 1851 by Sr. Theresa Hackelmeier who emigrated from Vienna, Austria to Indiana for this purpose. The order to which Sister (later Mother) Hackelmeier belonged was a German-speaking order, thus Marian University has a strong German heritage.

The Department of Languages and Cultures is a small department with five full-time faculty members: three in Spanish, one in French and one in German. Since I became a full-time faculty member at Marian University in 2012, my responsibilities for German have comprised only half of my duties (of a 4/4 teaching load), as I was also director of study abroad and department chair. Currently, the department offers a major in Spanish and minors in the Classics, French, German and Spanish. Two years ago, French/German/Spanish for the Professions minors were successfully introduced alongside the existing language minors to offer coursework that would complement the curriculum of business and nursing students. In addition, the department is planning on proposing a Languages and Cultures major for students who would like to advance their studies in French or German beyond the minor level. A languages major would allow students to broaden their linguistic abilities by taking courses in more than one language and would include a community-engaged learning or study abroad requirement.

When I started my position, one of my primary goals was clear: to revitalize a German program that consisted of introductory classes and just one student in third-semester German. For the past eight years, the German program has grown and averages between 15–20 minors, many of whom have studied abroad in Salzburg, Heidelberg or Eichstätt, Germany. Three years ago, my application to establish a chapter of the German Honor Society, Delta Phi Alpha, at Marian University was approved, and since then, we have inducted 17 new student members. Many of Marian University's German minors have been successful in competitions for external scholarships and national awards such as the Fulbright ETA to Germany, the USTA program to teach English in Austria, the DAAD summer scholarship, the Delta Phi Alpha study abroad scholarship and the national Gilman Scholarship for a study abroad program in Austria. One German minor completed a paid year-long internship at the German American Chamber of Commerce in Chicago and another was offered a full-time position at his internship location in Austria at the end of his semester abroad. It is gratifying that although German is just a minor, it has played such a prominent role in the students' post-graduation professional experiences.

Structural challenges and opportunities

As those in small language programs well know, there are a plethora of innate structural obstacles to program growth. Because there is just one person responsible for the program (or in my case, 50% of a person), there are automatic limitations on the number and variety of courses that can be offered as well as on all extra-curricular activities. As the only representative of the culture, the professor must be skilled in connecting to students and creating a sense of German identity on campus. Scheduling and students' time conflicts are another barrier. Since Marian University's five most popular majors (nursing, business management, biology, marketing and accounting) are all B.S. degrees with a 60-credit requirement (or higher), adding a double major or even a minor can be a challenging scheduling puzzle. Students' course conflicts have frequently prompted me to change my course meeting times, to work independently with students, help students enroll in German courses at neighboring institutions or complete course requirements while studying abroad. In addition, our department found that some program advisors were encouraging students to take their language requirement later in their studies, which made it impossible for interested students who began learning the language in the introductory level to add a major or minor.

Marian University's vision aims to be global: As published on the Marian University's website "Vision, Mission, and Values," we strive "to provide an education distinguished in its ability to prepare transformative leaders for service to the world." However, despite this formal commitment to providing "service to the world," the language requirement is just one course. Students meet with their academic advisors mid-semester to plan their schedules for the subsequent semester, so at this point, students have decided whether they will continue in the language beyond the requirement or not. Having just a one-course requirement means that the first half of the semester is a vital time in which the professor must spark the student's desire to continue learning the language. In terms of what the second course "counts for" once the general education requirement has been filled, the course could be taken as an elective, but generally, the students who continue beyond the first semester decide to minor in the language. Recognizing that declaring a language minor after just eight weeks of instruction is a big step, the department has lowered the six-course minor requirements in French and German to begin with the first introductory language course. This provides a sense of accomplishment and an incentive to continue for students in even the first semester, who can say that they have completed one-sixth of the minor requirements.

Fortunately, recent changes to the general education curriculum have created opportunities for all languages which have increased enrollment in intermediate and advanced classes as well as the number of students who sign up for a minor. One change is the requirement that students complete a minor or equivalent in an area outside of their major fields. Another change is the elimination of the "test out" option of the one-semester language requirement. The new general education requirement stipulates that students take a language course on campus at the level into which they placed or take an introductory course in a new language. Parallel to this, our department proposed and instituted a policy of offering "back credit" for up to two courses for students who place beyond the 101 level. This serves as an incentive for students to take the placement test seriously and makes completing a minor more feasible. Since the large majority of Marian University's students decide to continue in the language they had in high school (i.e., Spanish), the introduction of "back credit" was a highly successful strategy for the Spanish program which saw its enrollment numbers shift away from the introductory courses into intermediate and advanced courses. German and French, which have a dozen or so students test into intermediate and upper-level courses each year, also now see more students enrolling in courses they would have previously tested out of. For these students, the minor has become more easily achievable, something that is especially important for students pursuing a B.S. degree.

Another frequently cited challenge in the United States is the nationwide decline in interest in learning foreign languages. The MLA's most recent report, *Enrollments in Languages Other Than English in United States Institutions of Higher Education*, shows an overall decrease in modern language enrollments since 2006 and in German, a decrease from 95,613 students in 2009 to 80,594 students in 2016 (32). The national trend reflects an urgent need for language programs to reconsider their goals and how they align with the current generation's motivations for learning in general and, in particular, in the multi-year commitment needed to learn a foreign language.

In *How Learning Works*, Susan Ambrose and her coauthors (2010) remind us that student motivation is *the* key to successful learning and that motivation "influences the direction, intensity, persistence, and quality of the learning behaviors in which students engage" (68–69). What motivates today's students? Jean Twenge's (2017) study of the current generation, *iGen: Why Today's Super-Connected Kids are Growing up Less Rebellious, More Tolerant, Less Happy – and Completely Unprepared for Adulthood* confirms that today's students have a highly practical and transactional attitude towards the value of learning. She summarizes:

> Even in college, where students have more of a choice about being there, a similar pattern emerges: compared to previous generations,

iGen'ers are more focused on getting a better job and less focused on getting a general education. iGen college students believe they are in class so that they can get a better job once they are out of class. Learning is less important. (172)

The consequences, as Twenge points out, are seen in recent public discussions on the value of higher education and the liberal arts: "to Boomer, GenX'er, and even many Millennial faculty and administrators, college is a place for learning and exploration" whereas "iGen'ers disagree: college, they feel, is a place to prepare for a career in a safe environment" (172–173). Ambrose et al. (2010) remind us that, more than ever, there are "many competing goals that vie for [the students'] attention, time, and energy, it is crucial to understand what may increase or decrease students' motivations" (69).

If practicality and skill application have become the most important measures of academic value, then connecting students with local organizations and communities is a logical way to show the real-world application of our field. As Sandy Cutshall (2012) points out in her article "More than a Decade of Standards: Integrating 'Communities' into Your Language Instruction" in *The Language Educator*, "involvement with target-language and target-culture communities is the culmination of nearly all language learning goals" (32). The opportunities of using the target language and engaging with the target culture reflect the practicality of language learning and thereby increases iGen's perception of the field's value. Furthermore, Ambrose et al. (2010) outline six strategies in order to "establish value" of the subject matter in the student's eyes. Each of these strategies to increase the perception of "value" can be directly reached through a variety of community-engaged learning or experiential learning course activities. These strategies are:

- Connect the Material to Students' Interests
- Provide Authentic, Real-World Tasks
- Show Relevance to Students' Current Academic Lives
- Demonstrate the Relevance of Higher-Level Skills to Students' Future Professional Lives
- Identify and Reward What You Value
- Show Your Own Passion and Enthusiasm for the Discipline (83–85)

Ambrose et al. (2010) posit that the possibility of applying learned skills helps shift student motivation from attaining "performance goals" (i.e., getting good grades) to "learning goals" (mastering the course material) (71). Cutshall points out that the Standards themselves connect student motivation to the application of the language: "students are highly motivated to excel in their study of a second language when they see immediate applications for the skills they learn" (37). "Applying learned skills" by using the language and cross-cultural skills gained with speakers of the language is the ultimate goal in language acquisition courses, therefore, giving students the opportunity to practice this at different levels should be integrated into each course in the form of community-engaged assignments.

Community engagement at Marian University

Marian University's roots as a school designed to serve others (initially children of German immigrants) means that community-engaged learning, service-learning and experiential-learning opportunities are strongly promoted. As a small institution embedded in a diverse urban environment, the importance of connecting students to the community is apparent everywhere. Marian University's billboard signs along the highway, the university's admission's webpage and publications from the Center for Teaching and Learning all promote the concept that "not all learning takes place inside the classroom." From Marian University's "Day of Service" during freshmen orientation to service-focused alternative spring break trips in Haiti, Guatemala and Honduras, opportunities for community-engaged learning can be found across the campus. In the Department of Languages and Cultures, my colleagues in Spanish and French have been able to show the immediate relevance of their languages by having students engage with local Spanish-speaking and French-speaking immigrants as part of course-related service-learning and community-engaged projects. Under the supervision of their language professors, Spanish and French students could practice and improve their language skills while volunteering as interpreters at local schools on parent-teacher conference nights or at free legal and medical clinics. French students helped French-speaking African and Haitian children with their homework in weekly tutor nights and even interned at the Alliance Française. These personal interactions give a human face to the language and the hands-on experiences clearly motivated the students to continue their language learning, even for those for whom studying abroad was not a feasible option.

I was eager to show the local relevancy of German but had no training in how to incorporate community-engaged learning experiences into my classes. Like many, I had completed my doctoral degree at a large research university in a department which did not incorporate or address community-engaged pedagogies or experiential-learning opportunities in its curriculum. Seeing my Marian colleagues' initiatives, however, inspired me to consider ways to overcome this gap in my training and connect students to the German community here in Indiana. The only question, considering that the German community does not share the needs of the new Spanish- and French-speaking immigrants, was how?

In-class community events

Like concentric circles, our "language communities" begin with a sense of class community at their center then emanate outward to incorporate the broader campus, local, regional and even global communities. Since there were only introductory German (and one intermediate) students when I started at Marian University, I could not rely on upper-level students to organize German Club-type activities or model the possible academic paths for the beginning language learners. The "inner circle" for the potential community was small and thus community-building needed to begin in German 101. Knowing how tightly planned the students' schedules are and how many competing priorities vie for students' attention, I made several planning decisions early on which have made the various events successful. While German Club activities, which are both fun and educational, are often relegated to the world of non-essential "extra credit" offerings (the organization of which is frequently delegated to a lecturer or graduate assistant), I decided it was critical for students to recognize the value of German activities. Thus, almost all activities I have organized have been tied to the course curriculum and many have been directly included in assessments of student learning. Because of this, participation is required. In order to make attendance feasible, I try to schedule the events during regular class meeting periods. By tying events to class content and assessments, I (unknowingly) was following two of the "strategies to establish value" outlined in *How Learning Works* by "identifying and rewarding what [I] value" and "providing authentic, real-world tasks" (83–85). Since "extra credit" reflects neither the priority we wish students to ascribe to our events, nor the work involved in organizing such an activity, my emphatic advice is to *ditch the extra-credit* and make the activity required. This will result in German events being well attended, which provides the foundation to create a sense of German community among the students.

One activity I organize almost every year is a guided tour of Indianapolis' Athenaeum, a beautiful former German *Turnhalle* which is located in downtown Indianapolis, just six miles from our campus. Afterwards, the class has a three-course German meal at the attached Rathskeller Restaurant. The introductory German classes are scheduled to meet Monday, Wednesday and Friday, with a double period over the noon hour on Wednesdays, which allows me to hold longer activities, such as the above trip, without creating conflicts with the following period. During the tour, students learn about Indiana's rich German heritage and the influences of the German population on the state – something even local students are often unaware of. During lunch, students experience an authentic German meal (complete with *Brezel*, *Senf* and *Sachertorte*) and have the chance to practice some basic restaurant vocabulary. While I might time the tour to take place when we are studying a food chapter, I have typically held it in the weeks before midterm, so the experience is fresh in their minds as they consider whether to continue with their study of German. Questions about the information they learn during the tour and at lunch are included on a test, but another possibility for assessing engagement would be, as suggested in Cutshall's article, to have students reflect on their learning in "community reflection portfolios," journals or through a LMS Discussion Board.

It is not necessary to leave campus, though, to have students use their German to "engage with authentic, real-world tasks." In fact, it may not even be necessary to leave the classroom! Inviting on-campus international students from Germany, Switzerland or Austria to our classes for students to interview is one easy way to show the local applicability of the skills students are learning. As homework prior to the class visit, students prepare interview questions based on topics recently covered. I supply German pastries and the lesson becomes a hybrid of a structured *Kaffeestunde*. In a similar vein, I invite students who have studied abroad in a German-speaking country to give a presentation about their experiences to my German classes, or – in the case of one student – share newly acquired baking skills during an Austrian lunch (with *Linzer Torte*!) held in the kitchen of a student dorm. I plan to formalize this student role by designating the returnees as "study abroad ambassadors" who are financially compensated for their class presentations. Hearing from a peer who has studied abroad motivates students to consider this as a viable opportunity for themselves.

Similarly, during semesters when we have students studying abroad, I plan a Skype session with them during our class period. Since the study abroad program is open to all students (not just those currently taking German), I hold the Skype session in a central location on campus and advertise it widely in advance through campus media venues. This visibility benefits both the German and the study abroad program. These Skype sessions can also be tied to course content and facilitate a human connection to current European events. For example, in the fall of 2015, students in the advanced *Written Communication* course followed the refugee crisis coverage in the German-language news, then Skyped with two Marian students studying in Salzburg who shared their first-hand impressions of the refugee crisis on the Austrian border to Germany. Additional assignments for this class included writing an email (in German) to the students who were studying abroad prior to the Skype sessions and writing an article about the refugee crisis for the end-of-semester newsletter. In addition, each year I organize an annual study-abroad fair, which is held in conjunction with a "Taste of Nations Lunch" hosted by the International Office. The event usually falls on one of our class days, but rather than cancel class, I have students attend the fair and meet with the program representative from our partner program in Austria to learn about the program and ask questions about topics we have covered in class.

Departmental and university-level community engagement

The next "step out" of the concentric circles of community engagement takes place at the departmental and university level, where students from each language program can see the work of students studying other languages. Our department collaborates with other departments and offices to organize a number of high-visibility language events each year which showcase student work to the entire university community. Over the past few years, we have held an annual World Poetry Day Celebration, an annual Cross-cultural Research Symposium and a semester-long celebration of international cinema.

World Poetry Day, 21 March, was designated by the UNESCO to celebrate "one of humanity's most treasured forms of cultural and linguistic expression and identity with the aim of supporting linguistic diversity through poetic expression and increasing the opportunity for endangered languages to be heard." At this festive evening event with international food, students, faculty and staff recite poems (in either English or another world language). The program contains the poem in the original language and its English translation. Recited poems may be by a published author or the student's original work. Collaboration with the International Office, the English Department and the Peer Tutors Office has made this a vibrant and popular cultural event in which students sample international dishes while listening to poems in as many as ten different languages.

While the World Poetry Day Celebration is more loosely connected to our class curriculum since it is not required in all courses, the annual Cross-cultural Research Symposium is directly aligned with the general education goals for our language courses, which stipulate that students be able to "explain world cultural similarities and differences." In order to ensure that this goal was met equally in each of the language courses, our department introduced a cross-cultural research project across all introductory and intermediate language courses. Working in groups, students research a cultural topic of their own choosing and make evidence-based, cross-cultural comparisons. Students have conducted cross-cultural research on everything from educational systems, to religious celebrations, to the penal codes and recidivism rates in different countries. During International Education Week in November, students make formal poster presentations as part of the Cross-cultural Research Symposium (Fig. 2.1–2.4). The format of this project fulfills three of the Association of American Colleges & Universities' "High-Impact Educational Practices": Diversity/Global Learning, Collaborative Assignments & Projects and Undergraduate Research. Held in the most central location on campus and covered in university media, the symposium is a true community event. Faculty, staff and upper-level students judge poster presentations, the dean provides welcoming remarks and announces the award recipients and attendees include the university's provost and president. In addition to fulfilling general education goals through high-impact practices, this event builds both a sense of program and departmental identity, while raising the academic profile of languages on campus.

The Cross-cultural Research Symposium raised the campus-wide awareness of the language department's culturally engaged work and opened the door for inter-departmental collaboration. The Communication Department's interest in formally incorporating community-engaged courses as part of its curriculum created a strategic opportunity for the Department of Languages and Cultures to cross-list a community-engaged language course with a

Figure 2.1 During International Education Week, students make formal poster presentations as part of the Cross-cultural Research Symposium (Fig 2.1–2.4)
*All photographs were taken by the author

Figure 2.2

Communication course. The more flexible nature of our *Oral Communication* language courses, with their general learning goals of improving oral ability in the language, allowed us to design assessments around community-engaged activities. Examples of these assessments include: a campus tour in German for local German high school students, a formal individual interview with a native speaker and German culture lessons for children in local after-school programs. The campus tour for local high school students fills two purposes

Bringing global and local together 33

Figure 2.3

Figure 2.4

by giving the German students in both high school and college a chance to use their German skills outside of the classroom and by allowing high school students to tour a local university. The Admissions Office provides the "talking points" of the tour (and, naturally, recruiting materials for our guests) and the students translate it into German and add their own personal stories. The high school teacher and her students had also collaborated with the Marian art professor on a project involving illustrated German letters, so a visit to the exhibition was included in the tour.

Another successful course activity is to conduct a formal interview with a native speaker of German. I "connect the materials to students' interests" (Ambrose et al. 2010, 83) by matching the students according to their majors with German-speaking community members. Students record the interview, transcribe a portion of it and present on the experience to the class. This activity can be used in other courses as well. For example, I have had students in the *Business German* courses interview German members of the local business community to learn about the differences in job interview etiquette in Germany versus the United States.

Furthermore, teaching lessons on German holidays (*Martinstag* and Christmas) to the local school children as part of an after-school program has become a vital part of the *Oral Communication* course which is especially appealing for students majoring in education. Marian University participates in a "College Mentors for Kids" program in which children from the Holy Angles Catholic School, a Notre Dame ACE Academy for under-served communities, are bussed to campus each week where they are partnered with their own college mentors and engage in supplemental learning opportunities. Students in the *Oral Communication in German* class prepare cultural lessons on St. Martin's Day and German Christmas traditions for the elementary school students. Activities for the lesson include reading and acting out the story of St. Martin, learning a German St. Martin's song and making St. Martin's lanterns. For the lesson on Christmas traditions, the German and American Christmas traditions are compared. Children leave their shoes outside the door and *Nikolaus* visits while they are in class. Since the best way to learn something is to teach it, college students gain a deep understanding of the cultural material as well as an introduction in basic pedagogical strategies and classroom management in this activity. In response to the evaluation question as to what the "most valuable" aspects to the *Oral Communication* course were, one student commented in the course evaluation that "giving the tour and teaching the lesson to the kids were more interesting and engaging assignments." As a variation of this activity in this year's class, the German students were invited to teach German holiday and language lessons to Burmese Girl and Boy Scouts who were working towards their "culture badge" (Fig. 2.5–2.8). The connection to the Burmese Scout groups arose through a German student who works closely with the local Burmese community. The power of serendipity and the flexibility to take advantage of community opportunities like these as they arise is key to being able to keep a one-person program fresh and interesting for the students.

Connecting to local organizations

Because of Indiana's strong German heritage, there are a number of organizations which actively promote German cultural education and have been willing to partner with Marian University. These organizations include: the Warburg Chapter of the American Council on Germany, the Indiana German Heritage Society, the German-American Klub, the Athenaeum Foundation,

Figure 2.5 German students teach holiday language lessons to Burmese Girl and Boy Scouts working towards their "cultural badge" (Fig. 2.5–2.8)

Figure 2.6

the *IGeL Schule*, the German *Samstagschule*, the *Carmel Christkindlmarkt*, the Indianapolis-Cologne Sister City Partnership and the German sister city partnerships of other cities and towns. This is not to mention the committees behind the countless *Oktoberfeste* and German heritage celebrations that take place throughout the state. Other organizations, like the International Center are not focused specifically on German-American relations but cosponsor German professional conferences like the 2018 Germany-Indiana Business Conference. Of these organizations, it is the Indiana German Heritage Society (IGHS) which has proven to be the greatest partner and through which I was

Figure 2.7

Figure 2.8

able to connect students to German events in the community. Because of the sense of community IGHS offers, I feel fortunate, both professionally and personally, to have been invited to join the board of directors. Through IGHS, I met many German professionals who have been generous in their willingness to speak on campus or host Marian students at their events, or even as interns. For example, for my *Collective Memory* course, an IGHS board member gave a guided walking tour of Indianapolis' German-American architectural history (Fig. 2.9). By examining German-designed monuments such as the Soldiers' and Sailors' Monument, students reflected on how

Bringing global and local together 37

German immigrants impacted America's contemporary collective memory. One student reflected in the end-of-semester evaluation: "I never realized how much debate, controversy, and intention was put into memorials, so I don't think that I will look at a monument or memorial the same way again! I also enjoyed opportunities to go out of the classroom and off campus, such as taking a walking tour of Indy with a focus on German-Americans and architecture." In addition, many of the German guest lecturers I have hosted on campus I met through the Indiana German Heritage Society. For example, the (German) CEO of the International Center gave a lecture on Marian's campus to the German and Business students about German-American business relations. A local German-American author who had written about her experiences as a child in a WWII American internment camp for Germans and Japanese shared these experiences with the German classes and my *First Year Seminar* class which was learning about the stories of refugees (Fig. 2.10). A graduate student from IUPUI's program on museum studies spoke about his research project on memorials in Berlin to my German *Collective Memory* students. While each lecture was tied to course content and held during class time, I "made an event" of each and increased the visibility of the German program by partnering with other classes (Business, First Year Seminar, History), opening the lecture up to

Figure 2.9 Walking tour of Indianapolis' German-American architecture

Figure 2.10 A guest speaker relates her experiences as a child in a German internment camp

the campus community and offering German refreshments. This visibility brought even the university president to several of the German lectures.

Beyond providing connections to others in Indianapolis' German and German-American community, the IGHS has hosted a number of special cultural events to which I was able to take Marian's German students. One event was the 2019 rededication of a former German *Turnhalle,* the Athenaeum, as *"Das Deutsche Haus"* on the 100th anniversary of the changing of the name as a result of post-WWI anti-German sentiments. The ceremony included a keynote speaker who spoke about WWI, a formal dinner and a reception with both local politicians and a representative from the German Consulate in Chicago. Perhaps the most venerable guests that the Indiana German Heritage Society has hosted were the Archduke of Habsburg, Markus Salvator von Habsburg and the Archduchess Hildegard. IGHS hosted them during their visit to Indiana in 2014 and organized a formal luncheon reception to which I was able to bring twenty fortunate German students from Marian University. In addition to welcome addresses and the exchange of gifts, there was a keynote lecture on the historical significance of the Habsburg Empire, a catered German meal and a chance for the students to speak with the Archduke and the Archduchess (Fig. 2.11–2.12). This, I am certain, is a day that the students will never forget, as it brought representatives from the pages of their history books to life.

While most of the educational programs organized by the Indiana German Heritage Society focus on German-American culture rather than the German language, there is an annual essay contest in which students research and write an essay about a German-American topic in German. Taking part in this contest is a built-in requirement for students in my *Written Communication in German* course, which focuses on improving students' writing skills.

Figure 2.11 Marian students at the IGHS reception for Archduke Markus Salvator von Habsburg (Fig. 2.11–2.12)

Figure 2.12

Participation in the essay contest fills two of the strategies that Ambrose et al. (2010) cite as establishing "value" in the course material: "provide authentic, real-world tasks" and "show relevance to students' current academic lives" (83–85). The possibility of receiving an award provides a strong incentive to students. Marian University award recipients are recognized in the university's campus newsletter and, like the awards they receive for their posters at the Cross-cultural Research Symposium, they can list the awards in their professional résumés. Furthermore, contest winners are invited to attend the IGHS *Stammtisch* and program when they receive their awards, which provides another chance for them to connect with members of the local German-American community.

Some German organizations may be able to provide financial support for educational German events on the university's campus. One such organization in Indianapolis is the Eric E. Warburg chapter of the American Council on Germany (ACG). The ACG is a strong supporter of academic German events and the Warburg chapter, through the active engagement of Sven Schumacher, the Honorary Consul General to Germany, has hosted dozens of lecturers in Indianapolis. In the fall of 2019, for example, the ACG and *Netzwerk Deutsch* generously cosponsored a trans-generational panel discussion with Germans from the East that I organized at Marian University to commemorate the 30th anniversary of the Fall of the Wall. Small programs generally have a correspondingly modest budget and it is partnerships with organizations like the American Council on Germany, the DAAD and the AATG (though its *Netzwerk Deutsch* grants) which make it possible for even small programs to host larger German events on campus.

Community connections in the greater region

If the center of the concentric circles of community begins with our classroom, then emanates outward to include the university and the local German community, the next "ring" to the circle is the larger regional community. Using the greater region around Indianapolis has been a useful strategy in the promotion of community since cities such as Chicago and Cincinnati have many German resources offering the potential for intercultural connections. Once a year, I plan a larger trip for the German students which is tied to course content and which "demonstrates the relevance of higher-level skills to students' future professional lives" (Ambrose et al. 2010, 83–85). These trips mean that students miss classes for the day, but the supportive faculty at Marian University have always excused students from their classes and students have regularly reported that the field trips are among the "most valuable" aspects of the courses. Examples of the field trips I have organized for students include tours of the CANDLES Holocaust Museum in Terre Haute to hear Holocaust survivor, Eva Kor, speak, a tour of the "Over the Rhine" German district of Cincinnati (Fig. 2.13–2.14) and a trip to Chicago for the Business German students (Fig. 2.15–2.16). In Chicago, we visited the German quarter around Lincoln Street, toured the DANK Haus, had lunch at the Chicago Brauhaus, visited the Goethe-Institut and had a tour of the German American Chamber of Commerce. Because of the amount of German used, students described the day as a "mini-immersion" in German language and culture. Serendipity once again played a role in our trip to Chicago and the ability to connect to different German communities. One of the German minors who attended was later offered (and accepted) a full-year paid internship at the German American Chamber of Commerce.

Bringing global and local together 41

Figure 2.13 Touring Cincinnati: The Over-the-Rhine District, Berlin Wall Memorial and dinner at the *Hofbräuhaus* (Fig. 2.13–2.14)

Figure 2.14

Connecting to the global community

As shown in the fall 2019 issue of *Unterrichtspraxis*, "Teaching German Studies in a Global Context," making a global connection to the German-speaking world is more important now than ever and studying abroad provides a strong motivation for students to learn German. Global connections can be facilitated through faculty-led study abroad program offerings or a standing study abroad partner in a German-speaking country. Marian University has a partner program in Austria and the continuity of having Marian

42 Wendy Westphal

Figure 2.15 Visit to the German American Chamber of Commerce, Lunch at the Chicago Brauhaus and walking from the Goethe Institute to the GACC (Fig. 2.15–2.16)

Figure 2.16

students at the same location year after year encourages timid new travelers to consider studying abroad. In addition, this program offers students the option of a homestay, in which they can connect more directly with Austrians, and an internship with a company in the city, which allows students to gain global work experience before they enter the job market. Through yet another serendipitous connection, last year I was able to establish a shadowing internship for Marian pre-med students at a German teaching hospital in northern Germany (Fig. 2.17). One of our German students had a connection to the head vascular surgeon and proposed a partnership between Marian University and the hospital. We invited the surgeon to campus for a week of lectures and meetings and last summer, he supervised eight students during the shadowing internship over the summer. Not only did the students who participated in the program connect with the community in northern Germany, but the students at Marian University had the opportunity to meet him during his visit and learn about public health issues in Germany. Even though the undergraduate students (pre-med majors) did not enroll in German language courses on their return from the internship, I hope that the awareness of how German can directly impact their major-area studies will provide the incentive for more pre-med biology students to choose German for their language requirement.

Conclusion

Although it is hard to assess whether students have become *life-long* language learners, as is outlined in ACTFL's Standard 5.2, community connections tend to be extremely well-received by Marian University's students who frequently cite the experiences as one of the "most valuable" course activities. While studying abroad on the other side of the ocean might be the ultimate goal for many students in their German Studies, connecting to local and regional German organizations shows the relevancy of language learning closer to home. In addition, community engagement, as Japanese teacher Lynn Sessler notes, is "a way of advocating on behalf of your language program," which is an increasingly important aspect of language programs (Cutshall 2012, 37). Community-engaged learning is an especially effective vehicle in involving practically minded iGen'ers. By providing authentic, real-

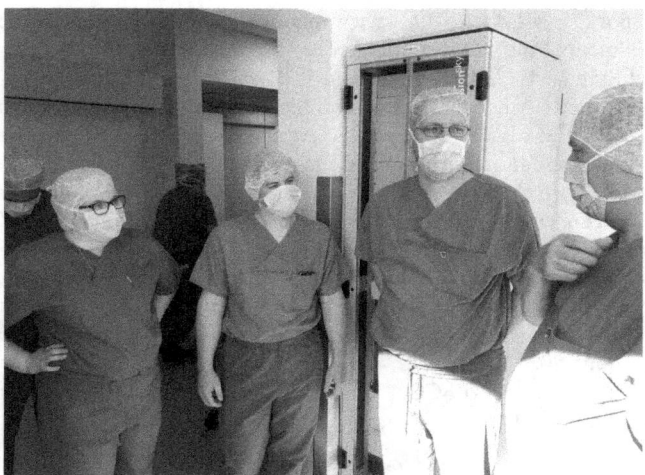

Figure 2.17 Shadowing internship for pre-med students at a German teaching hospital in northern Germany

world tasks which are relevant to the students' academic and future professional lives, community engaged activities naturally incorporate the strategies which "establish value." These community activities represent a variety of ways to bring the global and local together in order to promote global learning and they show that global learning starts in one's own backyard – indeed, it starts with the relationships built in our classes. As one graduating senior sums up the experiences in her last German course evaluation: "I am going to miss the fun, thought-provoking courses and the sense of community that I enjoyed while in Dr. Westphal's classes."

Bibliography

"A Decade of Foreign Language Standards: Influence, Impact and Future Directions." U.S. Department of Education. *Title VI: International Research and Studies Program*, April 2011, www.actfl.org/sites/default/files/publications/standards/StandardsImpactSurvey.pdf. Accessed 2 June 2020.

Admission Requirements. Marian University, www.marian.edu/admissions/admission-requirements. Accessed 2 June 2020.

Ambrose, Susan A., et al. *How Learning Works: 7 Research-Based Principles for Smart Teaching*. Jossey-Bass: A Wiley Imprint, 2010.

Cutshall, Sandy. "More Than a Decade of Standards: Integrating 'Communities' into your Language Instruction." *The Language Educator*, vol. 6, no. 6, 2012, www.actfl.org/sites/default/files/publications/standards/Communities.pdf. Accessed 2 June 2020.

Kuh, George. D. "High-Impact Educational Practices." *Association of American Colleges & Universities*, 2008, www.aacu.org/node/4084. Accessed 2 June 2020.

Learning Experience Framework for Marian University. Marian University, www.marian.edu/docs/default-source/Center-for-Teaching-and-Learning/marian-university-learning-experience-framework.pdf?sfvrsn=0. Accessed 2 June 2020.

Looney, Dennis, and Natalia Lusin. "Enrollments in Languages Other Than English in United States Institutions of Higher Education, Summer 2016 and Fall 2016: Final Report." MLA, 2019, www.mla.org/content/download/110154/2406932/2016-Enrollments-Final-Report.pdf. Accessed 2 June 2020.

The National Standards Collaborative Board. *World-Readiness Standards for Learning Languages*. 4th ed., American Council on the Teaching of Foreign Languages, 2014.

This is What We're Made Of: Admissions: At a Glance. Marian University, www.marian.edu/admissions/at-a-glance. Accessed 2 June 2020.

Twenge, Jean M. *iGen: Why Today's Super-Connected Kids are Growing up Less Rebellious, More Tolerant, Less Happy – and Completely Unprepared for Adulthood*. Atria, 2017.

Vision, Mission, and Values: About Marian. Marian University, www.marian.edu/about-marian/vision-mission-and-values. Accessed 2 June 2020.

Where will you go?: Admissions. Marian University, www.marian.edu/admissions. Accessed 2 June 2020.

World Poetry Day. UNESCO, en.unesco.org/commemorations/worldpoetryday. Accessed 2 June 2020.

3 Learning German in and for the 21st century

Birgit A. Jensen, Susanne Lenné Jones, David L. Smith and Jill E. Twark

College students need an education that prepares them to succeed in their future careers and private lives. Nowadays, educators release their graduates into a world in which ever-evolving technologies interconnect global communities and economies at lightning speed, yet a new wave of political isolationism and tribalism[1] threatens the study of other cultures at a time when we need it most. An education fit for the 21st century equips learners with the skills to tackle these civic and global crises confronting them. Successful graduates know how to (see Figure 3.1).

All these competencies are transferable skills, not knowledge retained by rote memorization. They are the outcomes of a progressive education, i.e. instruction in which learners experience or "do" what they are expected to acquire.[2] This type of learning focuses on students, engages them by inviting them to discover answers for themselves and is assessed through performance, not tested on paper (Nehring et al. 2019, 36). Contemporary progressive pedagogy includes features that transcend the individual, such as communal cooperation, social responsibility and civic accountability. To foster these traits and develop learners' abilities to effect social change, progressive teaching emphasizes cooperative learning,[3] service learning, experiential education and learning by doing (Sun and Yuan).

As graduates enter workplaces that evolve faster than ever before, they will be asked to solve problems that are constantly changing, requiring different approaches and solutions. Thus, they must be able to adapt swiftly and bring creative and innovative thinking skills to these ever-changing tasks. As the European University Association concludes in a recent report: "The complex questions of the future will not be solved 'by the book,' but by creative, forward-looking individuals and groups who are not afraid to question established ideas and are able to cope with the insecurity and uncertainty that this entails" (6). Some of the challenges facing humanity today – such as food security, global health, social inclusivity or ecological sustainability – require the efficient collaboration of individuals who are attuned to cultural differences in communication and open to possible solutions that may seem radical within their national contexts. Such individuals are products of an

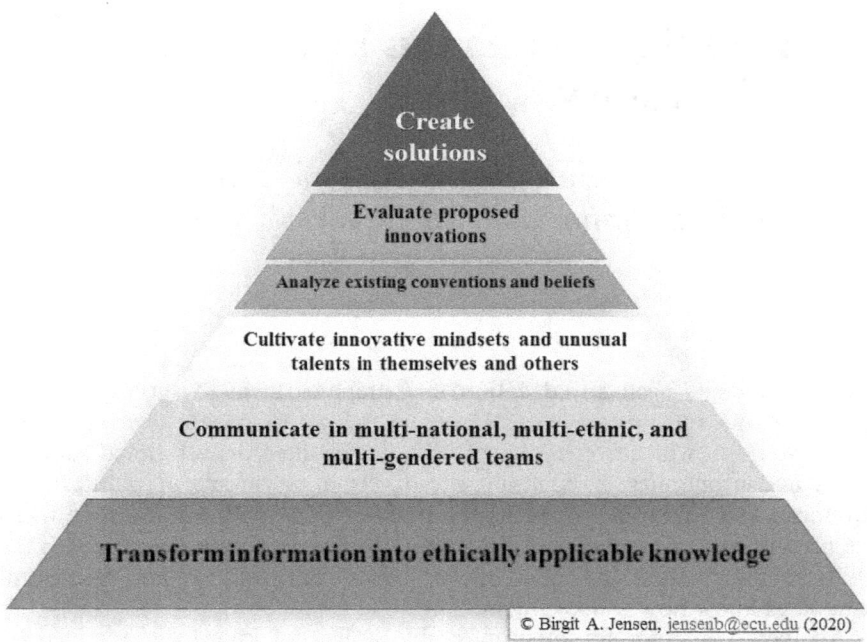

Figure 3.1

educational process that emphasizes open-mindedness and embraces the challenges of ambiguity.

Industry and government, in contrast, have increasingly criticized the education sector for its failure to produce the creative leaders essential for technical innovation, economic growth and international competition (Kim 2011; Helding 2011; Rampersad and Patel 2014). This criticism calls on educators to become creative, innovative participants in the 21st-century learning community. This means that educators must design courses that teach students to work together to find novel solutions to ever-changing problems. Traditional ("first generation" or "big C") notions of creativity conceive of it as an innate quality of gifted and artistic individuals. But the creative process is linked with the ability to work in partnership with others (Paulus et al. 2018). "Second generation" or "little c" models thus describe creativity as collaborative, purpose-driven processes that can be taught (Leonard-Barton and Swap 1999; Runco 2004, 21–30). Several scholars, including McWilliam and Dawson (2008), Feinstein (2006) and Jackson et al., (2006) have reflected on ways educators may design curricula that develop their students' creative capital and align closely with the central tenets of progressive pedagogy.

Instructors who rely on these teaching approaches orient themselves along three frameworks: the making of relevant personal meaning;[4] collaborative learning[5] and cognitive scaffolding.[6] With the digitalization of educational

Learning German in the 21st century 47

technology, progressive practitioners and learners alike began sharing and expanding their contributions to a more hands-on education. This fusion of contemporary progressive education and instructional technology undergirds the concept of 21st-century pedagogy and helps students flourish in today's fast-evolving intellectual, technological and professional landscapes.

After acknowledging the profound shift from an industrial to a knowledge economy, the U.S. Department of Education advised the nation in 1983 to become a "Learning Society." Since then, a coalition of prominent organizations and businesses has urged educators to cultivate students' problem-solving skills, commitment to life-long learning and digital literacy.[7] The most influential of these partners in educational reform is P21, the non-profit organization Partnership for 21st Century Learning. P21 identified a spectrum of competencies to be placed "at the center of learning."[8]

A degree in German (language, literature or education) successfully supports its graduates in attaining the characteristics of a 21st-century global denizen when the curriculum goes beyond "just German." Providing such an education and marketing its benefits to students and administrators is crucial for the survival and growth of smaller programs such as ours at East Carolina University (ECU). Home to a German program of four tenured professors and one part-time lecturer, ECU is a semi-rural institution boasting an enrollment of 23,000 undergraduates and 6,000 graduate students.

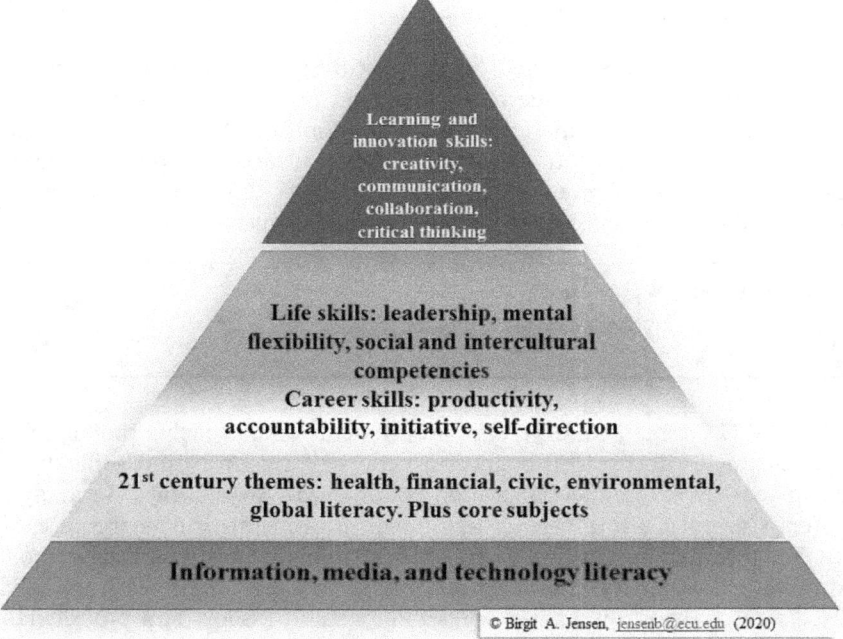

Figure 3.2

Undergraduates can complete a B.S. degree, which typically does not require language study, or a B.A. degree, which requires 12 semester hours of coursework in a foreign language. Students who enroll in language classes usually take Spanish, partly because of the dearth of other languages offered in high schools in our region. Since 2008, the university has undergone permanent budgetary cuts in excess of $165 million, resulting in the elimination of programs and faculty positions. Our Foreign Languages and Literatures Department responded to these institutional pressures by consolidating our three B.A. and three B.S. in Education degree programs into one degree, with concentrations in three languages (Spanish, French and German) and language education.

To maintain a competitive, relevant curriculum, we German section faculty members continuously adjust our teaching and outreach efforts. Three of our most impactful and innovative instructional practices are: teaching creative collaboration strategies through film production (Susanne Lenné Jones); introducing professional preparation and service learning into the curriculum (Jill E. Twark) and encouraging Flipped Learning 3.0 (Birgit A. Jensen). David L. Smith describes some of our outreach events that have helped draw attention to our program, thereby increasing possibilities for scholarship and activity funding as well as student recruitment.

Autonomous cultural production: developing student creativity and collaborative skills

In early 2005, the US Council on Competitiveness (COC) announced that "innovation will be the single most important factor in determining ... success through the twenty-first century" (Wince-Smith 2006, 12–14). The report calls for a national educational strategy that teaches innovation, risk-taking and collaboration. In order to grow their students' creative capital, McWilliam and Dawson (2008, 639–640) suggest that instructors:

Explain less and welcome errors

Promote coinvention/cocreation with separation

Lead and follow

One ECU German course that invites students to approach a problem from different angles, to use and connect a variety of resources and skills and to exchange ideas through collaboration is our third-year offering, Germany on Screen: Current Cultural Trends and Social Movements.[9] It incorporates the P21 learning and innovation skills (critical thinking, communication, collaboration and creativity) into tasks and projects such as film reviews, research-based film analyses, discussions, presentations and a short film project. How the film project in particular encourages students to collaborate and contribute creatively is discussed here.

From day one, the film project runs parallel to the viewing and discussion of contemporary German short and feature films. Students learn basic German vocabulary of film analysis, discover how film techniques create meaning and discuss these films in terms of the representation of current trends and social movements. Films about National Socialism and justice (*Sophie Scholl: Die letzten Tage* and *Das Labyrinth des Schweigens*); the end of the GDR (*Good Bye, Lenin!* and *Das Leben der Anderen*); migration (*Almanya: Willkommen in Deutschland* and *Willkommen auf Deutsch*); or anarchy, populism and terror (*Die Welle*) allow students to think about topics such as resistance, civil disobedience, political engagement, historical perspectives, concepts of home and the reasons for migration or the resurgence of populism and terror attacks in today's society, while growing increasingly literate in visual media and film analysis.

These skills are honed as students produce their own film. During the first week, three groups of students each choose a topic and write a brief synopsis which they pitch to the entire class in a brief group presentation. After the final topic is selected from the three options, participants sign up for various filmmaking roles and begin working first on the storyline and then on the screenplay. To encourage artistic freedom, no word requirement is given for on screenplay, though a minimum of 15 minutes is set for the film's duration. Instead, the rubric calls for a creative plot and dialogues that tell an interesting, logical, complete and easy-to-follow story in three parts, one provided by each group. The story must have a well-developed theme and recognizable point of view. Each of the three screenplay sections undergoes multiple reviews by peers and the instructor before filming and editing begins.

Explaining less and welcoming error

By reducing the number and length of lectures to increase collaborative class time, the instructor encourages students to learn by experimenting, making errors and helping each other to resolve issues. Some such opportunities to learn from mistakes are built into the project given that individual students write sections of the screenplay and then revise each other's portions; other occasions to learn from mishaps may arise spontaneously. In all cases, students have full autonomy and are encouraged to work together inside and outside the classroom to find solutions to the issues they encounter, such as team time management, conflicting ideas about the creative process or work-sharing.[10] By dedicating an entire semester to this process, team members have the time to discover problems and experiment with possible solutions.

Cocreating with separation

In order to reap maximum benefits from the collaborative, creative processes, students need to learn how to be "both separate from and attentive to those they work with and rely on" when completing a project (McWilliam and Dawson 2008, 640). Thus, each student takes responsibility for a specific filmmaking role, such as director, camera operator, editor, stage director (including props), lighting, sound director (including music) or make-up and costume artist. After researching their role with provided handouts and online readings, learners explain its function to their peers in formal presentations that include analyses of a film scene of their choice in which that film technique is instrumental to the creation of meaning.

Students collaborate closely in writing and editing the screenplay as well as during filming. Three teams write the manuscript after the storyline has been established. After each team has finished its portion, the other two teams edit and revise it, giving them the opportunity to practice providing, receiving and implementing constructive feedback for the benefit of the common project. After the film script is complete, each student expert adds *Director's Notes* explaining how his or her chosen task should be handled in each scene to support the character portraits, the mood, the significance of certain details or the film's overarching message. Finally, each expert is responsible for carrying out the duties of the chosen role during filming and post-production editing so that all collaborate with the other crewmembers to create the finished product.

Leading and following

Because each student becomes an expert in one or more filmmaking technique(s), he or she is empowered to take leadership over its implementation during filming. As participants rely on each other's growing expertise, timeliness and quality of contribution, they feel highly motivated to perform their parts to the best of their ability. By creating their own authentic cultural product, students also discover the various tools employed by the visual arts and literature to pose questions, create meaning and engage the viewer or reader. They learn how to pool their ideas and talents in creative, collaborative and purpose-driven ways to complete a project that fills them with pride and confidence. This experience can be expanded: at the end of the semester, students can share their final film product with the language section, department or even university in a public showing followed by a Q&A roundtable in which the film producers further engage with others.[11] All in all, the creative process encountered in Germany on Screen: Current Cultural Trends and Social Movements converts learners into more critical consumers of visual and textual media thanks to the analytical tools they acquired, which, of course, are salient components of 21st-century learning.

Promoting student professionalism: communicating and collaborating to succeed

Students and professors of foreign languages are frequently asked about job prospects after graduation. Successful recruitment, instruction and nurturing of students must thus be tied to educational programs that ensure students are equipped to find and perform in 21st-century professions. A multi-pronged approach that provides students with hands-on professional experiences as well as connections to local businesses and the wider community can facilitate these goals.

Modeling professional achievement

One way to forge paths for German students to careers is to organize alumni presentations on how language proficiency and intercultural competence enhance one's ability to secure employment. At ECU, we coordinate such presentations with other departments, which increases the number of students served and magnifies the scope of publicity for our small program. Previous alumni visitors have included a professional German-to-English translator, a senior buyer for a large German factory located nearby, an immigration lawyer and a public- relations officer in the U.S. Air Force.

In order to provide students with hands-on experience in the teaching profession, we invite them to apprentice-teach in beginning German language courses. The professor mentors the student as he or she coteaches a class, with the student assuming ever more responsibilities throughout the semester. We pioneered using independent study credit to offer this professional teaching internship (Twark et al. 2018, "Benefits"). Professional networking, apprentice teaching and other inventive answers to institutional constraints have proven vital for recruiting and retaining students.

Preparing for professional success

Applied professional experiences can additionally be offered in courses designed to showcase international careers or careers with foreign companies in the U.S. These courses assess students' individual aptitudes and educational backgrounds and guide them through the application process. Once rare, such courses are now becoming more common at U.S. universities, often under the blanket title German for the Professions. The benefits of this course, piloted at the senior level in spring 2019 at our university, derive from its emphasis on intercultural competence, interpersonal cooperation and community outreach. Students gain these proficiencies by traditional academic means (reading and discussing texts),[12] by engaging in job-seeking activities and by participating in a group service-learning project.

The specific 21st-century learning outcomes for German for the Professions anticipate that students are able to:

Demonstrate the ability to collaborate with other professionals in companies and non-profit organizations in the German-speaking world and the US and appreciate their alternative views.

Navigate the job search and future workplace by offering innovative résumés, writing culturally appropriate business letters, and communicating successfully in oral presentations and interviews

Analyze intercultural differences inherent in professional interactions in Germany versus the U.S. and offer creative solutions to intercultural challenges

---

In order to enable students to acquire these skills, they are guided through a series of interlocking activities over several weeks. First, the instructor presents a set of German companies and industries such as Deutsche Bahn, Deutsche Bank and the automobile or tourism industry. Course participants explore these companies' positions advertised online, ranging from technical, to administrative, to social media jobs. Students then perform their own job search in a series of steps that engage authentic material such as current job descriptions and sample U.S. and German applications. After selecting a company and writing a "company brief" on its history and current business model, they present the chosen industry in individual class presentations and receive feedback by means of an oral presentation rubric. For the company brief and presentation, they analyze a company's recent innovations that have led to a reformulation of its job descriptions and requirements, as well as their ramifications for employers, employees, society and, if applicable, the natural environment. After next producing a résumé and cover letter tailored culturally and linguistically to a specific position, learners peer-review and improve these texts as a group in class, with the professor facilitating the discussion and providing feedback. Such a step-by-step, collaborative curriculum improves students' self-confidence in seeking and applying for a job. They also practice the 21st-century skills of evaluating workplace innovations and their ethical ramifications in the professional world, as well as communicating interculturally and professionally. Linking these activities together in a chain improves their job-seeking skills, boosts their self-confidence and allays many fears associated with "taking the leap" of applying for a professional position.

Reflecting on preprofessional experiences through service learning

In addition to job-seeking activities, students engage in another collaborative, communicative activity in German for the Professions by performing a service-learning project in stages. Students research and present a German cultural topic or artwork to constituents outside the university, such as at a school or non-profit organization. After finding project partners, students write a half-page *Project Proposal*, and later a two-page *Production Plan* outlining their goals, objectives, target audience, production and distribution formats, group responsibilities, client responsibilities and timeline. Throughout the semester, students provide *In-Class Status Reports*, speaking briefly about the work completed, in-progress and still to be done. They also create, administer and summarize the results of an *Audience Survey* in their project presentations. At semester's end, they write a *Reflection Paper* and submit all project materials in a *Service-Learning Portfolio*.

Most student groups choose an activity suggested on the syllabus and give a PowerPoint presentation on an aspect of German culture – such as its social-welfare system or history of castle-building – to classes at local schools. One recent group, however, drew on the expertise of a student group member (a music major) and organized a *Musikbrauerei* concert with six other music majors singing German *Lieder* (songs) at a local pub. Another group member created and distributed marketing flyers about the event on campus and banners on social media. Approximately 40 people attended the concert, modeled after "Opera on Tap" productions held regularly throughout the U.S. (see "History").

Performing this service-learning project not only improves students' communication and organizational skills, but also raises their self-confidence in carrying out an extended, project-based activity in a group. Working in teams helps learners identify and develop talents in themselves and each other. These benefits accord with research on the advantages of service learning when compared with traditional methods of teaching and assessment (Hébert and Hauf 2015). This project also allows our language students to engage in a valuable outreach activity intended to spark interest about German culture in schools and the wider community.[13]

Flipped Learning 3.0: increasing learners' opportunities to think critically across cultures

In fall 2019, the ECU German program adopted the first textbook designed for the flipped learning of German as a foreign language, titled *Impuls Deutsch 1*. *Impuls Deutsch 1* explicitly embraces the four C's of 21st-century learning: collaboration, communication, creativity and critical thinking. It thus will further innovate our teaching across the German section.

Between spring 2013 and fall 2019, only the fourth semester Beginning German classes were flipped. This necessitated the development of additional materials to augment our previous textbook. Although this was a time-consuming undertaking, it helped recruit new majors and minors because this new learning direction has purposely promoted *cross-cultural critical thinking* (CCCT), a necessary skill for 21st-century learning that students also desire. CCCT expands learners' intercultural awareness by inviting them to:

Critically analyze features of L1 and L2 culture
Evaluate the purpose and practicality of related cultural practices
Decenter previous cultural norms, thus creating personal agency through reflection

The following describes the three stages of flipped instruction and how CCCT can enrich any curriculum.

German in the flipped classroom

Coined as a published term in 2012, *flipped classrooms* invert the traditional delivery of content (in the classroom) and its practical application (as homework). Students are exposed to content in their private learning spaces and apply it in the group space with the instructor nearby to guide teams through difficult processes. The most salient benefit is an immediate gain of improved instructional time because a flipped classroom is no longer teacher-centric, but instead differentiates to "reach every student" (Bergmann and Sams 2012).

"Flipped" ECU students (either in the older anticipatory teaching model or now with the new textbook) receive grammar and vocabulary lessons at home (through the *Impuls Deutsch 1* online unit readings, PowerPoint presentations and various assigned YouTube videos). Instructors who wish to adapt their current textbooks should ensure that their learners do, indeed, prepare ahead of class. This can be done by creating worksheets that are filled out with the grammar and vocabulary introductions that are necessary to prepare learners for class activities. At ECU, these worksheets (called *Lernblätter*) were uploaded to the Learning Management System for a time stamp that encouraged accountability. Learners then brought their printed sheets to class for further application of the preabsorbed content. Each *Lernblatt* concluded with a self-evaluation of that day's learning which was formulated as can-do statements (see ACTFL's performance indicators). Instructors who use a flipped textbook such as *Impuls Deutsch* will benefit from structured preclass activities that learners complete online to prime them for planned in-class work.

Flipped learning of German

Flipped learning occurs when the additional classroom time gained is purposefully restructured to increase learner efficacy in the classroom and transform the educator into a fellow learner, both inside and outside of this classroom (Jensen 2019, 52). By participating in (rather than "supervising") their students' learning processes, flipped instructors gain pedagogical effectiveness as they reflect on and innovate their instructional approach. They also deepen their disciplinary expertise as learners engage more with the material and ask ever more complex questions.

For maximum benefit, ECU learners join *Familien* (learning groups) for the entire semester. Each *Familie* comprises both strong and struggling learners, thus providing a more adaptive differentiation than in a standard class. Group unity can be fostered by adopting (silly, famous or ordinary) German last names and by playing review games early in the semester via Kahoot, Quizlet or on the whiteboard where families compete against each other. This synergy then fuels more enriching topical explorations than the cultural "factoids" in the textbook. A former textbook snippet on the *Bauernmarkt*, for instance, can be expanded into a two-week unit on nutrition, food-related legislation, sustainability and behaviors related to the consumption of material goods in Germany. The curiosity kindled by preparatory cultural readings and viewings inspires *Familien* to cowrite dialogues, act out culturally appropriate scenes and discuss their cultural findings in depth. Our new textbook contains such farther-reaching cultural activities already, but instructors with standard textbooks can expand the often superficial cultural content by using the flipped learning approach.

Flipped Learning 3.0 in German classes

The next evolution of the old flipped classroom, *Flipped Learning 3.0*, serves as a meta-strategy for 21st-century learning. It employs many active learning approaches (e.g. project-based, gamified or experiential learning), which are all supported by "flipping" content absorption out of the classroom to concentrate on creativity, collaboration, communication and critical thinking inside the group learning space. In other words, discipline-specific content is explicitly subordinated to the practice of these skills.

In Flipped Learning 3.0, backward-designed units employ higher-cognition activities (analyzing, evaluating, creating) to reach specific 21st-century outcomes (Wiggins and McTighe). Students in a classroom based on these principles encounter thematic units in which the linguistic elements (lexicon and grammatical structures) play a supportive role. Language production becomes a *communicative tool* for concrete practical purposes; it is no longer the end goal of language instruction. Each culturally organized module invites learners to negotiate meaning as they think critically across two cultures and cognitively process information that is scaffolded carefully for maximum comprehension.

In a unit on healthcare, for instance, students can be guided toward creating solutions to soaring personal and national healthcare expenses in the U.S. and toward understanding the connections between medical costs, personal well-being and national economies. Their private and public use of the higher-cognition competencies found in Bloom's Revised Taxonomy (Sweet et al. 2016) is one of the most important unit outcomes. For the final unit project, learners may collaborate to publish their findings in a manner they choose. They may create posters for the ECU library or write a report to the U.S. Surgeon General in which they compare both nations' approaches to healthcare.

Collaboration

A frequent obstacle to learning a foreign language is the fear of speaking (García-Palacios et al. 2018). In traditional classrooms, the instructor may call on one student at a time to hear a reply, a practice that can paralyze learners who suffer from xenoglossophobia. Because flipped learning relies on group or partner work, public responses are nearly eliminated (except for voluntary questions at the beginning of class). All communication takes place in the group or when the instructor consults with a group collaborating on a task. The classroom becomes learner-centric, loud and even chaotic as the groups seek to finish their daily tasks.

When mastery learning (the insistence that a preestablished level of proficiency must be reached before a learner can move on) is employed in addition to Flipped Learning 3.0, groups quickly learn that an unfinished task will have to be completed outside of class (Emery et al. 2018). Such performance pressure:

Keeps groups focused on the work at hand

Motivates learners to acquire the necessary grammatical structures before class to collaborate successfully in their *Familien*

Promotes L2 use to succeed at a task (not just to produce language for practice's sake)

Because speaking the target language is necessary for attaining a practical goal, and because others at the table are pursuing the same objective at the same time, the foreign language loses the frightening dimension of public performance.

Continuous collaboration, when undergirded by flipped learning, thus serves to endow foreign-language learning with several benefits that are commensurate with 21st-century learning. It emphasizes good communication in the encouraging realm of one's *Familie*, it replaces the anxiety-causing factor of public performance with the reflective construction of personal meaning and it differentiates the assessment of L2 proficiency in end-of-module group projects where all members can creatively contribute according to their strengths. Moreover, collaborative learning and flipped learning allow higher-order thinking outcomes to be incorporated into language courses that traditionally have been seen as skills-building classes (see Figure 3.3).

Two striking results of pursuing 21st-century learning by flipping L2 instruction at East Carolina University have been: 1) the increase in learner success (and ultimately motivation!) and 2) in students' ability to examine their hidden cultural biases and thereby to gain greater intellectual autonomy. In numerous surveys, a large majority of students expressed an appreciation of the pivot away from the standard L2 teaching approach and the increased focus on critical thinking, particularly cross-cultural critical thinking, which uses language as a tool to explore a topic instead of as an end in itself. As one student explained in an anonymous survey (fall 2015):

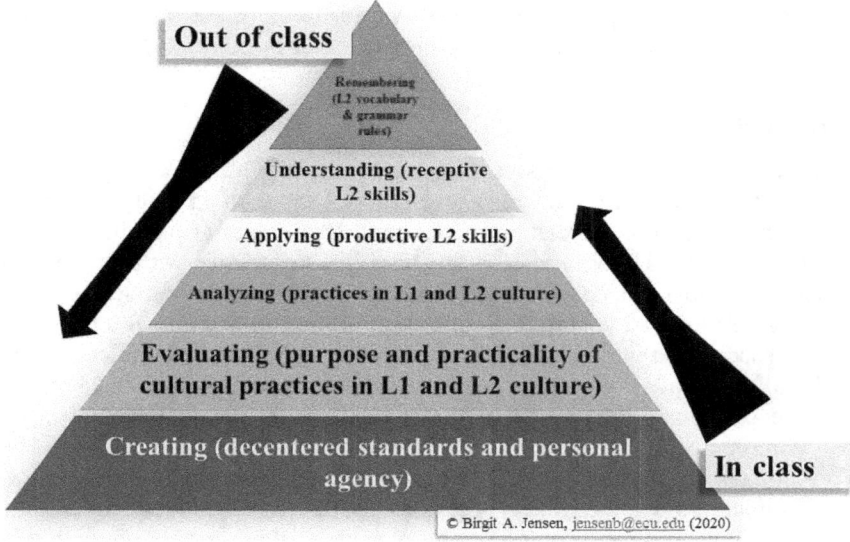

Figure 3.3

One of the biggest benefits of flipped learning for German was the fact that we were learning more how to speak the language instead of just memorizing verbs and vocabulary. This instead came more natural as we learned the language. We also had more time to dive into the culture which for students like myself who are planning to travel abroad was the biggest advantage. While it definitely remedied the problem of assigning too much homework, there is a level of accountability that you need to have to succeed in this class because it is still hard work. It is work that challenged how we think which is better than having to memorize anything.

Promoting German culture in the 21st century: innovative outreach

When students are encouraged to collaborate and exercise their creativity in the classroom, they become instrumental in suggesting and organizing outreach activities and service-learning opportunities of their own. Those students become our program's best advocates by talking with parents, peers and even administrators about the experiences they have initiated to address current topics of societal concern. Such events involve the campus and local communities and incorporate students' personal and academic interests. Though our program hosts small and large events throughout each semester, we have found that sponsoring one large signature event per academic year contributes most to promoting our brand as an innovative and robust program that prepares students for a meaningful life in today's world. Four recent initiatives undertaken by students and faculty at ECU provide cases in point.

Outreach abroad

A German Club discussion about the refugee crisis in Germany in spring 2016 led club officers to envision a spring break service trip with a faculty member to understand the complex societal, political and legal issues at play in Germany and the European Union and later to share this knowledge with members of the campus and local communities. With faculty guidance, the spring break interest group found a volunteer organization partner in Munich. Students then wrote a successful funding request to our university's Office of Student Affairs for $20,000 to cover the airfare and lodging in a youth hostel for 11 undergraduate participants. In addition, the students raised another $2,500 in the local community to purchase educational supplies for the 150 men from Iraq and Afghanistan supported by the local volunteer organization.

In Munich, students engaged in a daily routine that included tutoring the young men in rudimentary German, playing frisbee and basketball with them, interviewing them about their hobbies with the help of translators so the volunteers could plan free-time activities for them accordingly and sharing lunch. To contextualize the trip, the volunteer organization arranged for the ECU group to interact with: 1) a Bavarian politician involved in refugee affairs; 2) state-employed social workers charged with ensuring the welfare of refugees in the city; 3) representatives from other volunteer organizations and 4) a reporter from *Süddeutsche Zeitung*. The resulting article in the *Süddeutsche Zeitung* attracted the attention of the U.S. Consulate, which invited the students to discuss their outreach efforts with U.S. State Department representatives.

A post-trip voluntary survey of students revealed that all six respondents "strongly agreed" with the following statement: "Participating in the service trip to Munich has made me want to continue with my German language studies," and all six noted that their enthusiasm for working to produce positive social change was "much better" than before. Five of the six students indicated that they were "much more" inclined to participate in social outreach initiatives in their own community. Later, these students organized and hosted a well-attended roundtable discussion of their experiences for ECU students and faculty and gave interviews about their work to local media and university officials. Several students remain in touch with, and have visited, volunteers from the Munich partner organization since the collaboration in 2016.

International outreach on campus

In spring 2017, our program took advantage of the support garnered by the Munich trip to host a four-day symposium on migration titled

"[IN]Voluntary Migration Around the Globe: The Good, the Bad, and the Unknown." This multi-disciplinary workshop encouraged students, faculty and community members to explore, broaden and reconstruct narrow political visions of the "Other." Events included a historical overview of refugee and migrant bans in the U.S., a screening and discussion of the feature-length film *The Land Between*, a keynote address by the Consul General of Mexico, a roundtable discussion featuring representatives from local aid organizations assisting refugee and migrant communities in North Carolina and a student panel speaking about their experiences as immigrants to the U.S. The event was received enthusiastically, and surveys indicated that over half of the attendees thought they had been exposed to information that made them reconsider their assumptions about refugees and migrants.

Campus outreach

In addition to the four-day symposium on migration, our program also hosted an interdisciplinary symposium marking the 500th anniversary of Martin Luther's "95 Theses" titled: "Here I Stand: Showing Civil Courage in the Face of Controversy." Aside from examining the complexities of Luther's character, the two-day workshop featured presentations by faculty and undergraduates, including a panel discussion by students on their efforts to facilitate positive change in people's lives. These students represented the Honors College, the LGBT Resource Center, African and African-American Studies, the Arab Student Union, the Muslim Student Association and the Collegiate Recovery Center, an organization that assists students in leading sober lives.

Regional outreach

In fall 2019, our program organized an interdisciplinary symposium on "Democracy and its Discontents in Germany and Across the Globe" inspired by current events and anniversaries which are key for understanding German democracy as it exists today (e.g. 30 years since the fall of the Berlin Wall). The workshop featured a keynote presentation on historical and current challenges to American democracy and a faculty panel on issues confronting democracies around the world (e.g. voter apathy, populism, social media influence). In preparation for the symposium, and using project-based learning, students in a Contemporary German Culture course researched German political parties and conducted discourse analyses of their platform stances toward refugees and migrants. Students created posters to showcase their research findings and displayed them during the event.

While outreach can take many forms, we have found that events connecting current controversies and student contributions are most empowering for sharing the principles of 21st-century learning with others on campus and in the surrounding community. Such events display our German program's educational benefits for learners and provide them with opportunities to build their skills in communicating across cultures, ethnicities and genders, to collaborate in disseminating meaningfully constructed knowledge, to think critically about old approaches to current problems and to propose possible solutions.

Conclusion

This chapter urges educators to focus on 21st-century learner needs. If students are to graduate as creative problem solvers, we must support them in their quest for agency throughout their undergraduate experience. Teaching German and offering extracurricular activities must go beyond the standard presentation and practice of a grammatical topic or the obligatory campus *Oktoberfest*. Instead, instruction must be informed by a process of cocreation and exploration, with students emboldened to practice the language without fear of mistakes as they learn also to negotiate working in diverse teams. Because we encourage students to make connections between German Studies and other areas of study, our program has successfully developed relationships with constituencies both on and off campus (who have reciprocated by donating to our scholarship fund). These improved connections, combined with a 21st-century student-focused curriculum, attest that our program is vibrant, engaged and relevant. These attributes serve as an important rejoinder to detractors who may not readily value the importance of learning about other cultures or polishing the soft skills required by today's economy.

Notes

1 A development that affects education as well as its funding (Foster and Fowles).
2 The concept of a progressive education has been promoted since the 18th century in Germany, England, France, Italy, the United States and India. Early reformers hoped to rouse the intellectual curiosity of children so that they develop self-discipline voluntarily. Most notable among them were Johann Bernhard Basedow, Johann Heinrich Pestalozzi, Friedrich Fröbel, John Locke, Jean-Jacques Rousseau, John Dewey, Helen Parkhurst, Rudolf Steiner, Maria Montessori and Rabindranath Tagore.
3 Also consult http://www.co-operation.org/.
4 Based on Jean Piaget's philosophical constructivism. For current research affirming the positive effects of constructivist teaching, see Zabihi and Khodabakhsh (2019).
5 Based on Lev Vygotsky's educational psychology; also see Daneshfar and Moharami (2018).
6 As conceived by Jerome Bruner. For a practical application, see Banister (2018).
7 Among them: the OECD, the AACU, MIT and Harvard University, the National Governors Association and several U.S. Fortune 500 companies.
8 P21 further insists that the instruction of these skills must be supported by four pillars: assessments based on standards and mastery learning; curricular planning based on empirical research data; instructors' commitment to continuing their education; and active-learning pedagogies informed by differentiation, progressive ideals and constructivism.
9 When first taught, this course presented a case of creative problem-solving in that it grew out of a budget-mandated necessity to combine an under-enrolled mid-level Composition and Conversation course with an upper-level German topics course.

The seminar comprised students with mixed levels of German proficiency who might not have fared well in a traditional course, where the same tasks would have been undertaken uniformly.
10 Though meeting times can be challenging, especially for students working full-time, gathering in small teams, communicating digitally and allocating some class time for group work typically provide enough opportunities to collaborate.
11 This would necessitate English subtitles which students were not expected to provide.
12 The readings included articles on intercultural competence (e.g. Deardorff 2006) and select chapters from *Communication Between Cultures* (Samovar et al. 2013) and *Understanding German and American Business Cultures* (Schmidt 2003).
13 When catering only to upper-level German students, this course can be under-enrolled. Our department thus decided to open the class to all majors and explore international careers in their respective countries of interest.

Bibliography

Almiron, Núria, and Jordi Xifra, editors. *Climate Change Denial and Public Relations: Strategic Communication and Interest Groups in Climate Inaction.* Routledge, 2020.

Banister, Chris. "Scaffolding Learner Puzzling in Exploratory Practice: Perspectives from the Business English Classroom." *Profile Issues in Teachers' Professional Development*, vol. 20, no. 2, 2018, pp. 17–33.

Bergmann, Jonathan, and Aaron Sams. *Flip Your Classroom: Reach Every Student in Every Class Every Day.* International Society for Technology in Education, 2012.

Bruner, Jerome. *Child's Talk: Learning to Use Language.* Oxford University Press, 1983.

Creativity in Higher Education. European University Association, 2007, eua.eu/resources/publications/653:creativity-in-higher-education.html. Accessed 5 April 2020.

Daneshfar, Samran, and Mehdi Moharami. "Dynamic Assessment in Vygotsky's Sociocultural Theory: Origins and Main Concepts." *Journal of Language Teaching and Research*, vol. 9, no. 3, 2018, pp. 600–607.

Deardorff, Darla K. "Identification and Assessment of Intercultural Competence as a Student Outcome of Internationalization." *Journal of Studies in International Education*, vol. 10, no. 3, 2006, pp. 241–266.

Emery, Alyssa, et al. "When Mastery Goals Meet Mastery Learning: Administrator, Teacher, and Student Perceptions." *The Journal of Experimental Education*, vol. 86, no. 3, 2018, pp. 419–441.

Feinstein, Jonathan S. *The Nature of Creative Development.* Stanford UP, 2006.

Foster, John M., and Jacob Fowles. "Ethnic Heterogeneity, Group Affinity, and State Higher Education Spending." *Research in Higher Education*, vol. 59, no. 1, 2018, pp. 1–28.

Frameworks and Resources. Battelle for Kids, www.battelleforkids.org/networks/p21/frameworks-resources. Accessed 5 April 2020.

García-Palacios, Azucena, et al. "The Effect of Foreign Language in Fear Acquisition." *Scientific Reports*, vol. 8, no. 1157, 2018, pp. 1–8.

Gardner, David P., et al. "A Nation at Risk: The Imperative for Educational Reform. An Open Letter to the American People. A Report to the Nation and the Secretary of Education." United States Department of Education. The Commission, 1983.

Gray, Lacey. "Providing Direct Aid: ECU German Club Spends Spring Break Assisting Refugee Efforts in Germany." *ECU*, 12 March 2016, news.ecu.edu/archive/2016/03/24/providing-direct-aid/. Accessed 5 April 2020.

Grundner, Hubert. "Das Engagement hier ist erstaunlich." *Süddeutsche Zeitung*, 7 March 2016, sueddeutsche.de/muenchen/neuperlach-das-engagement-hier-ist-ersta unlich-1.2896587. Accessed 5 April 2020.

Hébert, Ali, and Petra Hauf. "Student learning through service learning: Effects on academic development, civic responsibility, interpersonal skills and practical skills." *Active Learning in Higher Education*, vol. 16, no. 1, 2015, pp. 37–49.

Helding, Lynn. "Creativity in Crisis?" *Mindful Voice. Journal of Singing*, vol. 67, no. 5, 2011, pp. 597–604.

History. Opera on Tap, 2019, www.operaontap.org/about/. Accessed 5 April 2020.

Ibrahim, Karim. "Foreign Language Practice in Simulation Video Games: An Analysis of Game-Based FL-Use Dynamics." *Foreign Language Annals*, vol. 52, no. 2, 2019, pp. 335–357.

Jackson, Norman, et al. *Developing Creativity in Higher Education: An Imaginative Curriculum*. Routledge, 2006.

Jensen, Birgit A. "Using Flipped Learning to Facilitate Cross-Cultural Critical Thinking in the L2 Classroom." *Die Unterrichtspraxis*, vol. 52, no. 1, 2019, pp. 50–68.

Johnson, David W., and Roger T. Johnson. *Cooperative Learning Institute*, 2019, www.co-operation.org/. Accessed 5 April 2020.

Kim, Kyung H. "The Creativity Crisis: The Decrease in Creative Thinking Scores on the Torrance Tests of Creative Thinking." *Creativity Research Journal*, vol. 23, no. 4, 2011, pp. 285–295.

Leonard-Barton, Dorothy, and Walter C. Swap. *When Sparks Fly: Igniting Creativity in Groups*. Harvard Business School Press, 1999.

Masterson, Mary. "Self-Discovery through the Experiential Co-Construction of Life Stories in the Foreign Language Classroom." *Journal of Experiential Education*, vol. 41, no. 4, 2018, pp. 341–355.

McWilliam, Erica, and Shane Dawson. "Teaching for Creativity: Towards Sustainable and Replicable Pedagogical Practice." *Higher Education*, vol. 56, no. 6, 2008, pp. 633–643.

"NCSSFL-ACTFL Can-Do Statements."American Council on the Teaching of Foreign Languages, 2017, www.actfl.org/publications/guidelines-and-manuals/ncssfl-a ctfl-can-do-statements. Accessed 5 April 2020.

Nehring, James, et al. *Bridging the Progressive-Traditional Divide in Education Reform: A Unifying Vision for Teaching, Learning, and System Level Supports*. Routledge, 2019.

Paulus, Paul B., et al. "Enhancing Collaborative Ideation in Organizations." *Frontiers in Psychology*, vol. 9, 2018, pp. 1–12.

Rampersad, Giselle, and Fay Patel. "Creativity as a Desirable Graduate Attribute: Implications for Curriculum Design and Employability." *Asia-Pacific Journal of Cooperative Education*, vol. 15, no. 1, 2014, pp. 1–11.

Rauschert, Petra, and Michael Byram. "Service Learning and Intercultural Citizenship in Foreign-Language Education." *Cambridge Journal of Education*, vol. 48, no. 3, 2018, pp. 353–369.

Runco, Mark A. "Everyone Has Creative Potential." *Creativity: From Potential to Realization*, edited by Robert J Sternberget al., American Psychological Association, 2004, pp. 21–30.

Samovar, Larry L., et al. *Communication Between Cultures*. 8th ed., Cengage Learning, 2013.

Schmidt, Patrick L. *Understanding German and American Business Cultures: A Manager's Guide to the Cultural Context in which American and German Companies Operate*. 3rd ed., Meridian World Press, 2003.

Sun, Peijian, and Rui Yuan. "Understanding Collaborative Language Learning in Novice-Level Foreign Language Classrooms: Perceptions of Teachers and Students." *Interactive Learning Environments*, vol. 26, no. 2, 2018, pp. 189–205.

Sweet, Charlie, et al. "Why the Revised Bloom's Taxonomy is Essential to Creative Teaching." *The National Teaching & Learning Forum*, vol. 26, no. 1, 2016, pp. 7–9.

Tracksdorf, Niko, et al. *Impuls Deutsch 1: Textbook Series for College/Adult Learners*. Klett, 2019.

Twark, Jill E., et al. "The Benefits of Apprentice Teaching with Undergraduates in German Language Classes." *Die Unterrichtspraxis*, vol. 51, no. 1, 2018, pp. 1–14.

Twark, Jill E., Birgit A. Jensen, and Susanne Lenné Jones. "Erfolgsstrategien zur Wiederbelebung eines universitären Germanistikstudienganges in den Vereinigten Staaten." *Aussiger Beiträge*, vol. 5, 2011, pp. 23–34.

Wiggins, Grant, and Jay McTighe. *Understanding by Design*. Expanded 2nd ed., Association for Supervision and Curriculum Development, 2005.

Wince-Smith, Deborah L. "The Creativity Imperative: A National Perspective." *Peer Review*, vol. 8, no. 2, 2006, pp. 12–14.

Zabihi, Reza, and Mina Khodabakhsh, "L2 Teachers' Traditional versus Constructivist Teaching/Learning Conceptions and Teacher Burnout." *Current Psychology*, vol. 38, no. 2, 2019, pp. 347–353.

4 Diversity programming, student outreach and the politics of visible inclusivity for small German programs

Ervin Malakaj

In an article devoted to strengthening undergraduate German programs at North American institutions of higher learning, James C. Davidheiser (1999) articulates faculty labor conditions as the biggest challenge for innovation: "the fact that many instructors are under heavy academic pressure to excel in the areas of service and scholarship in addition to teaching may be a reason that faculty have been reluctant to take the time to examine and implement ways to make their programs more attractive for students" (60). This conundrum of, on the one hand, generating new structures for student learning and success, and on the other, not having the time to do so, places an extraordinary burden on faculty in small programs. Nonetheless, as Davidheiser notes, "unless they [excel in all three areas] the number of students taking German may continue to decline" (60). In fact, "one of the chief reasons German programs are cut back or dropped at small undergraduate institutions is low enrollment" (65). Although Davidheiser's article describes the field of German Studies in 1999, the broader structural challenges informing the labor conditions of faculty working in small German programs twenty years ago persist into the present. That is, faculty in small programs, in particular, are often expected to orchestrate multiple institutional curricula (i.e. the basic German language sequence, the German minor, the German major and/or other certificate programs) while concomitantly working under stifling staffing and budgetary conditions (Lewis 2015; Pancrazio 2011). In addition, these programs, as Davidheiser states in his article, would best attract students by generating an expansive series of cocurricular programs along with innovative curricular structuring. Such innovative curricular and cocurricular offering, in tandem, would shape student interest, guide students through the social stations of college or university life and would facilitate an intellectual and social home for students within the purview of the German program on campus.

However, even the best of such efforts of German program curricular innovation and cocurricular planning only marginally attend to diversity and inclusion, if they consider them at all. Davidheiser's article, for instance, lists a strong series of programming efforts to strengthen small German programs, but does not mention how attending to the needs of historically marginalized and structurally disadvantaged learners figures in the list of curricular and cocurricular planning for the future of German Studies. Some such diversity initiatives exist in the field. In fact, the work of the scholarly collective Diversity, Decolonization, and the German Curriculum (DDGC) has shown how the last thirty years of German Studies in the United States have had moments of devoted effort to theorizing and modelling plans attentive to the intellectual and structural needs of disadvantaged learners; however, those efforts have not generated a sustained commitment to serving the needs of structurally disadvantaged and minoritized learners. In an open letter to the largest scholarly association devoted to the teaching and learning of German in the United States, the *American Association of Teachers of German* (AATG), which was signed by 240 German Studies professionals and supporters from across North America and beyond, DDGC articulates a structural critique of the field's failures to center the needs of an already diversified higher education landscape. The collective recognized the extensive work of scholars such as Ingeborg Henderson (1991) and George Peters (1995), who among others involved with the creation of the AATG scholarly task force to attend to the needs of minoritized learners, advocated throughout the early 1990s and into the 2000s for more resources and scholarship in teaching and learning supportive of such learners. Nonetheless, DDGC noted that a meaningful systemic shift in the field with regard to the place of diversity and inclusion "remains announced, but not enacted." What is more, the collective critiqued that when minoritized learners are considered in the curricular and cocurricular planning of German Studies, they are done so within the purview of initiatives, which "appear opportunistic and fear-driven, directed more toward an effort to 'save German Studies' than toward creating a more just world."

In this chapter, I will attend to the impulse for innovative programming at small German programs by focusing on diversity and inclusion outreach initiatives. I will ground these initiatives in the scholarship on critical diversity studies, critical pedagogy and critical language studies. My aim is not to offer a technology to funnel minoritized students into the German Studies classrooms in order to make up for the damage caused by structural shifts in the neoliberalized higher education landscape, which have caused a stark decrease in German program enrollment and have also led to the closure of 86 German programs between 2013 and 2016 (Johnson 2019). As noted above, the DDGC scholarly collective has criticized such an approach by foregrounding its self-serving aims without being grounded in genuine commitment to student learning and success. Instead, my aim is to demonstrate on the basis of a case study how efficient and equitable diversity programing in a small German program can create an intellectual home for minoritized, structurally disadvantaged and historically underrepresented students.

Diversity work and German studies

In her work on diversity, Sara Ahmed (2012) critiqued the corporatization of diversity work at postsecondary institutions. Calls to diversification, inclusion and equity have, according to her research, generated a higher education administration landscape in which diversity serves as a shield institutions hold up when charged to be non-diverse, non-inclusive and unequitable. In this light, diversity language "*can be* a way of maintaining rather than transforming existing organizational values" (57). Being able to point to diversity initiatives and inclusion offices on campuses, colleges and universities can misuse diversity in the service of sustaining institutional authority instead of generating more equitable settings for structurally disadvantaged community members (which includes students, faculty and staff). Many advocates of diversity and equity at postsecondary institutions have thus become wary when diversity language is used by university administrators. As Ahmed notes, "when words such as 'diversity' get repeated by officials, becoming official words, they acquire a life; they have further to go. What is being achieved by the mobility of these terms remains another question" (60). Here, the function that such diversity initiatives can serve is that they change the terms of critique. Take, for instance, Ahmed's example of an institution being critiqued for being too white. As she notes, such critique generates the conundrum of the so-called killjoy, whereby the articulated problem is not the problem but rather the person articulating it: "rather than responding by accepting this perception (and assuming the task of modifying the thing perceived as white) the perception becomes the problem. The task becomes changing the perception of whiteness rather than changing the whiteness of the organization" (184). Here, diversity initiatives come to support the very thing they seek to dismantle.

Such processes of coopting diversity work have done a lot of damage to diversity initiatives at institutions. They are perceived by some once-supporters to be dubious endeavors as a result of easily being mobilized by university administration to protect the institution, while long-time critics relish the ambiguous position such endeavors take in institutional life. "Diversity work," as Ahmed notes, "thus requires insistence" (186). Misappropriation of this work requires extensive commitment and rhetorical labor to undo the damage done to the core endeavor of diversity work, which is to establish equitable learning and working conditions at institutions of higher learning. Such misappropriation of diversity language requires a tripartite approach to undo the misuse and abuse of this language, a process of what Yuliya Komska, Michelle Moyd and David Gramling have described as an act of "linguistic disobedience" (13). That is, in the face of creative misuse of diversity language in institutional life, diversity practitioners and scholar-teachers committed to equity and inclusion on campus are hard pressed to critique, correct and care for diversity language and insist in its core values (13–19).

To recover diversity work for German postsecondary language and culture studies means first to recognize the glaring problem that whiteness poses for the field. As I discuss with my coeditor Regine Criser in our volume *Diversity and Decolonization in German Studies* (2020), Henderson and Peters pointed out already in the early 1990s that the field's overwhelming whiteness in terms of student and faculty demographics points to a structural barrier for non-white students. What the DDGC scholarly collective has in shorthand described as uncritical "flag-and-castle-emblazoned promotional materials, with little Multikulti on the side" works in tandem with and along the systems of whiteness that signal to students that German Studies offers a particular type of intellectual home for a particular type of student. The question of relevancy for non-white students and their relationship or non-relationship to German Studies is immediately recognized as cultivating an exclusive environment. Henderson's work is instructive here, too, for she pointed out in 1991 that students of color are, for instance, more drawn to those disciplines in the humanistic social sciences that relate to their lived experience than they would be to German Studies (6; cf. Malakaj 2020, 92–93). More recently, Priscilla Layne has shown in a similar vein and in response to the problems articulated by Henderson that course offerings in the subfield of Black German Studies, for instance, can increase enrollment by POC students in the German program and could lead to further study in the discipline (Layne 2020, 83–87). In Layne's experience, articulating for students of color how German Studies can attend to their personal experiences and be relevant for their lives goes a long way toward nurturing a more diversified student body in the German program on campus.

Another way to recover diversity work for German postsecondary language and culture studies is to acknowledge the limitations and dangers of its current ideological underpinnings. The last decades have shown that the realm of language learning and culture studies in North America is firmly aligned with both nationalist as well as globalist attitudes about the value of such learning. That is, as Claire Kramsch (2019) has shown, "despite the rhetoric of transdisciplinarity and post-colonial rhetoric, [foreign language] departments are still heavily nationally oriented and are often seen by their national sponsors as colonial outposts" (60). In the same vein, such departments articulate the goals of their own programs of study frequently in terms of shaping students in the mold of a "global citizenry" that contributes to, benefits from and sustains the global capitalist network. Such ideological underpinning is problematic for a number of reasons ranging from troubling core principles (Tochon 2019) to, as Timothy Reagan and Terry A. Osborn (2019) have shown, unpersuasive skill development in the limited context of reduced language exposure in language programs (80–84). At the core, these modes of conceiving language and culture studies programming come at the expense of students' positionality in their local, regional, state, national and international communities. The core principle of such nationalist and globalist language education strives to professionalize and optimize students while leaving little room to consider their own life narratives, their structures of feeling and their systems of belonging and being in the world.

The small German program cocurricular ideas I will introduce in the next section are not oriented according to nationalist and globalist language and culture studies paradigms, but rather draw on the insights developed in the scholarship and practice of student affairs in North American colleges and universities. The intellectual programming and student outreach are not necessarily bound up with mandates enforced by disciplinarity: that is, I am less interested in generating German-Studies-specific content and persuasion mechanisms that articulate to students why German Studies is valuable to them, than in meeting the student where they are. Such an approach is grounded in the insights in educational theory regarding the notion of the "whole student," a holistic approach to education, which takes into account the student, not merely as a learner in our courses, but one with a complex life narrative informing learning and social performance (cf. Byrd 2020).

In their work on the history and transformations of the educational ideal of the whole student, Lisa E. Wolf-Wendel and Marti Ruel (1999) have shown that faculty plan and expect a type of student they ultimately do not encounter in their programs. They note, "compared to college students in the past, today's undergraduates are more likely to be older (over age twenty-four), to be from diverse economic and cultural backgrounds, to be in debt, to work, and to have external responsibilities beyond their academic pursuits" (40). Such a range of different experiences, backgrounds and statuses does not correspond to the image of the idealized learner faculty at postsecondary institutions are in some studies shown to expect (39–40). As Wolf-Wendel and Ruel note, "it is important for us in American higher education to remember that every college student is unique. The essence of these students is not easily captured in demographic snapshot" (41). The venues on our campuses which have a strong understanding of this need to attend to the personal life narratives of the whole student, are in the realm of student affairs. The clubs, organizations and scholarly communities on campus housed outside of our department that stem from student affairs are all structured around the idea of providing students with social and intellectual homes by considering their experiences, backgrounds and statuses.

A cornerstone of such cocurricular planning attentive to student-life narratives is the extension of what bell hooks (1994) has termed "engaged pedagogy," a holistic approach to teaching and learning in close proximity to the intellectual history informing the scholarship on the "whole student." For hooks, engaged pedagogy establishes a set of relations among learners and instructors, which serve to empower students to seek out their own learning and subsequently come to understand "education as the practice of freedom" (20). In a symbiotic process, instructors and learners come to empower one another in their pursuit of freedom, which is a transgressive force that combats various oppressive structures in our society. hooks, in her discussion of the generative effects of engaged pedagogy, notes that such approach to teaching "also sanctions involvement with students beyond that setting. I journey with students as they progress in their lives beyond our classroom experiences" (205). It is this extension of engaged pedagogy, attentive to the life narrative of the whole student, that provides the foundation for cocurricular programming capable of generating an intellectual and social home for minoritized, structurally disadvantaged and historically underrepresented students in the purview of the German program on campus.

Programming and the politics of visibility at Sam Houston State University

In a recent study on German program size and enrollment, Per Urlaub (2014) determined that a dataset of elite liberal arts and research universities across the United States offers an insight about curricular and cocurricular planning that paints small German programs as more efficient in carrying out program goals because of their small size. In the category of staffing and student enrollment, "programs at smaller institutions outperform larger departments at large institutions with respect to the ratios of faculty members to German majors and to the student population as a whole" (128). Although the average number of total student enrollment in larger programs exceeded the total enrollment of students in the programs at small, liberal arts colleges, the total number of majors exceeded that of large programs. In this regard, Urlaub lists as example that "Bowdoin produces over 13 times as many German majors per 1,000 students as does Harvard University" (127). One of the reasons for such strong enrollment numbers in the major are the flexibilities afforded by small undergraduate programs. That is, because of staffing limitations, faculty in small programs generally teach students across several levels of instruction, repeatedly engage with students from semester to semester and thus generate lasting bonds among faculty and students, which help sustain student interest. Moreover, the liberal arts setting is known for its strong cocurricular offering: the extensive opportunities students have to generate intellectual and personal connections to faculty shape their sense of belonging in a given program. It is not the case that large programs at larger institutions are unable to generate a similar sense of belonging for their students; rather, it is more challenging for larger programs to sustain such close-knit communities as a result of diffused faculty labor – programs with graduate programs, for instance, rightfully draw the attention of research faculty to graduate curricula. Most importantly, Urlaub explains that the tightly knit communities among faculty and student in small German programs also make for more flexible venues in which curricular and cocurricular innovation could take place. For instance, "compared with large departments, small programs have a structural advantage toward developing, implementing, and sustaining integrated language and culture curricula" (129).

It is in the context of such flexibility that I developed an integrated German language and culture studies curriculum at Sam Houston State University (SHSU). Prior to my appointment at the University of British Columbia (UBC), I coordinated the SHSU German program. Initially, I was the only faculty on staff, joined in my second year at SHSU by a part-time colleague. I began work at SHSU in 2015 right out of graduate school. My position was a one-year Visiting Assistant Professorship on a 4/4 teaching load. However, upon my arrival in the program, only two courses were on the books. There were not enough students enrolled in the program to justify four courses. I was in the fortunate situation that my department chair provided me with a course release for two courses in my first semester under the condition that I use that time to build the program. The person who was in my position in the previous year, was denied tenure. With this person's departure, all information about the German program left SHSU. To illustrate the dire sense of the situation, upon arrival I was able to determine which textbook students used in the second year – information that no one in the department knew prior to my arrival – only through a conversation with staff at the bookstore. I mention this context here not to articulate the challenges of working in such a context; on the contrary, I believe that the almost blank slate provided a rather unique opportunity for me to develop a program from the ground up, which efficiently provided students access to German Studies using most recent methods and topics alongside extensive cocurricular planning. It was this work of building the program in the first semester that ultimately persuaded my department and college administration to bring back the tenure line in German to SHSU (a position I got the next year and held until my move to UBC in 2018).

The integrated curriculum coupled with outreach initiatives helped sustain interest in the German program for a large number of students enrolling in first semester German, which ultimately tripled total enrollments in the German program over the course of two years. However, my interest here is less in the curricular programming or the sophisticated numbers the program could generate but more in the outreach and programming initiatives that spoke to a diverse student population. For it is the intellectual and social home that the SHSU German program could provide to diverse student learners that ultimately helped the program succeed and not its enrollment numbers. Of a total student enrollment of about 20,000 students, SHSU is proud that half of its student body are first-generation students – 70% of the student body is designated "at risk," either because of socioeconomic background or belonging to a historically underrepresented population on campuses that renders the student learner "underprepared" for college. 21% of the student body is Hispanic/Latinx and 19% African American. The majority of the student population stems from a low socioeconomic background.

Despite the university's four-semester language requirement, students were not enrolling in German when I first arrived at the university. Anecdotally, students communicated to the department that they were rather interested in Spanish or American Sign Language because of the practical applicability of both such languages in the Texas region. The other languages in the department, Arabic, French and German, had traditionally lower enrollments. In conversation with my colleague Regine Criser, who works at the University of North Carolina, Asheville, I came to realize that practical decision-making is one factor in students' program selection; the other one depends on whether the program offers the student an intellectual and social home. However, student outreach at a midsize university such as SHSU is not easy. The majority of the student body commutes to campus and leaves campus the moment classes are done to tend to family and work obligations. How does one communicate to this student body that the German program can be an intellectual and social home for students?

The first step I took was to find out more information about student habits, interests and culture on campus. Despite the commuter culture that shaped curricular and cocurricular planning at the university, a thriving Student Affairs Office orchestrated strong academic and social programming for students in the form of student groups and organizations. Reaching out to the Student Affairs Office on campus was an important first step for me to get to know student life better. I discovered that among the 200 organizations on campus, a number were dedicated to students based on their personal background, lived experience or status. These organizations are dedicated to bringing together queer and questioning students on campus, Black students, Hispanic/Latinx students, veteran students, etc. In addition to the information provided on the official website, the Student Affairs Office helped me get in touch with a number of such organizations to find out what times these groups met, what programming they offered to their membership and what motivated their selection of courses. Initially, I showed support and contained curiosity about this programming on campus. I communicated to the groups that I was there to support their efforts and that I would be glad to attend events should these be open to non-membership. This last part is very important: student groups on campus are, among other things, safe places where students can be among people like them. Invading these spaces leaves lasting marks.

Reaching out to student groups, even in the form of email or attending one of the public events the group hosts, is a powerful gesture of support and solidarity for their work. To me, this type of communication did the work of visible inclusivity in that I explicitly communicated to student groups that their presence was welcome on campus, their work important and that, should they decide to take my courses or attend programming in the German program, their presence would be respected and their input welcomed. Notably, my initial outreach work had little to do with the value and import of language and culture studies; my commitment was rather to support students and meet them where they were in order to shape rapport and develop lasting connections. Their events, when I was invited to them, were incredibly insightful about students' struggles in their daily lives at and beyond the university. For instance, I discovered that a substantial number of queer students on campus were eager to attend all sorts of academic programming but were unable to attend events for students if these were scheduled any time after 3p.m. For some groups, members' work schedules did not permit them to schedule their own organization meetings late in the evening let alone give them a chance to connect to campus life. So any programming that took place had to be cognizant of missing a substantial portion of students.

For me, the lesson was that programming could not take place during set times and that varied and flexible event planning (and sometimes multiple iterations of the same event) would need to be in place in order to reach a wide number of students. In fact, learning from student groups about programming provided me with a model for German program cocurricular planning that otherwise would have failed in that it simply always would have been scheduled at the most inopportune times for many students.

The engagement with these student groups led me, as faculty, to sponsor events related to the interests, struggles and realities of historically underrepresented student groups on campus. Initially, this work took place unofficially. Slowly, this interest led to my work with a newly formed diversity and inclusion committee in my college. The politics of visible inclusivity on campus, which I signaled through sustained connections with various student groups on campus, reached a new level of visible commitment in my role on the committee. There, within a semester, I became the cochair of the committee. As an entity, we felt that diversity and inclusion on campus were among the most important initiatives. In particular, we felt that we had to implement programming that helped study and hopefully dismantle the obstacles structurally preventing students from historically underrepresented backgrounds from succeeding at our institution. In this regard, we developed a number of initiatives devised to center student learning and outreach in our work. Chief among them was the diversity reading program. Modeled according to standard university reading programs common at many institutions across the United States, my collaborator and I fundraised for the initiative in various departments, our college and the Student Affairs Office. Our university already had a first-year reading program, which selected a book all incoming students would read and then discuss in a series of events throughout their first year. We wanted to take this model but center questions of equity, social justice and diversity in the selection of the book and any programming surrounding the initiative. The premise was simple: let's pick one book from which we can collectively learn about some of the most pressing social issues of our time, buy a bulk number of copies of the book, distribute it free of charge on a first-come, first-served basis and get together as a group a month later to learn collectively from it.

Initially, we secured funding for 150 copies of Ta-Nehisi Coates's *Between the World and Me* (2015). The publicity surrounding the inaugural event was quite powerful, as we had selected one of the most important books on the Black experience in contemporary U.S. history to appear that year – a text, which had received extensive coverage in the media – and we reached out to all constituents on campus. Student groups were most eager to partner up with us, which we welcomed. We reached out to a number of organizations of students of color or student groups with a commitment to advancing social justice. The interfacing with such various constituents took place over the course of a number of weeks, in anticipation of the event. On the day, we brought students, faculty and staff into small groups in a large auditorium. In these small groups, they discussed selections from the book in a discussion guided by my collaborator and me. Months after the event, I would run into students, faculty and staff on campus who were part of the diversity reader and who still wanted to carry on a conversation with me. The subsequent texts in the series, which we organized each semester, were: the third volume of John Lewis's graphic autobiography *March: Book Three* (2016); Sandra Cisneros's classic Chicana text *The House on Mango Street* (1984) and Claudia Rankine's *Citizen: An American Lyric* (2014). For the Lewis event, we were fortunate that John Lewis, as well as the graphic artists working on the book, came to campus under the auspices of the National Book Awards programming at SHSU. This expanded the reach of the program and helped us forge meaningful and lasting connections to various constituents on campus.

I mention my work with student groups on campus as well as the work with the diversity and inclusion committee because these were important ventures for me to connect to students from various backgrounds and develop relationships which would have otherwise been challenging to shape on a commuter campus. In these venues, I was able to get to know students personally, learn about their experiences on campus and learn about the structural barriers between me and them. Such work took place not instead of "traditional" programming for the German program, but rather parallel to it. With traditional programming I mean weekly conversation hours, film screenings, student and faculty lectures, a student symposium series, honors society programming, etc. However, at each juncture, I created connections between diversity programming on campus and the German program. That is, each diversity reader would figure somehow in my courses (e.g., mini lessons in German language courses, short excerpts of the reader were discussed in advanced anglophone German Studies courses) and would be a component of the cocurricular planning (e.g., conversation hours would be structured around a theme that connected to the themes in the reader). Such measures not only signaled to students from various backgrounds and statuses that I was an ally and supporter on campus, but also secured important space within the German program in which students could articulate how they positioned themselves vis-à-vis the social problems and social justice initiatives discussed in the diversity programming we helped shape on campus. The SHSU German program thus became an extension of the diversity initiatives in our college as much as it became a major supporter of over half dozen vibrant student groups dedicated to the personal and intellectual growth of minoritized, structurally disadvantaged and historically underrepresented students.

Bibliography

Ahmed, Sara. *On Being Included: Racism and Diversity in Institutional Life*. Duke UP, 2012.

Byrd, Vance. "The Whole Student, the Whole Campus." *Re-Imagining the Discipline: German Studies, the Humanities, and the University*, 1 May 2020, futurehumanities.wixsite.com/re-imagining/vance-byrd-grinnell-college. Accessed 9 June 2020.

Criser, Regine, and Ervin Malakaj, editors. *Diversity and Decolonization in German Studies*. Palgrave, 2020.

Davidheiser, James C. "Attracting and Retaining Students in Small Undergraduate German Programs." *Die Unterrichtspraxis*, vol. 32, no. 1, 1999, pp. 60–65.

Henderson, Ingeborg. "Addressing Diversity: A Call for Action." *Die Unterrichtspraxis*, vol. 24, no. 1, 1991, pp. 4–9.

hooks, bell. *Teaching to Transgress: Education as the Practice of Freedom*. Routledge, 1994.

Johnson, Steven. "Colleges Lose a 'Stunning' 651 Foreign-Language Programs in 3 Years." *The Chronicle of Higher Education*, 22 January 2019, www.chronicle.com/article/Colleges-Lose-a-Stunning-/245526. Accessed 2 April 2020.

Komska, Yuliya, et al. *Linguistic Disobedience: Restoring Power to Civic Language*. Palgrave, 2019.

Kramsch, Claire. "Between Globalization and Decolonization: Foreign Languages in the Cross-Fire." *Decolonizing Foreign Language Education: The Misteaching of English and Other Colonial Languages*, edited by Donaldo Macedo, Routledge, 2019, pp. 50–73.

Layne, Priscilla. "Decolonizing German Studies While Dissecting Race in the American Classroom." *Diversity and Decolonization in German Studies*, edited by Regine Criser and Ervin Malakaj, Palgrave, 2020, pp. 83–100.

Layne, Priscilla. "*On Racism without Race: Keynote Address.*" Diversity, Decolonization, and the German Curriculum Conference at St. Olaf College, 1 March 2019, www.stolaf.edu/multimedia/play/?e=2655. Accessed 2 April 2020.

Lewis, Philip E. "Beyond Program Closures, the Menace of Slow Defunding." *Profession*, December 2015, profession.mla.org/beyond-program-closures-the-menace-of-slow-defunding/. Accessed 2 April 2020.

Malakaj, Ervin. "The State of Diversity and Decolonization in North American German Studies." *German Transnational Education and Comparative Education Systems*, edited by Benjamin Nicklet al., Springer, 2020, pp. 85–102.

Open Letter to the AATG: A Ten-Point Program of the Diversity, Decolonization, and the German Curriculum (DDGC) Collective. *DDGC Blog*, diversityingermancurriculum.weebly.com/ddgc-blog/open- letter-to-the-aatg-a-ten-point-program-of-the-diversity-decolonization-and-the-german-curriculum-ddgc-collective. Accessed 2 April 2020.

Pancrazio, James J. "The German Major in Today's Fiscal Climate." *ADLF Bulletin*, vol. 41, no. 3, 2011, pp. 37–42.

Peters, George F. "Dilemmas of Diversity: Observations on Efforts to Increase Minority Participation in German." *ADFL Bulletin*, vol. 25, no. 2, 1995, pp. 5–11.

Reagan, Timothy, and Terry A. Osborn. "Time for a Paradigm Shift in the U.S. Foreign Language Education? Revisioning Rationales, Evidence, and Outcomes." *Decolonizing Foreign Language Education: The Misteaching of English and Other Colonial Languages*, edited by Donaldo Macedo, Routledge, 2019, pp. 73–111.

Tochon, François Victor. "Decolonizing World Language Education." *Decolonizing Foreign Language Education: The Misteaching of English and Other Colonial Languages*, edited by Donaldo Macedo, Routledge, 2019, pp. 264–282.

Urlaub, Per. "Departmental Contexts and Foreign Language Majors." *ADFL Bulletin*, vol. 43, no. 1, 2014, pp. 123–134.

Wolf-Wendel, Lisa E., and Marti Ruel. "Developing the Whole Student: The Collegiate Ideal." *New Directions for Higher Education*, vol. 1999, no. 105, 1999, pp. 35–46.

5 Southern Illinois University Carbondale
One public university's experience with international studies in the Midwest

Mary A. Bricker

Introduction

The New York Times reported in 2019 that public universities in small rural communities throughout the United States faced a crisis with declining enrollments, decreased public spending and a declining local population (Smith 2019). Thus, the general outlook for public universities in these small college towns has reached a critical point. Nationwide the overall trend in higher education includes decreased public spending, which significantly impacts small public universities that contribute greatly to the economic growth within remote towns and regions. Decreased public spending has to be made up somehow and increased tuition has been one response. To keep overall costs down, universities allow positions to go unfilled, and former employees are forced to move elsewhere for employment. On campus, this cycle impacts many departments, but it is felt particularly among foreign language departments that have a smaller number of majors and a service-oriented curriculum which entails enabling students from other majors to fulfill their language requirement. Remaining staff struggle to produce the same amount of work in teaching, service and research as before. Professors may be forced to make hard choices that prioritize research over teaching or service, especially untenured professors, and curriculum offerings are subsequently cut. Professors strapped for time try to come up with solutions to recruit more students and retain those in the program while fending off the outside threats within the university that consider downsizing the department to make up for lost revenues.

The above description depicts the case at Southern Illinois University in Carbondale (SIUC). Even with rather substantive student enrollment in languages, including a respectfully high number of German majors, world language departments such as at SIUC remain vulnerable, in part because of the small number of overall majors compared to those of other larger departments. According to Gikand (2019), "[f]oreign language departments are easy targets – and the reductions have had devasting consequences" (2). German enrollments in the basic language program decreased dramatically at SIUC within the last decade and parallels an overall decrease in students at the university, which dropped from approximately 17,989 in fall 2014 to 11,695 enrolled for fall 2019 (Fuller 2014; Courtois 2019). Though overall enrollment in first-year German is down by roughly 75%, the number of majors in German has remained constant and hovers around 14 to 16 in any given year.[1]

Annually at SIUC, when the internal list of the numbers of majors within the College of Liberal Arts is available, we consider our numbers in comparison to other departments to see what risk we are facing. We tend to act proactively to make internal changes, such as in 2014 when we combined all of our majors into one – called Languages, Cultures, and International Studies – within the department to strengthen our numbers, and by doing so, fended off any potential future threats associated with numbers of majors. Not all German students want a major called Languages, Cultures, and International Studies with a specialization in German, though. Already aware of its dire situation in 2009/2010, the language department at SIUC added international studies to its curriculum in 2011 as a way to promote foreign languages, to increase the number of majors and to maintain high enrollments.

As a public university in a rural setting, SUIC was very forward thinking in acting on the educational trend of preparing students to work in an increasingly globalized world. The field of international studies emerged as a response to the need to educate global citizens, and the new program acted accordingly as a remedy to boost student enrollment. As Dana Zartner, associate professor of international studies at the University of San Francisco notes, international studies accomplishes many goals that other majors do as well, such as language learning, critical thinking and encouraging students to go abroad, but it has the advantage that "each individual skill becomes more marketable when combined into a complete package through international studies" (149). The creation of international studies programs also responds to a recent trend to make education more interdisciplinary at the college level (Stone et al. 2009, 322).[2] Interdisciplinary efforts are applauded as a way for universities to break through the traditional disciplinary restrictions and recognize the global harmony of elements, thereby preparing students to consider a changing world. This awareness reflects the distant echoes of the education of the Renaissance man who is well studied in a range of fields that complement one another. Further, the diversified skill set that international studies offers prepares students for an array of professional opportunities.

In this chapter I discuss the international studies program at SIUC and the strategies our language department used when establishing the program. Specifically, I address the key role that our introductory course played in adding cohesion to an otherwise fragmented interdisciplinary curriculum. It acted as the unifying element for students in their pursuit of an individually tailored international studies degree outsourced to a variety of departments, mainly within the College of Liberal Arts. As I will explain, as long as the introductory course was offered, the program maintained its position as the largest program within the department.

Description of SIU Carbondale and its international studies program

Southern Illinois University in Carbondale is a public rural university with roughly 12,000 undergraduates, 75% of whom are from Illinois and the other 25% from other geographic locations in the United States and worldwide. Students within the College of Liberal Arts take languages for a variety of reasons, including the need to satisfy a one-year language requirement. In the past, 100- and 200-level courses were part of the core curriculum, and students enrolled in the first-year language course to fulfill the language requirement.[3] Currently, American Sign Language, Chinese, French, German, Japanese, Latin and Spanish are offered in the Department of Languages, Cultures, and International Trade (LCIT)[4] in addition to the signature programs foreign language and international trade (FLIT) and international studies, with a total of 53 majors. In 2019–20, 72 students enrolled in fall semester and 67 students in spring semester German courses which were taught by two assistant professors and two graduate students. There were a total of 16 majors in German Studies (or equivalent): ten in German Studies; one in International Studies-German; one in FLIT-German and four in the Teacher Education Program-German. In addition, German graduated four students in May 2020. There are generally two to five minors in any given year.

Like many other similarly situated programs, our department has faced several existential challenges over the past decade. In fact, the international studies major was born from crisis: roughly ten years ago a former dean, hostile to the importance of language study, proposed the elimination of the college-wide language requirement. After resolving the issue by gathering support from other department heads in the college, our department created the international studies undergraduate program at SIUC as a lifeline to increase enrollment in modern languages and to secure the existence of its foreign languages department. As detailed in this essay, the international studies program strengthened our department, yet over the past several years, language learning at SIUC has faced additional existential challenges due to a series of financial hardships facing the university. From 1 July 2015 to 31 August 2017, Illinois state schools experienced a financial crisis that was caused by the inaction in approving an annual budget. Public state schools went without state funding for two years, which resulted in a general sense of uncertainty concerning the future of education in Illinois (Strayer 2016). Drops in attendance were felt statewide across disciplines and compounded the sense of instability. Already in 2014, 16,461 residents left for out-of-state universities while only 2,117 out-of-state students came to Illinois for college, according to the U.S. Department of Education (Strayer 2016). Additionally, the Illinois Board of Higher Education suggested plans to eliminate all undergraduate majors that graduated fewer than five students per year, which led the department to consolidate all individual majors (such as German, East Asian Language and Culture, French, Spanish, international studies, and foreign language and international trade) into one larger departmental languages major, as mentioned briefly in my introduction.

Compared to other universities, SUIC's international studies program stands in a relatively unique position, in that its major and minor are housed in the Department of Languages, Cultures, and International Trade. Created by a former LCIT chair and German professor, Anne Winston-Allen, to help prevent future crises similar to the one that had threatened the potential elimination of the college-wide language requirement, international studies increased enrollment in language classes after the faculty senate had approved the creation of the program within the department. Even though most programs include some language learning element that world language departments offer (Brown et al. 2006, 208)[5] many international studies programs are housed in political science departments, as Robert G. Blanton (2016) notes in his article "Surveying International Studies Programs: Where Do We Stand?" (229). Ishiyama and Breuning's (2004) study of 66 international studies programs in Illinois, Missouri and Iowa generally found that programs existed at institutions with religious affiliations or in which international relations, a subfield in political science, was offered as a graduate program (145). In their study, foreign language departments were not found to be high contributors to international studies programs, which is problematic when considering the unquestionable role languages play, as "there is perhaps no skill more important for our students than second-language acquisition" (Zartner et al. 2018, 150). By housing the international studies program in a languages department, SIUC made a statement on the importance of language within its curriculum. As a program with a strong language focus anchored within the language department, international studies at SIUC promises a broad, internationally informed education that highlights the importance of language skills.

During their studies, students take global and international comparative coursework, select a region of the world as a specialization (Europe, Asia and the South Pacific, Latin America and the Caribbean or Africa and the Middle East) and take language instruction within their region. In the department, coursework is offered in Chinese, French, German, Japanese and Spanish that counts toward the language requirement.[6] Following Zartner et al., who found that "if foreign language study is built into the requirements of the international studies major, as it is in many programs, this ensures that students take more language beyond general university requirements provided the resources are available" (153), students in international studies are required to take three years of language training, thereby sustaining robust enrollments in even third- and fourth-year language classes. Thus, the strong language component in the international studies program indeed strengthened enrollments in the modern languages classes. In addition, other courses can be taken both in and outside of the department to complete the regional as well as the global and international comparative issue coursework[7] with one exception: the introductory seminar which, as the only mandatory course, constitutes the core of the international studies program.

International studies introductory seminar as a cohesive academic core

As Blanton notes in 2009, an academic core is vital to the health of an international studies program, to hold the multidisciplinary major together and to avoid administrative challenges due to the lack of a designated department or resources. Following the research that advocates for "an introductory course, methods training, and a senior capstone course" (Blanton, "What Makes International Studies Programs Successful?" 137), we at SUIC created an introductory course that would be housed in LCIT to help provide a cohesive identity and foundation for the program in Carbondale.[8] Since many students in international studies tend to take classes in anthropology, economics, geography, history and political science (Brown et al. 2006, 208), the program is dependent on other academic units with their own competing curricular needs (Blanton 2016, "What Makes International Studies Programs Successful?" 136). An introductory course is therefore of great importance since it constitutes a curricular core that contributes to a sense of community among the students within the international studies program.

As the director of international studies at SIUC from 2012 until 2016, teaching the international studies introductory seminar was one of my annual teaching duties[9] and was instrumental in growing the program. Under my leadership, international studies grew from the first student who signed up for the major in 2011 to over 40 majors which was more than double the number of majors in any individual language major. The introductory course fostered a sense of community and brought majors and minors together while also being popular with non-majors, who often wanted an internationally guided course to complement the content in their own programs. More than 75% of all students who enrolled in the introductory course for international studies were associated with LCIT. German majors only comprised around one-fifth of the overall students.[10] Students either majored or minored in international studies or one of the languages offered through our department and ranged from freshmen to seniors, with seniors representing the largest percentage of students, followed by sophomores, freshmen and juniors in that order. Over the four years that I was the primary instructor, the combined division of undergraduates by class were: 18 freshmen, 25 sophomores, 17 juniors and 29 seniors.

The general goal of the international studies introductory course, apart from bringing students together, was to provide an overview of the academic field of international studies. Students analyzed global issues and developments by incorporating the disciplinary perspectives of history, geography, political systems, economic structures and socio-cultural milieu into their work. The course topics covered ranged from, but were not limited to, forms of material religious expression, cultural contributions of refugees and the impact of foreign aid to developing countries. In addition, the introductory course engaged students in several ways, from regular guest speakers, to preparing chapter readings, to conducting independent research for presentations, to researching opportunities abroad. The activities I assigned correlated with suggestions concerning best practices to educate international studies students (Zartner et al. 2018, 148–169), e.g., the importance of engaging students educationally on a variety of levels as well as the significance of preparing students for professional employment.

Main learning objectives of the introductory course

Following Zartner et al.'s advice, my introductory course was built around three important learning objectives: 1) learning about international research sources; 2) improving presentation skills and 3) identifying international opportunities for work abroad. Over the course of the semester, students read about the contributions of various disciplines to international studies, became familiar with theories in the field and began to critically evaluate their findings. The knowledge gained from the readings was the foundation for examining and analyzing a number of case studies later on in the semester. Furthermore, I focused on the improvement of students' presentation skills with the help of multiple guest speakers who served as role models for the students. Lastly, after having reflected on their individual goals, students researched and identified international programs and grants to which they could apply for self-advancement opportunities involving internships, study abroad and scholarships. With these learning objectives, I aimed to help prepare students for professional life, as the research skills and the public speaking skills were transferable to any career after graduation, including an international one.

Another objective that stood out to me was to provide students with an introduction to all things international within our community in order to highlight Carbondale's multicultural elements. In my introductory course, students learned about the United Nations Association Southern Illinois Branch and the various language club activities, volunteer opportunities with local migrant workers as well as international resources available to them at SIUC's Morris Library. Hence, this course served as an outlet to communicate with the international studies majors concerning international student clubs, international volunteer work and study-abroad information. Though not required, students who elected to follow up and participate in these opportunities could gain an appreciation of cultural identity and multicultural diversity on a first-hand basis.

Case studies as a window to the world

The presentation of case studies was one of the most substantial projects assigned for the class, and fulfilled many learning objectives of the course mentioned above, including learning about international research sources, improving presentation skills and identifying international opportunities for work abroad. Students were asked to select their topics from readings in our textbook which addressed important global issues such as "International

Terrorism," "Turkey and the EU: The Crossroad from Europe to Asia" and the "Global Population Projection." In groups, students read and summarized the case studies and performed additional research to determine which human rights issues were at stake, e.g. by consulting the Universal Declaration of Human Rights. After they had identified potential human rights violations with the help of the United Nation's Global Goals for Sustainable Development, their subsequent task was to find organizations that promised to alleviate those issues. My goal was for students to learn about individual challenges facing specific regions of the world, to become familiar with the Universal Declaration of Human Rights and to research organizations that work to address such problems.[11] Their findings led to critical discussions in their groups about the needs of people worldwide and subsequent presentations of those findings to their peers.[12]

Placing a fair amount of emphasis on presentations not only helped students to become more engaged and to think critically, but it also honed their public speaking skills for the workforce. Zartner et al. argue, "[a]s educators, it is our job to help our students understand how to link what they are learning in the classroom to the broader skill set that employers are looking for" (149). As the students worked in groups, the presentations validated their work and helped to broaden the general interest in the material while creating new questions for future research.

The widespread enthusiasm within the class led me to develop an additional assignment in which students identified scholarships to study abroad or internships with an international focus on humanitarian concerns and civic engagement that they could apply to during their college years. The assignment followed guest lectures hosted by the Office of Study Abroad and board members from the United Nations Association Southern Illinois Branch with the goal of sharing general benefits of studying abroad and breaking down the application process. One board member of the UN Association, a retired professor from the SIUC School of Medicine, talked about her experience as a Peace Corps volunteer in Malawi and her volunteer efforts in northern India to help eradicate polio. Through this exercise, students took the first step toward an international career by considering the different types of global opportunities and how to apply for them.

As Zartner et al. note, "study abroad, of course, builds a large number of skills that are beneficial to students, including intercultural and cross-cultural communication skills, independent thinking, critical analysis, adaptability, flexibility, and foreign language" (153). The authors further suggest that the internships, independent research and community engagement offered abroad can even increase students' marketability (153). By being asked to research and apply to scholarships or internships, students gained confidence in their ability to succeed in real life, which was greatly enhanced when students actually were offered positions, such as an internship in Germany at Coutinho Ferrostaal GmbH in 2013 or multiple grants to continue their Arabic language training in the United Arab Emirates in 2014. Thus, it did not come as a surprise that on their end-of-the-semester evaluations each year, students mentioned how this part of the project helped them beyond the expectations of the classwork. In addition to the substantive issues, students appreciated the practical element, as one student from my 2014 course commented that the class "gave me a great view into some of the possible jobs I could get when I graduate. I'm a senior so that helped me a lot!" and in 2016 another student remarked that she/he liked "hearing about job opportunities related to my major."

Overall the introductory course structure was well received; students stated on the 2016 evaluations that they benefited greatly from: "getting to know about other subject areas relevant to international studies," "learning about all regions of the world and not just our focus area" and "learning about past and present issues in different regions of the world." In 2015, they praised the course by discussing "so many different topics from all across the world" and in 2014, they valued "learning about different cultures." In particular, the inclusion of guest speakers was appreciated as students enjoyed "finding out about other people's professions" and liked to "hear the experiences of professors from different departments focusing on different countries or regions." Seeing the nuanced perspectives of the guest speakers gave the students models to think critically about issues relating to global developments. There was a synergy effect that resulted from the inclusion of these scholars. Incorporating lectures from interdisciplinary experts gave students a chance to meet professors whose courses they could count for their major and equally gave the professors an opportunity to promote their international courses and clubs to potential new members. On a larger scale, students specifically gained an awareness of the Universal Declaration of Human Rights and the Global Goals for Sustainable Development – information to guide well-informed citizenry, both locally and globally, in their decisions concerning justice, gender equality, poverty, hunger, illiteracy and the environment.

In my last two years as director of international studies, I also started asking students to present their senior projects in the international studies introductory course as a way for the beginning students to learn about the wide variety of projects students worked on in the major.[13] The senior projects allowed students the opportunity to bring together various components of the major that included comparative issues and a regional focus. For example, one student wrote about terrorism in European countries and the freedom of movement granted through the Schengen Agreement, another focused on Syrian refugees and ethnic cleansing and a third student read news sources in French about Ebola – a topic that originated from a United Nation's Association talk the student attended at SIU Carbondale's School of Law. The inclusion of the presentation of projects gave senior students the chance to practice their own presentation skills that would help them on the job market in addition to mentoring the new students in the program.

Conclusion

As the university faces continued challenges, the international studies program is forced to make changes to the curriculum. Overall university enrollment in fall 2019 was 11,695, down 8.75 percent from fall 2018 (Courtois 2019, 1). With the departures of students, faculty departures have followed. Key faculty from other departments who had offered international courses that counted for the international studies major have gone unfilled for a number of years, which in turn has hurt a multidisciplinary program that depends on international courses being offered by a variety of departments. The administration is no longer filling positions simply because someone leaves. The introductory course that I described in this chapter has not been taught since 2016, as the international studies directors after me did not offer the course and waived the requirement for majors. By not offering the introductory course – the only aspect of the program required for all majors – international studies ultimately lacked the sense of community that is needed for a program to thrive, and the number of majors has dwindled. Once the largest major in the department, the number of majors has now dropped to a point at which the department has to decide whether to revamp or eliminate the program.

The new international studies director, Satoshi Toyosaki, associate professor of Japanese who recently joined our department, has proposed and passed promising widespread curricular changes to the original major. The result of the reshaping of international studies will make our language department less dependent on the regular offerings of other international courses from departments beyond our own. Luckily, there is not only one set model of an international studies program, as Blanton notes in his study of international studies programs throughout the country ("Surveying International Studies Programs" 224). To keep the program at SIUC viable, changes to the international studies curriculum allow students to count more courses from the Department of Languages, Cultures, and International Trade for the major. The new program also does not have a language requirement, making language study instead one of several electives. These changes will help ensure that students can take enough courses required for graduation, as our own language course offerings have also decreased due to a downsizing of language sections.

The importance of collaboration across disciplines cannot be stressed enough, yet there is also much to be said for intradepartmental support that the new version of international studies major enjoys these days. Whereas, before, the international studies program with its social science leanings left many language and cultural humanities scholars in the department as mere observers, the new curricular changes allow many faculty members to play an active role in the program. Courses that are already taught can now be counted toward the major, thereby generating a new interest in the international studies program among existing faculty. Thus, while faculty tended to be less involved in the initial creation of the program, they are now much more familiar with the international studies program and have been willing and able to contribute to the discussion that preceded the introduction and vote of changes at the departmental level.

Teaching the introductory course was one of my regular annual teaching assignments in the department in addition to the German language and culture courses that I taught for the German section. The addition of international studies as part of my service assignment increased my interaction with students outside of the German language and broadened my perspective in terms of departmental needs and sensitivities. For example, I gained insight into what and how other language students wanted to learn about international issues outside of their own regional specializations. In my role as international studies director and as instructor of the introductory seminar, I was fortunate to interact with a wide variety of students from within and outside of our language department on a number of levels: student adviser, administrator and recruiter for the program. Ultimately, it did not hurt German for me to be involved in an interdisciplinary program, as we had two other tenured/tenure-track faculty members who focused only on the students in the German major. However, the directorship did reorient my service away from activities that were entirely German-language focused and toward those activities that were centered on international studies.[14]

As international studies remains housed within LCIT, the introductory course itself is being replaced in the revised curriculum with another culture course that may be able to act as a cohesive element of the program.[15] The international studies program's potential for renewed success should show Germanists at other institutions the promise of interdisciplinary programs as a way for German programs to remain viable during this time of unparalleled uncertainty in higher education.

Notes

1 This is due in part thanks to a highly generous ongoing scholarship from Dr. Helmut and Mary Liedloff, who since 1986 have offered scholarships for undergraduate majors in German, funding three new German majors annually with full tuition scholarships for three years. The recipients of these scholarships are new recruits selected from Illinois high schools and community college programs.
2 The MLA reported already in 2007 the need for a more interdisciplinary curriculum to foster the teaching of culture in "Foreign Languages and Higher Education: New Structures for a Changed World," a report that spurred widespread discussion in the scholarly community. Including, but not limited to the following, were responses by Germanists Cathy L. Jrade in *ADFL Bulletin*, Carol Anne Costabile-Heming in *German Quarterly*, Lisabeth M. Hock in *Die Unterrichtspraxis/Teaching German (UP)*, and Heidi Byrnes in *Modern Language Journal*.
3 The basic language program in German decided to withdraw from the core curriculum in AY 2016–2017, which may also have caused the drop in enrollment by 75%. The two German intermediate courses offered at 200-level have remained in the core curriculum.
4 The former Department of Foreign Languages and Literatures, changed its name to the Department of Languages, Cultures and International Trade preemptively

to help comply with the expected new directive adopted by the State of Illinois Board of Higher Education that called for Illinois public universities to eliminate majors that did not graduate a certain number of majors every year. Few languages had that requisite number of graduating majors. The department took the additional step of combining all of the department's seven majors into one broader major, called Languages, Cultures and International Studies, and made our former majors into specializations. This new directive was ultimately not put into effect, however.

5 SIU Carbondale was not included in their 2004 study, as the program did not begin until 2011.
6 Other languages such as Arabic, Korean and Russian are taught separately in the Linguistics Department on a one-year basis depending on graduate assistant staffing. Students who begin language training in a language outside of the department's offerings may finish the language requirement abroad. For example, one student went to Jordan in the summer of 2012 to live with a host family and finish her language training in Arabic. It is possible for students to use other languages not offered at all at our university to meet the language requirement. For those languages not taught at our university, students could fulfil the requirement at another intensive language program approved by the department, such as the one offered at Indiana University in the summer months or go abroad to receive credit for their language training.
7 Students take five courses in both their regional specialization and in global and international comparative issues. International law or world history are examples of global and international coursework offered in other departments. Several of our language courses that focus on culture also count toward the international studies degree, typically within the regional focus rubric. For example, my course on the European Union taught in German counted toward students European regional specialization.
8 Though not a course, students of international studies have an additional required senior project. This focused research served as senior capstone experiences. The senior projects are individually planned in coordination with a faculty advisor.
9 My position as international studies director was a central component of my appointment as assistant professor of German. I received a two-credit hour course release for the work. In my role, I tried a number of projects to help make the major cohesive and give it its own identity, such as starting a monthly newsletter, creating and administering exit interviews and creating the International Studies Job Series.
10 The ratio for students of German was around 17% three of the years and at 7% in 2014.
11 The Universal Declaration of Human Rights was created in 1948 by the United Nations' General Assembly. The document identifies fundamental human rights that all people and nations should protect. More information is available on the United Nations' website: https://www.un.org/en/universal-declaration-human-rights/.
12 Adopted in 2015, the 17th United Nations' Sustainable Development Goals target issues concerning poverty to literacy in ensuring peace and prosperity for the planet by 2030. More information is available on the United Nations Development Program: https://www.undp.org/content/undp/en/home/sustainable-development-goals.html.
13 In addition to teaching the introductory course, I directed senior projects each semester, mentoring over 25 senior projects during my tenure as director. A capstone experience is a common element of undergraduate international studies programs (Brown et al. 2006, 275). It gives students the chance "to integrate, apply, and actively learns as an appropriate conclusion to the four-year model" (Levinson 1998, 109). Mentoring students lasted over a semester and involved regularly

meeting individually with each student to discuss their senior projects. Though each of the projects did not specifically entail a language component, using sources from the target language was encouraged.

14 The German section had very mixed support for international studies: though the section was able to count the many international studies majors within its own totals for reporting purposes, the international studies program took away teaching and service time that I would otherwise have devoted to German. Yet, at the height of the program under my leadership there were over 40 majors – much more than any other major in the department. So while the international studies majors did not help German specifically, they did boost the overall departmental numbers, which helped maintain resources within the department.

15 A proposed university restructuring has resulted in the removal of the two largest majors from the College of Liberal Arts (psychology and criminal justice) in 2019. These former departments have now been placed in independent schools that do not have a language requirement. This restructuring plan is being advanced and the Department of Languages, Cultures, and International Trade is scheduled in the next round of departmental eliminations to cease as a department as we merge with one or two other departments to become a new school.

Bibliography

Anderson, Sheldon, et al. *International Studies: An Interdisciplinary Approach to Global Issues*. Westview, 2013.

Blanton, Robert G. "Surveying International Studies Programs: Where Do We Stand?" *International Studies Perspectives*, vol. 10, no. 2, 2009, pp. 224–240.

Blanton, Robert G. "What Makes International Studies Programs Successful? A Survey-Based Assessment." *International Studies Perspectives*, vol. 17, no. 2, 2016, pp. 136–153.

Braunbeck, Helga. "Competition, Connection, and Collaboration in Smaller German Programs." *Die Unterrichtspraxis*, vol. 44, no. 2, 2011, pp. 146–153.

Brown, Jonathan N., et al. "Consensus and Divergence in International Studies: Survey Evidence from 140 International Studies Curriculum Programs." *International Studies Perspectives*, vol. 7, no. 3, 2006, pp. 267–286.

Byrnes, Heidi. "Perspectives." *Modern Language Journal* vol. 92, no. 2, 2008, pp. 284–287.

Chernotsky, Harry I. and Heidi H. Hobbs. *Crossing Borders: International Studies for the 21st Century*. Sage/CQ Press, 2013.

Condray, Kathleen. "Thriving in the New Normal: Meeting the Challenges of Doing More with Less in the Twenty-First-Century German Studies." *Taking Stock of German Studies in the United States*, edited by Rachel J. Halverson and Carol Anne Costabile-Heming, Camden House, 2015, pp. 71–88.

Costabile-Heming, Carol Anne. "Responding to the MLA Report: Re-Contextualizing the Study of German for the 21st Century." *German Quarterly*, vol. 84, no. 4, 2011, pp. 403–413.

Courtois, Brandi. "After Another Dip in Enrollment, Administration Talks Retention." *The Daily Egyptian*, 5 Sept. 2019, dailyegyptian.com/95464/uncategorized/a-smaller-dip-in-enrollment-could-show-siu-heading-in-the-right-direction/. Accessed 20 June 2020.

Fuller, Jennifer, and Brad Palmer. "SIUC Enrollment Up for Fall 2014." *WSIU News*, 3 Sept. 2014, www.news.wsiu.org/post/siuc-enrollment-fall-2014#stream/0. Accessed 20 June 2020.

Gikand, Simon E. "President's Column: Language Matters." *MLA Newsletter*, vol. 51, no. 2, Summer 2019, pp. 2–3.
Hock, Lisabeth M. "Information Literacy across the German Studies Curriculum." *Die Unterrichtspraxis*, vol. 40, no. 1, 2007, pp. 46–56.
Ishiyama, John, and Marijke Breuning. "A Survey of International Studies Programs at Liberal Arts Colleges and Universities in the Midwest: Characteristics and Correlates." *International Studies Perspectives*, vol. 5, no. 2, 2004, pp. 134–146.
Jrade, Cathy I. "Assessing the Present Foreign Language Major and Offering Strategies to Improve It." *ADFL Bulletin*, vol. 41, no. 2, 2000, pp. 83–87.
Kagel, Martin, and William Collins Donahue. "An Immodest Proposal: Reenvisioning German Studies through European Integration." *Taking Stock of German Studies in the United States*, edited by Rachel J. Halverson and Carol Anne Costabile-Heming, Camden House, 2015, pp. 272–301.
Levinson, Nanette S. "A 'Globaliberal' Arts Approach: The International Studies Major and the Next Millennium." *International Studies in the Next Millennium: Meeting the Challenge of Globalization*, edited by Julia S. Kushigian and Penny Parsekian, Prager, 1998.
Looney, Dennis, and Natalie Lusin. "Enrollments in Languages Other Than English in United States Institutions of Higher Education, Summer 2016 and Fall 2016: Final Report." MLA, 2019, www.mla.org/content/download/110154/2406932/2016-Enrollments-Final-Report.pdf. Accessed 20 June 2020.
Matos-Ala, Jacqueline de, and David J. Hornsby. "Introducing International Studies: Student Engagement in Large Classes." *International Studies Perspectives*, vol. 16, no. 2, 2015, 156–172.
MLA Ad Hoc Committee on Foreign Languages. "Foreign Languages and Higher Education: New Structures for a Changed World." *Profession*, 2007, pp. 234–245.
Schroeder, Charles C. "Collaboration and Partnerships." *Higher Education Trends For The Next Century: A Research Agenda For Student Success*, edited by Cynthia S. Johnson and Harold E. Cheatham, American College Personnel Association, Washington D.C., 1999.
SIU Enrollment Numbers. SIU. irs.siu.edu/interactive-factbook/students/full-part-time-enrollment.php. Accessed 25 June 2020.
Smith, Mitch. "Students in Rural America Ask 'What is a University without a History Major?'" *NYT*, 12 January 2019, www.nytimes.com/2019/01/12/us/rural-colleges-money-students-leaving.html. Accessed 20 June 2020.
Stone, Tammy, et al. "Launching Interdisciplinary Programs as College Signature Areas: An Example." *Innovative Higher Education*, vol. 34, 2009, pp. 321–329.
Strayer, Nick. "The Great Out-of-State Migration: Where Students Go." *NYT*, 26 August 2016, www.nytimes.com/interactive/2016/08/26/us/college-student-migration.html. Accessed 20 June 2020.
Zartner, Dana, et al. "Knowledge, Skills, and Preparing for the Future: Best Practices to Educate International Studies Majors for Life after College." *International Studies Perspectives*, vol. 19, 2018, pp. 148–169.

6 Designing a language lab that encompasses cultural and interdisciplinary experiences

Martina Wells

Introduction

Language programs large and small at institutions of higher education in the United States are reevaluating the role they play in the undergraduate liberal arts curriculum. This self-examination is a response to what the Modern Language Association (MLA) report on foreign languages from 2007 calls a "changed world." It has resulted in lively academic discussions highlighting the shift in both institutional and student needs over the past two decades. Concerns about the viability and future of language programs are at the core of the discussions and drive many of the approaches to situate foreign languages (FL) in this new academic environment. While the factors motivating the recalibration of curricula and programs cannot be reduced to a single one, it is the teaching of culture in FL education that takes center stage. Ever since the MLA (2007) report, as the authoritative voice of the profession issued the challenge to systematically "incorporate cultural inquiry at all levels" (239), cultural competence as a pedagogical objective is considered fundamental to preparing world-ready students. In fact, the promotion of cultural competence is understood to inject new life and purpose into language programs.

Designing FL curricula that turn MLA recommendations into practice is difficult to achieve, particularly at small language programs. Limited course offerings in the languages, limited resources and institutional support due to dragging enrollment numbers cripple transformation efforts. Yet, despite the limitations and obstacles, I argue that by tweaking existing program features and by making use of resources provided through units outside of the languages, such as the Offices of Multicultural Affairs and International Affairs and the library, and engaging in community outreach, curricular changes can be successfully implemented. Without upending an entire program, they can signal a step towards meeting the goals outlined in the MLA report.

This chapter introduces a redesigned language lab course as an example of such small-scale curricular changes. Different from a traditional language lab focused on linguistic skills, this one-credit lab course – a corequisite to every language course – creates opportunity for cultural experiences outside of the classroom and complements in-class language learning. The chapter provides an overview of the theoretical and pedagogical frameworks underpinning the course. What follows is a description of the course design, moving from its institutional context to its conceptual framework. Course content with practical examples of specific activities will be discussed. These activities inform a lab model that can readily be adapted and applied to any language and to any level. It is my hope that instructors and coordinators of small language programs seeking low-cost ways to update their course offerings and enhance the extra-linguistic cultural experience of their students might find inspiration in this model.

Literature review and theoretical underpinnings regarding cultural competence

While the MLA report is a key reference point for the design of the language lab course, the course as a tool to teach culture is informed by a number of theoretical and pedagogical concerns about the role culture plays in language education. The urgency to promote and emphasize cultural instruction is widely acknowledged (Schulz et al. 175; Windham 2017, 79; Costable-Heming 2011, 403; Furstenberg 2010, 329; Wurst 2008, 57; Boovy 2016, 140; Kramsch 2014, "Teaching Foreign Languages" 296). However, the question of how to effectively integrate culture in the foreign language curriculum remains a crucial discussion point (Furstenberg 2010, 329; Arens 2010, 322; Byram and Kramsch 2008, 20). Raising the question as to whether it is possible to make culture the core of the language class, Furstenberg highlights a central problem: the lack of a consensus on how to define culture and associated competencies. After all, culture is, to use Furstenberg's explanation, "a highly complex, elusive, multi-layered notion that encompasses many different and overlapping areas and that inherently defies easy categorization and classification" (329). Byram and Kramsch (2008) best summarize the conundrum when proposing to teach language *as* culture, rather than language *and* culture (21). This very idea resonates with calls to bridge the language/literature and culture divide (Wurst 2008, 57; Furstenberg 2010, 329) – a division rooted in a narrow understanding of culture with consequences for the traditional curriculum: it prioritizes canonical literary texts reserved for upper-level language study over cultural texts linked to products and practices. Yet, describing culture from an anthropological perspective as a way of life, i.e. the practices, perspectives and products of a group (Schulz et al. 174; ACFTL Standards), characterizes reform efforts. It forces educators to pay attention to all kinds of texts traditionally not included in FL curricula and alerts them to the way they shape identities. Arens' notion of language as a social field within which individuals function and construct their identities is useful. She reminds us that "learning culture means learning the pragmatics of identity formation within the target C2, not just language, facts, institutions, or objects" (322), thus promoting learning targets around embodied ways of being.

Cultural competence is the operative term capturing a learning objective connected to identity formation. The National Standards (2014) broadly define cultural competence as the learner's capacity to relate cultural practices and products to perspectives and use language skills to investigate and reflect on those relationships. It hinges on the ability to read a variety of cultural texts, to recognize the patterns that inform identities revealed through these texts to then make comparisons with one's own culture. Furstenberg describes the learning behind this ability in terms of an acculturation process, where the teacher guides students in making sense of the jumble of products, practices and perspectives of the target culture (332).

Giving students the opportunity to engage with a range of textual sources not included in their textbooks becomes key to translating Furstenberg's concept into practice. Relevant for this lab project are those approaches concerned with facilitating cultural experiences and engagement with different texts. Sederberg (2013) gives the practical example of interactive and experiential learning through content-based language classes (258). While her model relies on "museum-based learning" to include virtual, on- and off-campus visits to museums, Hellebrandt's model advocates the benefits of hands-on experiences for students through direct contact with German communities off-campus. Similarly, in Boovy, teaching culture takes the shape of engaged and experiential learning by taking students off-campus and connecting them with local communities affiliated with German. Favoring an analogous focus on language learning in context, Euler (2017) discusses the "project method for teaching culture and intercultural competence" and action-learning: working with authentic subject material relevant to the students' life experiences is expected to boost cultural competence (67).

Inherent in these methods is the idea of pleasure – a feature Kramsch deems vital to language learning. Kramsch (2012) values pleasure, because it is a sensual experience engaging the whole person. Importantly, she "encourages teachers to focus much more on the visceral, physical, subjective experience of learning and using a language" ("*Im Gespräch*" 74). Equally valued are the affective factors in language learning and their impact on student motivation. They feature in theoretical examples (Davidheiser and Wolf 2009, 61; White 2011, 20) and find their practical application in Prager and Kramer's (2014) model of an extracurricular culture-oriented program called "*Kulturpass*" (42). Creating different kinds of cultural experiences for students emerges as a priority in these approaches and forms a foundation for efforts to reconceptualize the role of culture in language education.

Learner autonomy

Espousing this concern for diverse cultural experiences, the lab course draws on the pedagogy of learner autonomy as both a method and practice for teaching culture. Learner autonomy has been credited with promoting student motivation and self-initiative, accommodating different learning styles and types of learners and allowing control over the learning process, to name just some of the benefits of individual learning (Benson 2013; Godwin-Jones 2019,

"Riding"). But learner autonomy is a highly complex construct; its meaning has shifted over the last 30 years from an association with independence, to interdependence, to being a social construct (Murray 2014, 5) and may even vary in different national or institutional cultures (Godwin-Jones 2019, "Riding" 11; Benson 2013, 840).

A common thread in research on learner autonomy is the role of technology and how emerging technologies challenge definitions and practices. In particular, the "rise of informal language learning online" (Godwin-Jones 2019, "Riding" 8) points to changes in the way autonomous language learning occurs. No longer reducible to the notion of self-paced learning, autonomy should be understood within the social context where it takes place, i.e. the dynamic environments found in the interplay between learner, tools, materials and settings (Godwin-Jones 2019, "Riding" 8). It is a "construct developing through interdependence and collaboration in the social setting of the language classroom" (Murray 2014, 6).

The definition of autonomous learning thus expanded premises Reinders and Benson's (2017) concept of language learning beyond the classroom (LBC) as one form of autonomous learning (561). Their argument problematizes the setting, i.e. the context where learning takes place. Building on Kramsch, they propose viewing settings "as potential elements within broader 'social ecologies' of language learning" (563). Settings understood as a myriad of possible spaces, including face-to-face or Skype communications, language tables, heritage learning in the community, digital gaming or podcasts, online TV dramas or study abroad (Reinders and Benson 2017, 565), become a useful critical term to think about learner autonomy and the cultural experiences the lab offers. Adopting the notion that learner autonomy is a function of its social setting and contextual embeddedness, the course outlined in this chapter provides the scaffolding that facilitates active student involvement in the pursuit of cultural competence.

Institutional context and course design

The lab course was developed at Chatham University, Pittsburgh – a regional, urban liberal arts university with a co-ed student body of 2,200 and with 60 undergraduate and graduate programs centered around its areas of excellence in sustainability & health, business & communications and the arts & sciences. The course originated in response to two distinct institutional needs: first, administrative changes affecting the delivery model of the language courses, and second, the overhaul of Chatham University's internationalization efforts. The course framework applies to all six languages (Arabic, Chinese, French, German, Japanese and Spanish) offered, although course content caters to the specifics of each language and course level taught. They are housed in Modern Languages within the Department of History, Political Science and International Studies. Any of the languages are taught only at the introductory and intermediate levels for a total of four semesters of language study.

Administrative decisions about Chatham University's weekly course schedule grid in 2015 required the language program to shift from a four- to three-credit on-site language course model. To offset the loss in face-to-face instructional time, curricular adjustments became necessary. The one-credit lab course framework was designed to complement each of the on-site language courses to form a 3+1 credit delivery model. Because the lab course is managed online via Chatham University's course management system (Brightspace), course delivery is not affected by the constraints of the weekly scheduling grid and the desired four-credit curriculum for language courses could be maintained.

Additionally, the creation of the lab course was driven by the push to internationalize the undergraduate student experience, mainly through study abroad. Internationalization is defined in the International Programs' (2019) mission statement on Chatham University's website in terms of "providing students with a strong global perspective ... providing curricular and co-curricular experiences on campus and abroad, and involving all students regardless of major." Understanding a culture through experience is the hallmark of study abroad to the effect that cultural literacy becomes integral to a student's linguistic repertoire. While financial incentives have helped increase the number of students studying abroad, the vast majority are unable to seize the opportunity. Most commonly, reasons are of financial and timing concerns. Without a language requirement or language major in place, many students don't find their way into the language classrooms until later in their college careers when it is no longer feasible to build study-abroad experiences into their coursework. The lab course with its focus on cultural and interdisciplinary experiences as part of the foreign language curriculum thus fills a void. Goodman's (2009) argument that "innovative language teaching and cultural experiences on campus can play a critical role in gaining exposure to other cultures" (611) when study abroad is not feasible is salient. The underlying notion of "local internationalization" thus informs the overall lab course rationale: facilitating greater student engagement with another culture locally and beyond the classroom in an effort to boost cultural competence. Moreover, since language study is commonly the primary pathway to study abroad, the lab course seeks to pique student interest in Chatham University's study-abroad offerings.

Conceptual framework

An initial goal for the course design was to construct a flexible framework for cultural experiences that connect students to their language learning in-class and, importantly, to web-based and already existing resources on campus and beyond. These experiences take the shape of weekly activities for a total of 14 weeks over the entire semester. Occupying a hinging position between in-class language instruction and out-of-class activities, the course functions as a vessel that holds all activities together in a structured format. This feature of structural embeddedness counters concerns that the teaching of culture is often done in ad hoc formats which are disjointed, lacking cohesiveness and integration with language learning (Furstenberg 2010, 329; Schulz et al. 175). It also addresses pedagogical concerns to not leave students to operate in a vacuum when performing independent learning tasks. To ensure regular engagement, separate activities are assigned and completed on a weekly basis, ranging in their setting and content. They are grouped into two categories: those that make up the "common" activities required from all students and those constituting the "individualized" activities, which allow students to choose according to their interests and preferences. Within these two categories, activities are characterized by different modes of engagement: independent work, online social interactions and face-to-face interactions. Irrespective of the mode, students' weekly assignments are graded based on task fulfillment rather than on notions of correctness, which helps students focus on the activity and instructors with marking, respectively.

Our course goal aligns with research that emphasizes the importance and impact of broadening the institutional footprint of a small language program through outreach and collaborations with academic and non-academic communities on and off campus (Gelhaar 2009; Wurst 2008; Prager and Kramer 2014, Costable-Heming 2011; Boovy 2016). This holds true for a stand-alone German program as much as for a small language program like ours where several languages are combined. The importance of outreach is a reminder that language programs exist within a network of relations (Braunbeck 2011, 146), which can be made mutually beneficial to the constituents. The impact of outreach speaks to the much richer learning environment for students as a result of operating in a network – much richer than a small language program could otherwise afford. Making creative use of resources not directly linked to language study is therefore integral to the success of the lab course as a space for socio-cultural explorations. An additional benefit of such networking addresses the greater visibility of the program on campus, by documenting activities in pictures and updates with the help of newsletters and social media.

A second course goal was to design a framework that is grounded in sound pedagogical practices. Unlike learning a language with its focus on grammatical correctness and vocabulary memorization, cultural competence requires a different set of skills, as the MLA report showed. Paramount is the act of reflection when engaging with the products, practices and perspectives (ACTFL Standards) of the target culture. In our model, this kind of reflection can occur at the level of a single activity, while keeping in mind that the composite of individual reflective acts will deepen cultural knowledge and cultural sensitivities over the course of the semester. Based on this premise, the pedagogical objectives are: 1) to gain a basic understanding of the products, practices and perspectives that inform the target culture; 2) to motivate students to be active and autonomous in exploring the target culture; 3) to develop a mental frame of reference that includes values and perspectives outside of students' own culture.

Course content and activities

The broad frame of possible settings and networks has resulted in the mosaic-like quality of activities and cultural texts included in the course. In designing the activities, we wanted to be mindful not only of the institutional context, but also of our particular student body. According to Costable-Heming (2011), the "survival of German Programs lies with recognizing who our students are and identifying what their needs are" (409). There is agreement that student needs in higher education have changed (MLA report). Low enrollment numbers and diminishing student interest in in-depth language study are indicative of such changes. This is no different at Chatham University. Most of the students who find their way to language study don't commit to more than the introductory or intermediary sequences, or portions thereof. However, they want to learn about the other culture from day one – "it's fun and different" as students have put it – despite the limitations their rudimentary linguistic skills create. We can't afford to not tap into this curiosity early on – a duty Davidheiser and Wolf (2009) aptly describe as "fanning the flames" (60). It challenges us to engage students in ways that bring the culture alive and allows them to gain access regardless of the linguistic barriers typical of the early language acquisition phase. Hence, we need to move away from the idea that a monolingual, i.e. German-only classroom and cyberspace, is essential for gaining cultural competence. Quite to the contrary, it is imperative to use English strategically to facilitate both cultural literacy and enthusiasm for learning the target language. Furthermore, it is also important to remember that our typical student, fresh out of high school, has never traveled abroad or lived in a community with diverse populations. Thus, even socio-cultural encounters or experiences that seem trivial to us educators, who often have diverse cultural backgrounds and are versed in all things international, can make an imprint on a student.

With this in mind, my next step is to introduce activities as examples of successful cultural engagement. A common thread in these exercises is the blending of learning modes – independent work, face-to-face and online socio-cultural interactions – and their relationship with in-class language study with its primary focus on developing linguistic skills. Concordantly with Reinders and Benson's "fluid, and dynamic view of the classroom," the classroom and lab combined form an "interconnected web of learning opportunities" (574).

Independent work

Within the category of independent work fall those activities that students complete without social interactions. Required resources are linked to technology, in particular the Internet. Because assignments are web-based, students enjoy some discretion and therefore control over the learning process. The on-demand format of such text types allows for flexibility in timing and self-paced learning. Materials include watching instructor-suggested video clips and films but are not limited to these tried and tested tools. Podcasts have proven to be a valuable addition to the repertoire, especially when offering "pedagogically assisted content" (Godwin-Jones 2011, "Autonomous" 6). *Deutsche Welle* (DW) publishes news podcasts which are perfect to introduce students to current affairs related to Germany. A popular staple of the lab course is "Germany in the News." The *DW* English language podcast is particularly useful for the first-year students. While the *DW* English language version is critical to the success of the activity at the novice level, the *Deutschlandfunk* podcast "*Nachrichten leicht*" works for intermediate students. At either level, students select news items of interest to them, search for coverage of the same events in U.S. media outlets and write comparisons of the coverage in English. Vocabulary work using the sites' built-in resources complements the writing.

Other activities provide more narrowly defined guidelines for the online research. Here, specific topics directly relate to textbook[1] units from the onsite course and extend vocabulary and content learned in class. Examples are the creation of a weather map for a particular week, a virtual shopping spree at a department store or a virtual museum visit, a rental apartment search for an imagined study abroad in Germany or the mapping of a weekend trip to a city in Germany including train travel and hotel reservations. Always popular is the creation of a personal profile in presentation format, the parameters of which can be adapted to any language level. Recording their profile presentation on Voicethread and sharing it with peers not only elevates the work into the realm of publication, but also adds an element of fun.

Online social interactions

If the "independent work" activities require students to work on their own using web-based tools, the second category of "online social interactions" asks them to use technology to connect with peers. With the heading "autonomous, not alone" Godwin-Jones (2011) gets to the point of the social aspects of learner autonomy ("Autonomous" 6). It recognizes sociability as an important factor in autonomous learning, one made possible by the growing inventory of tools available for digital literacies (Benson 2013, 839). This can take the form of a peer network established with the help of online resources, or simply of one-on-one online interactions. Best practices in online intercultural exchanges rely on the "facilitation of online interaction with peers and a tutor" (Nissen 2016, 11). Because facilitation enhances the effectiveness of the exchange, the online social interactions supported by the lab course are instructor-mediated. They involve asynchronous email exchanges and oral-synchronous Skype meetings with partners in Germany found through the instructors' personal connections, as well as synchronous text chats. Students prepare questions and research a particular topic from the current textbook unit to engage in a conversation with a partner abroad or a peer from the on-site class. Instructors facilitate partner matching, although some students choose peers through a network of their own. Given the limited German communication skills at the novice level, conversations are conducted in English. In the case of email exchange and text chat, students submit a copy of the conversation for feedback and grading. Skyping proves to be particularly popular when the partner is familiar. This is the case when students Skype with other students from Chatham University currently studying abroad, their familiarity making the discussions about their daily experiences in Germany easily relatable.

Face-to-face social interactions

Rather than relying on social interactions facilitated online, our third category concerns face-to-face learning experiences on and off campus. The German Language Table offered once or twice during the semester provides a less scripted and less structured format for using the language than the classroom. A different setting for practicing the language is made available through the Conversation Partner Program. Here, the Modern Languages Program collaborates with the English Language Program to facilitate one-on-one encounters between our international German students and students of German. From a pedagogical perspective, engagements of this kind promote intercultural exchange on campus and language practice. Our most visible and popular activity combining the dimensions of outreach and language use is the International Karaoke Night, held one evening a semester at the campus café lounge. Students from different language classes alternate to perform songs as a group in their target language. Preparation with the lyrics is done as a lab assignment via Moodle and includes vocabulary work, whereas practicing their songs takes place in out-of-class meetings and during class. With similar preparation requirements, our International Holiday Dinner and International Dessert Night at the end of fall and spring term introduce students of all language backgrounds to holiday and food traditions from around the world. Performing events like these as a unified program has its benefits: it demonstrates the vitality of the program, creates community and excitement and showcases in a public space the language learning done on campus.

Other forms of outreach on campus include the participation in the Study-Abroad Fair, the Global Mixer events offered through the Office of International Affairs, or ad hoc workshops,[2] e.g. the German elections workshop with political science students. Outreach within the community at large involves going off campus: a walking tour of the Deutschtown neighborhood tracing German immigration to the area, a visit to the local symphony's German composer-inspired concert followed by a meeting with its Austrian conductor Manfred Honeck or workshops and cultural events hosted by our academic partner institutions.

The opportunities to find synergies suitable for cultural experiences are numerous. Given that the semester allows for only 14 activities, choices must be made. A useful selection criterion is the overarching goal to expose students to a variety of cultural experiences. It is important that the instructor be nimble in adapting the curriculum, not only to accommodate learning styles, but also spontaneously arising learning opportunities such as local theater productions, foreign films or food festivals. This kind of flexibility also means that instructors must create alternative online learning opportunities for those students unable to attend events due to other commitments. Missing out on cultural experiences in person becomes less of a hindrance for students when able to bypass their time constraints in this learner autonomy-focused model.

Assessment and discussion

Research recognizes both the difficulty in assessing cultural competence in terms of quantifiable data and the prevalence of indirect measures to evaluate learning outcomes (Schulz et al.; Godwin-Jones 2013, "Integrating"). The lab course, too, relies on assessment tools of written student feedback and evaluations rather than data-driven testing structures common in assessing linguistic competencies. Student responses from weekly assignments combined with their final reflections provide insights into the learning process and their perceived values thereof. Since a larger sampling is desirable when determining patterns, comments from language labs other than German are considered.

Feedback collected from over the past three years points to a sharp learning curve regarding curriculum development. Instructors' discretion in designing activities for a cultural lab so different from their customary on-site language course has posed challenges. Students early on iterated that there was "confusion about assignments," and expressed their need for "announcements as reminders," or said it was "difficult to complete assignments for students who are not on campus the majority of time" or "this work load leans towards heavy, due to the time commitment that some cultural events require, for only one credit." Comments like these highlight pedagogical hurdles: the online course format, identification of appropriate settings and modes of learning, clarity of instructions and the adaptation of resources to fit with student needs. Because the lab course lives in cyberspace and involves autonomous learning, clear communication of expectations in all areas is thus key. Online resources required for independent work must be carefully curated and constantly updated to avoid losing students in the Internet jungle without a map, and activities tied to fixed events must be paired with alternative assignments. Instructors can provide models for particular assignments as a way to guide students. Adaptability and flexibility in choosing activities are important design factors.

The trajectory that has emerged in student feedback since making adjustments reflects the lessons learned. Many students mention the benefits of having choices each week and appreciate the range of activities included: "I like having multiple options to choose from for each lab," "this course has a great mixture of online and out-of-class activities," "it's helpful to be able to do the assignment in fits and spurts, when I have time around other commitments." As these comments suggest, the lab's effectiveness is linked to the mechanics of course design, not to content only. But, beyond addressing design issues, what do they say about the stated pedagogical learning objectives?

Reading student reflections through the lens of these objectives provides some answers. Comments consistently emphasized the value of working with current and authentic materials reflecting real-life issues. Here, activities related to independent work with podcasts and websites stood out. One student stated that "while listening to the podcasts I was able to tell how different French news is compared to American news; the French were not biased," and others offered that "listening to the news in another language ... means that additional aspect of learning about those news from the perspective of someone not even on this continent" or that "often the labs coincided with something that was currently going on in Germany." With reference to food culture, students noted, "it seems that Germans drink a lot of mineral/sparkling water instead of just plain tap water" or "I was surprised to learn how much coffee the French drink and how many courses there are in a meal." Responses like these reveal the discoveries made when engaging with the target culture. They demonstrate that students begin to construct a comparative framework allowing them to reflect on their own practices and viewpoints. This ability to recognize that there are other ways of being and doing in the world is one of the tenets of cultural competence.

The second course objective calls on students "to be active and autonomous in exploring the target culture." Students offered many comments addressing the lab's inspirational qualities. They mentioned "I love seeing the topic for the lab each time I open an assignment ... some of the lab content has influenced me to do further research outside of class" and another said "I don't think I would have done well in the on-site class without this lab. It pushed me to do more work away from class and constantly widen my radius" or "I used to shy away from websites in Spanish, but I have better learned to navigate them and feel more comfortable." Such reports are a reminder that guidance and contextualization of discoveries support autonomous learning outcomes (Euler 2017, 5). Motivation depended on trying out different learning modes and settings, leading students to make greater efforts – and efforts matter in learning. Fun and pleasure are thus factors not to be dismissed and contributed to student commitment. Students responded particularly positively to activities involving their senses: "My favorite activity was the international dessert party, because I could meet other students studying all kinds of languages and try desserts from around the world" or in the words of another, "having to find a German restaurant or activity in the city was the most fun, interesting and memorable for me." Examples like these suggest that the learning process was enhanced and more meaningful to the student when engaging in the experience with others. As one student put it: "The activities that truly helped me the most were some of the hands-on experiences, such as the karaoke night. Seeing all the language students and the variety of languages studied come together and having fun gives me hope for the entire world" or put differently, "taking a universal concept such as karaoke, but hearing it in a multiplicity of languages gave me a glimpse into other cultures in an enjoyable manner." The shared experience created a sense of community, joining students as members of a world so much bigger than their own. Recognizing the different cultures that their languages represent while finding in themselves the ability to belong is a valuable lesson learned. Being able to place oneself within a broadening frame of reference is an important function of cultural competence.

Conclusion

With this course, students venture into extra-linguistic experiential learning to explore the complex contexts in which their target language exists. Because culture is a dynamic field with meaning production always evolving, the course design needs to be adaptable to stay current and to fit program needs. It offers a practical framework for integrating a variety of cultural texts into the language curriculum, including those provided through partners on and off campus. In this sense, the course is a true laboratory, where new and unscripted discoveries can be made. Discoveries discussed show that students even at the novice level of language study are able to sharpen their cultural awareness and appreciate perspectives particular to the target culture, leading them to make connections with their own lives and the world at large. Importantly, students identified the lab activities as a motivator in furthering their language study – a welcome boost to our program that has influenced the decision to reintroduce language minors. Creating a sense of community among language students and lending the program visibility and vitality are net gains not only for German, but for all languages.

Notes

1 In both introductory and intermediate German, we use the textbook *Wie geht's* by Sevin & Sevin, published by Cengage.
2 In the past, workshops have been organized by a number of academic and non-academic units, such as Modern Languages, the library, the Office of Multicultural Affairs or the English Language Program.

Bibliography

Arens, Katherine. "The Field of Culture: The Standards as a Model for Teaching Culture." *The Modern Language Journal*, vol. 94, no. 2, 2010, pp. 321–324.
Benson, Phil. "Learner Autonomy." *TESOL Quarterly*, vol. 47, no. 4, 2013, pp. 839–843.
Boovy, Bradley. "German Beyond the Classroom: From Local Knowledge to Critical Language Awareness." *Die Unterrichtspraxis*, vol. 49, no. 2, 2016, pp. 140–146.

Braunbeck, Helga. "Competition, Connection, and Collaboration in Smaller German Programs." *Die Unterrichtspraxis*, vol. 44, no. 1, 2011, pp. 146–153.

Byram, Katra, and Claire Kramsch. "Why Is It so Difficult to Teach Language as Culture?" *The German Quarterly*, vol. 81, no. 1, 2008, pp. 20–34.

Costable-Heming, Carol Anne. "Responding to the MLA Report: Re-Contextualizing the Study of German for the 21st Century." *The German Quarterly*, vol. 84, no. 4, 2011, pp. 403–413.

Davidheiser, James, and Gregory Wolf. "Fanning the Flames: Best Practices for Ensuring the Survival of Small German Programs." *Die Unterrichtspraxis*, vol. 42, no. 1, 2009, pp. 60–67.

Euler, Sasha. "Utilizing the Project Method for Teaching Culture and Intercultural Competence." *Die Unterrichtspraxis*, vol. 50, no. 1, 2017, pp. 67–78.

Furstenberg, Gilberte. "Making Culture the Core of the Language Class: Can It Be Done?" *The Modern Language Journal*, vol. 94, no. 2, 2010, pp. 329–332.

Gelhaar, James N. "Of Course They Want Us at the Curriculum and Internationalization Table." *The Modern Language Journal*, vol. 93, no. 4, 2009, pp. 616–618.

Godwin-Jones, Robert. "Autonomous Language Learning." *Language Learning & Technology*, vol. 15, no. 3, 2011, pp. 4–11.

Godwin-Jones, Robert. "Integrating Intercultural Competence into Language Learning through Technology." *Language Learning & Technology*, vol. 17, no. 2, 2013, pp. 1–11.

Godwin-Jones, Robert. "Riding the Digital Wilds: Learner Autonomy and Informal Language Learning." *Language Learning & Technology*, vol. 23, no. 1, 2019, pp. 8–25.

Goodman, Allan E. "Language Learning and Study Abroad: The Path to Global Citizenship." *The Modern Language Journal*, vol. 93, no. 4, 2009, pp. 610–612.

International Programs. Chatham University, August 2019, www.chatham.edu/academics/international-programs/index.html. Accessed 4 April 2020.

Kramsch, Claire, and Sascha Gerhards. "Im Gespräch: An Interview with Claire Kramsch on the 'Multilingual Subject'." *Die Unterrichtspraxis*, vol. 45, no. 1, 2012, pp. 74–82.

Kramsch, Claire, and Sascha Gerhards. "Teaching Foreign Languages in an Era of Globalization: Introduction." *The Modern Language Journal*, vol. 98, 2014, pp. 298–311.

MLA Ad Hoc Committee on Foreign Languages. "Foreign Languages and Higher Education: New Structures for a Changed World." *Profession*, 2007, pp. 234–245.

Murray, Garold, editor. *Social Dimensions of Autonomy in Language Learning*. Palgrave Macmillan, 2014.

The National Standards Collaborative Board. *World-Readiness Standards for Learning Languages*. 4th ed., American Council on the Teaching of Foreign Languages, 2014.

Nissen, Elke. "Combining Classroom-Based Learning and Online Intercultural Exchange in Blended Learning Courses." *Online Intercultural Exchange: Policy, Pedagogy, Practice*, edited by T. Lewis and R. O'Dowd, Routledge, 2016, pp. 173–191.

Prager, Debra, and Daniel Kramer. "The Kulturpass: Strategies for Enhancing Cultural Engagement outside the German-Language Classroom." *Die Unterrichtspraxis*, vol. 47, no. 1, 2014, pp. 42–48.

Reinders, Hayo, and Phil Benson. "Research Agenda: Language Learning Beyond the Classroom." *Language Teaching*, vol. 50, no. 4, 2017, pp. 561–572.

Schulz, Renate, et al. "In Pursuit of Cultural Competence in the German Language Classroom." *Die Unterrichtspraxis*, vol. 38, no. 2, 2005, pp. 172–181.

Sederberg, Kathryn. "Bringing the Museum into the Classroom, and the Class into the Museum: An Approach for Content-Based Instruction." *Die Unterrichtspraxis*, vol. 46, no. 2, 2013, pp. 251–262.

White, Cynthia. "Inside Independent Language Learning: Old and New Perspectives." *Independent Language Learning*, edited by Bruce Morrison, Hong Kong UP, 2011, pp. 15–23.

Windham, Scott. "Culture First: Boosting Program Strength Through Cultural Instruction." *Die Unterrichtspraxis*, vol. 50, no. 1, 2017, pp. 79–90.

Wurst, Karin. "How Do We Teach Language, Literature, and Culture in a Collegiate Environment and What Are the Implications for Graduate Education?" *Die Unterrichtspraxis*, vol. 41, no. 1, 2008, pp. 57–60.

7 The courage to construct and experiment

Initiatives in updating the German minor program at Concordia University

Stefan Bronner and Regina Range

The current situation of the humanities and its effects on (small) German programs

The problems the humanities are currently facing are inextricably linked to the state of (small) German programs and their day-to-day challenges. In U.S. academia, the crisis is already showing severe consequences. Programs within the humanities face major cuts in funding, i.e. German departments lose their graduate programs, positions are frozen, and the student numbers drop due to increasing financial strain. Disciplines like religious studies, classics and other foreign languages do not fare better ever since universities started operating with terms such as "research" instead of "scholarship." Programs and departments consolidate, becoming large entities that only make sense in a corporate way but not academically, for example the combination of classics, linguistics and modern languages at Concordia University in Montréal, Canada. Already in 1977, Michael Fody, who established a small Portuguese program at West Virginia University, pointed out that language programs struggled, citing "the double pressures of decreasing enrollments and spiraling costs" (38). In the 1970s, German was one of the top three languages that were taught in the United States, along with Spanish and French (38). Since then, the conditions for language programs in postsecondary educational institutions have deteriorated. Despite challenging times, those of us who are teaching German and are dedicated to program building are aware of what the humanities can offer our students. Francine Prose's (2017) argument for the value of the humanities rings true:

> the ability to think critically and independently; to tolerate ambiguity; to see both sides of an issue; to look beneath the surface of what we are being told; to appreciate the ways in which language can help us understand one another more clearly and profoundly – or, alternately, how language can conceal and misrepresent ... [The humanities] help us learn how to think, and they equip us to live in – to sustain – a democracy.

To keep our German programs flourishing, we need to cultivate new and creative approaches, openness toward new forms of academic communication, a broad public audience, artistic formats and most importantly, the courage to construct and experiment.

In this chapter, we will provide an overview of the initiatives we undertook to revitalize the German minor program at Concordia University in Montreal between 2013 and 2018. We intend to shed light on the approaches we developed as successive program coordinators to invigorate a wilting program that was suddenly impacted by a university budget crisis and delineate how we collaborated to ensure that the overall vision of the program stayed on course. We will detail our, ultimately successful, strategy for saving the program, which focused on a rigorous curriculum overhaul that updated and broadened the appeal of course content at all levels of German language and culture instruction and included the introduction of a multidisciplinary minor in German. Moreover, we will discuss some of the teaching approaches we employed to increase students' intercultural competency levels. Other endeavors which we share in our chapter include local outreach, internal and external university collaborations, identification and pursuit of adjunct funding sources, enhancement of local and international program visibility and community building within the program itself.

Program description

Concordia University (CU) is a Canadian public university located in Montreal, Quebec. With a student enrollment of almost 47,000 students, it ranks among the largest in the country. The German program at Concordia University is part of the Department of Classics, Modern Languages and Linguistics (CMLL) and just one of the 300 undergraduate programs offered. Despite CU's large size, the German program remains relatively small and has struggled for a variety of reasons, but primarily due to its troubled history regarding an unstable, three-year non-renewable language coordinator position that led to the administration's resistance to further support the program. Ultimately, it took the development of a new curriculum, a long-term plan for the program and two dedicated consecutive language program coordinators to increase the program's visibility and the number of students.

The German minor at CU is a part of the modern languages program, which includes Arabic, Chinese, Spanish and Italian. While Italian, Spanish, Classics and Linguistics all offer a B.A., Arabic and Chinese only offer a minor and certificate option. The minimum admission requirements for CU students do not encompass a language. In 2004, the German program's major was suspended. Along with the introduction of the multidisciplinary minor in German in 2018, the credit hours were reduced from 36 to 30 in order to give students additional incentives to choose German as a minor. The CMLL Department at CU consists of 24 full-time and 35 part-time faculty members. German is the only program that hires a language program coordinator into a Limited Term Appointment (LTA) position, which does not allow for a stay beyond a maximum of three consecutive years, comparable to visiting faculty positions in the United States. The position, focused on teaching and coordination with no financial support for research or conference travel, needs to be renewed annually and is dependent on performance, available financial support and nationality of the candidate.[1] LTAs are responsible for the supervision of part-time faculty and teaching assistants, curriculum design, course scheduling and language placement.

The constant fluctuation of incoming LTAs has undoubtedly affected the program, the quality of instruction and, ultimately, the students' learning experience negatively.[2] With every new LTA hire come different ideas and plans regarding the program's profile and content. Instructors are immediately affected by such changes, as they are asked to adapt to the new standards of the LTA's plan, which might be replaced by the succeeding coordinator. Resignation and disillusionment among part-time faculty regarding their role and impact on the program are a logical consequence. Moreover, the necessity to work at multiple institutions presents a challenge in organizing meetings that all instructors are able to attend. However, finding the time to demonstrate to instructor colleagues that their input and dedication greatly contributes to the quality of the program is crucial. Instructors' motivation to participate in extracurricular events was initially low, due to their multiple appointments.[3] Since both LTAs were and continue to be convinced that in particular small language and culture programs require more engagement beyond the classroom, they made networking, organizing and promoting events to increase the visibility of the program and build a community within the university and the city their priority throughout their terms.[4]

Developing a five- to ten-year plan on a three-year renewal contract: curriculum (re)design

Designing a diverse array of extra-curricular activities was a key step in the creation of a solid, sustainable and up-to-date German program. These extra-curricular activities and community-building events were accompanied by the ambitious task of updating and restructuring the existing curriculum. This reconfiguration was in line with the 2007 MLA report that proposed a broader and more coherent curriculum in which language, culture and literature would be "taught as a continuous whole, supported by alliances with other departments and expressed through interdisciplinary courses" (237). The report suggested that such an approach would allow the reinvigoration "of language departments as valuable academic units central to the humanities and to the missions of institutions of higher learning" (237). Hence, Range instituted changes at all levels of instruction, with one major change being the switch from a German-German to the American-German textbook, *Sag Mal* with the aim to "incorporate cultural inquiry at all levels" in order to entice students to continue their language study (238).

The newly adopted textbook at the beginning level featured an online workbook with language lab-like features, allowing students to record themselves and providing opportunities for collaborative writing and speaking assignments. Every unit contained a wide variety of "authentic" texts covering different genres as well as a video component following the day-to-day interactions of a diverse group of German students in Germany. The textbook was both closer to the students' everyday experience and more age appropriate than previous books. The ability to insert and share additional materials with students and the option for instant feedback, via student-to-teacher and student-to-student chat options, were important components for introducing a more personalized and student-centered learning experience. The new textbook made room for a teaching approach that was more supportive of a "classroom flip" (Baker 2000, 17), also referred to as an "inverted classroom" experience (Lage et al. 2000, 32). Having students work through the material prior to class by "providing a menu of learning options for students" (Lage et al. 2000, 32), freed up valuable time for meaningful in-class communication and student presentations. These presentations focused on topics such as family, personal interests, differences and commonalities in the Canadian and German school systems.

In the second-year German classes, the textbook change to *Denk Mal!* was made to implement a more culture-driven approach, which "not only puts students on a trajectory toward intercultural competency ... [but also] helps boost program strength" (Windham 2017, 83). In addition to the textbooks, Range integrated a variety of digital sources such as YouTube and Vimeo videos, blogs and audio books that accompanied the new textbook. Her assignments included digital projects where students were tasked with creating a video to show Montreal to a fictitious German-speaking study-abroad student, finding and deciding on an apartment or *Wohngemeinschaft* close to a German-speaking university (PPT presentation) or differences between the Canadian and German recycling system (research poster). Often new ideas for topics came about by students' exposure to the weekly *Stammtisch* or to blog entries that the instructor and her German TAs posted on Facebook.[5] This emphasis on various forms of presentations provided CU's German students (as early as the elementary level) with the necessary skills to meet "audience expectations, anticipate questions and use visual aids effectively" (Rarick 2010, 68). Furthermore, the coordinators attempted to take advantage of the strong correlation between cultural study and increased enrollments as postulated by Goldberg et al. (2004, 45ff). Our intention was to enhance students' intercultural competence by updating the curriculum and finding pedagogical approaches that would be more appropriate to serve the needs of CU's diverse student population.

Ultimately, we wanted to build a program that would be sustained and "supported by alliances with other departments and expressed through interdisciplinary courses" (MLA 237). To this end, the upper-level curriculum received an even more rigorous redesign that served as the basis for the multidisciplinary minor Program in German. Offering courses which were interdisciplinary in nature and cross-listed with other programs and departments helped us expand the pool of potential German minors and increased the enrollment numbers for upper-level German courses. The four upper-level courses that Range developed in English were titled: Cyborgs, Robots and Automata in German Literature; Film and Video Games; Of German Witches, Ghosts, Daemons and Vampires; German Women Writers Across the Ages as well as German Exiles in Hollywood and which attracted students from various disciplines.[6]

Apart from the creation of new courses, which was a major focus for Range during her time at CU, Bronner introduced another pedagogical device, which he called Rhizomatic Response Projects (RRPs).[7] These online responses linked literary and theoretical texts to "real life" objects or academic discourses. A text on space theory, for example, could lead to an investigation of the architecture of a university library in order to study how discourses regarding the production of knowledge "translate" into the structure of the building. These team projects provided a broader understanding of the text as a cultural artifact that "communicates" with other discourses in the past and present. Moreover, students connected to other academic disciplines but also responded to texts in non-traditional, artistic and creative ways. During the first two sessions the instructor outlined the main structure of the class, including students' responsibilities and samples of previous RRPs. Class time consisted of two major parts: first, one team shared ideas for their RRP in progress with their fellow students and the professor; second, the class which had only read the departure texts responded with constructive criticism. One project on Johann Wolfgang von Goethe's *Faust*, with a particular focus on the Homunculus episode, initiated political as well as ethical reflections on the research of artificial life – starting with René Descartes and working toward Daniel Dennett's concept of consciousness. In dialogue with the *Faust* text students discussed and worked through questions regarding the essence of the self and the philosophical mind-body problem. Another RRP departing from Georg Büchner's text, *Lenz*, shed light on the notions and history of insanity, which students laid out with Michel Foucault's study, *Madness and Civilization*. With these interdisciplinary projects, students were encouraged to think "beyond" the text and its author and to consider the historical background and network of discourses in which it was embedded.

By the end of the semester, each student team compiled a written blog entry, consisting of traditional academic components, i.e. quotes from secondary sources, an abstract and a bibliography, but also incorporated non-traditional elements, for example, video sequences, images, drawings and installations. Bronner encouraged students to use digital tools, such as interactive maps or programs for digital storytelling. To assess students' comprehension and facilitate discussion, students commented on their peers' RRPs on the blog. This graded feedback consisted of at least one question, thought or reaction to each RRP. The reviews were graded on the basis of the level of abstraction, usefulness for the creators of the RRP and level of involvement. Peer reviews could consist of suggestions for additional readings, ideas, video material, art pieces, newspaper articles and other related cultural artifacts. They offered the possibility to creatively and academically engage with the course readings and projects of fellow students.[8]

Another advantage of the RRPs in comparison to traditional academic papers was the diversity of media that could be included. RRP projects were easier to "present" to and "digest" for fellow students, friends and possibly even parents, for they entailed texts, images, statistics, graphs and videos. Thus, students oftentimes linked their RRPs to their own social media channels or blogs. In class evaluations, students discussed the RRPs' diverse media inclusiveness, which motivated them more than a traditional academic response. In case of exceptional projects, they were published online.

In order to open up conversations between traditional scholarship in literary studies with other fields such as philosophy, media studies and biology, Bronner developed the course Dandies, Flaneurs and Tricksters: Crossover Figures in Modernism, which he cross-listed with the English Department. The course, as part of the newly established multidisciplinary German minor, introduced traditional literary texts and films but also real-life dandy- and trickster figures, such as Karl Lagerfeld, Anna Delvey and the German artist-entrepreneur Rafael Horzon. Students had to find ways to "read" their stories and connect them to the seminar's underlying set of ideas. When discussing dandyism, taste, for example, is a discourse, which connects knowledge in biology with reflections in philosophy. These new courses intended to meet the "changing needs of language learners as global citizens and teach translingual and transcultural competency by offering courses that would encompass German history, media, politics, contemporary society, film, and literature" (Davidheiser and Wolf 2009, 63). This interdisciplinary approach to teaching a literature course placed a clear emphasis on making visible the connections of fictional and theoretical texts to other disciplines and public discourses. In addition to showing students how to "apply" literature and theory, our courses introduced academia as a potential career path to students while also stressing the benefits of the academic skill sets acquired through these courses to others.

To promote the German program outside of CU, Range introduced students to the world of academic conferences in all of her content classes. Students were asked to imagine attending a conference where they briefly had to describe their research topic to a person outside of German Studies. When the University of Toronto published a call for papers for a German undergraduate conference, Range was able to build on her in-class projects and created a workshop for students on how to craft a conference proposal and turn a final essay into an oral presentation. All five students who sent in proposals to the University of Toronto were accepted, presented their research there and shared their experience with other students the following semester. Building on her success in Toronto, Range continued to develop other research projects with her undergraduate students that were collaboratively presented at the Kentucky Foreign Language Conference in Lexington, KY and at the International Conference on *Translation in Exile* in Brussels, Belgium. The skills gained as part of their German classes and their conference presentations prepared students for a variety of other situations (Rarick 2010, 69), among them the future job market or a career in academia.

All new course offerings were bolstered by strategic marketing, including eye-catching flyers and online posts (on Facebook, the German program blog and later on through the Concordia German Language Student Association's Instagram account), which explained the seminar's topic and offered a sneak-peak of the texts and films that were covered in class. As Costabile-Heming (2011) argues: "all language faculty need to become part of the selling game" (406). Yet, in order to keep the workload of the part-time instructors low, LTAs provided PPTs that featured video snippets and QR codes with additional insights. Both LTA and TAs showed shorter versions of these PPTs during their visits to all German classes which were part of the advertising campaign for tutoring and other German program events and offerings. Once again, the importance of actively reaching out was crucial to increase enrollment for these new course offerings. The revamping of the curriculum, the LTAs investment in students' successes and professional development, including the willingness to collaborate with students on projects and conference presentations, quickly became known and aided in convincing the administration to extend the German program even further.

Multidisciplinary minor in German

In the fall of 2016, Bronner introduced the idea of a new multidisciplinary minor program in German, which was approved by the administration and launched in the fall semester of 2018, right after Bronner's departure to the University of Connecticut. The intention behind the minor was to continue updating the existing curriculum and opening it to interdisciplinarity. Students were thus encouraged to branch out within the university and seek out additional courses that would add to German Studies, such as courses in history, philosophy, art history, cinema studies but also biology or neuroscience. This multifaceted and interdisciplinary work valorized students' diversity and showcased the versatility of German Studies. The general idea was to reflect current research trends in the field of German Studies in teaching. Old curricula often strongly focused on German literature and culture and tended to teach content in an isolated manner, such as German drama or film. However, German Studies scholarship today is interdisciplinary in its nature and includes cultural texts from various fields. A study on German right-wing populism, for example, cannot be limited to literary sources and national contexts anymore but must look beyond national borders and encompass diverse materials, such as blog posts, song lyrics or images of album covers. By looking into other fields, students are encouraged to use new tools from other disciplines to widen their analytical spectrum and are thus brought into conversation with other discourses as well.

Like other German programs, the multidisciplinary German minor encompasses language and content courses, taught both in German and English; however, 9 credits out of 30, which is roughly 1/3 of the entire course of study, must be chosen from related disciplines in consultation with the department and can include courses in history, philosophy, art history and religious studies.[9] Additionally, Bronner proposed two new courses, the aforementioned course Dandies, Flaneurs and Tricksters, and Outreach Experience Practicum. For the latter students are asked to develop a feasible project, e.g. organize a German film series at CU or apply for an internship at Montreal's Emile Berliner Museum of Sound or the Goethe-Institut. The goal of the course is to connect students with the wider community, to enhance CU's intellectual life with students' event projects and to support German cultural and educational institutions in Montreal. The practicum course is meant to be tailored individually according to the student's interests and the given needs of local institutions. If the Goethe-Institut in Montreal is hiring an intern for their library, CU's German students are encouraged to apply for the position. In general, the practicum course could be compared to a more individualized and hands-on version of a capstone course, known from German programs in the U.S., as it is also scheduled to be taken in the last year of the program. In case students might work for the Goethe-Institut, this approach is intended to improve their language proficiency level.

Aside from the tasks the students have to complete as interns at the Goethe-Institut, there are minimum requirements that need to be fulfilled to receive credit. Although the practicum course can look different for every student, there must be one collaborative aspect between the institution and CU's German program. For example, one event that a student organized consisted of an exhibition of children's books thematizing and comparing the architecture of cities and city-life in Germany and North America. The project included a day where families were invited to the Goethe-Institut to read German stories with their children and enjoy the exhibition. The student's task was to select the children's books, put together the exhibition, host the reading day and write a report, which included the presentation of the idea, learning objectives, as well as the benefits for German students who visited the exhibition, and also for the local German community. Other options for the practicum include a reasonable number of events organized by the students for other German students at their university. All events must have learning objectives for the student who takes the practicum course and the larger German student community of the university. Ideally, these events should include the local community to inspire interest in, and learning about, German culture and do not necessarily have to be conducted in the German language. The practicum course, therefore, guarantees a constant connection to the local German community and institutions while it, at the same time, increases the visibility of the German program.

Extracurricular activities in Montreal

From 2015 to 2018, Bronner not only continued the curriculum overhaul but he also created several successful extracurricular events to increase student enrolment. He collaborated with McGill University's German Department in organizing: 1) a reading tour for Swiss author Christian Kracht to four Canadian universities in 2016; 2) a talk with Austrian filmmaker David Schalko in 2017 and 3) a creative talk with the Weimar-based artist collective *Giegling* in 2018. German students were involved in all stages of the event planning, which included successful proposals for financial support to the Dean of Students and to the Swiss culture foundation "Pro Helvetia." Furthermore, students assisted with room reservations, the publicizing of the events and the communication with the artists. Their involvement made them a vital part of the program as creators and contributors in an intellectual network (Prager and Kramer 2014, 46). Through these events, students interacted with current authors, filmmakers and music producers of the German-speaking world and connected with them on a personal level. Involving students in the organization of cultural events amplified their interest in the German culture and ultimately enhanced their performance in the classroom. On a larger scale, CU's program benefitted greatly from such collaborative events, for our increased visibility and reputation as a lively part of the German cultural community within the city helped us later in our fight with the administration who wanted to close admissions to the German program.

As mentioned previously, the Goethe-Institut in Montreal was an essential player in our efforts to build the German program since it offered a great resource for information on all things German, including possible business and cultural contacts, and collaborated with CU's German program on multiple occasions. For example, it advertised our readings through their various channels within the city and beyond, thus attracting between 80 and 100 guests to our events. The attendance of both the Consul General of Germany and the Deputy Consul General of Switzerland was particularly relevant in forging a strong sense of community. The Goethe-Institut, furthermore, was instrumental in bringing German artists to Montreal, such as comedian and poetry slammer Till Reiners. Reiners, who also attended our advanced German conversation classes, performed a short poetry slam session and crafted a poem together with the students. Last but not least, the Goethe-Institut provided their rooms at no cost for the annual essay contest ceremony and the end-of-year party. Students submitted traditional prose texts, poems, rap songs, collages and objects in the German language and were honored during a ceremony at the Goethe-Institut where the winners were announced. Students were awarded gift certificates from a bookstore, cinema tickets for German films and German food baskets from a local Austrian butcher.

It is nearly impossible to trace the success of a program to individual components. We believe that only synergy-effects, namely the combination of the strategic curriculum redesign with its new emphasis on interdisciplinarity, new courses with appealing titles, including an outreach course, networking with regional cultural players of the German-speaking community as well as a rich and diversified extracurricular life can make a significant impact. In the following paragraphs we will provide more details on how we forged a community which we found to have an almost immediate impact on student retention and enrollment numbers.

Community building

It is no secret that enrollment in small programs depends to a great degree on the personal engagement of faculty members. Crucial factors are the approachability and presence of instructors, their passion for the field and investment in students' growth. Being relentless in one's dedication to create a community is critical, yet, knowledge of the program's history[10] is equally important to target specific problems. Communication between the administrative personnel, advisors, the chair, colleagues and students revealed that the German program at CU was lacking a sense of continuity and community and that prior to Range's arrival, the Concordia German Language Student Association (CGLSA) was not connected to the German program. As a first step, Range convinced the CGSLA members to join efforts – many of whom were dormant members and not even students of the German program at that point – to inform them about her ideas for extracurricular activities and to increase the visibility and appeal of the program. Although the enrollments at the 300-[11] and 400-level[12] were alarmingly low in 2013, students in the German program were curious about the newly hired LTA. Using this momentum clearly aided in receiving steadily growing numbers for events such as *Kaffeeklatsch, Stammtisch* and *Weihnachtsfeier*, film screenings, German trivia nights, a book club, a *Bergfest*, end-of-semester party and a traditional German breakfast, none of which had been offered in previous years. Involving the CGLSA also secured a funding resource for future activities, since the department offered no financial support for them, and CU's Student Union funded student associations and clubs. Initial event attendance at the *Stammtisch*, for example, was about four students and increased to a steady number of 20 and more within the first semester. The German breakfast event, initially funded by the LTA and then supported through the CGSLA in the following semesters, was attended by over 50 people. A listserv for event reminders, new classes, tutoring hours, etc. was created and continuously expanded.

Beyond our outreach experiences with the Goethe-Institut and collaborations with visiting artists, the undoubtedly most effective recruitment tool for our students was *Stammtisch*. The German *Stammtisch* showed that active engagement with students in and outside of class was key in the effective promotion of the program. While *Stammtisch* is a staple extracurricular activity which most German programs offer, we will share our philosophy behind it and what proved to be successful strategies for us as a means to forge a sense of community between students and the coordinator.

The German *Stammtisch*

Debra Prager and Daniel Kramer (2014) emphasize the importance of extracurricular activities in fostering community identification and raising the visibility of a small German program inside and outside the university, arguing that "language- and culture-oriented activities – outside class – can be vital to keeping our students engaged and motivated to learn more about the language, history, and culture of German speakers" (42). *Stammtisch* served all of those desired purposes and was a place of mutual learning. It presented an immersive environment and opportunity for our students to develop intercultural competencies. *Stammtisch* created a forum in which different cultures communicated, learned and inspired each other. For students who wanted to practice their German at the meetings, it represented an excellent opportunity to seek out language partners from German-speaking countries, which served as a major motivator to invest time and energy in language studies (Windham 2017, 87). However, it is important to note that German *Stammtisch* did not require students to speak German at all. It was rather a community space in which some students would complete their homework, while others practiced their oral proficiency or enjoyed talking with each other and meeting new people. Thus, German *Stammtisch* and the CGLSA at CU were not only about speaking and practicing the German language but aided in establishing a sense of community for non-native and native German speakers alike. Conversations ensued between Canadian students (many of whom had never traveled to Europe) and German, Austrian and Swiss students which not only challenged both sides' perception of "normality" but also ultimately taught our students that this very normality is a question of perspective (Jensen 2019, 55). While *Stammtisch* created a home-away-from-home for German, Austrian and Swiss members, it also instilled a sense of belonging and community in our Canadian students.

Stammtisch was an effective way to reach students from CEGEPs[13] and high schools to advertise individual programs by creating the opportunity to establish contact with teachers and students.[14] Recruiting in local high schools is a crucial aspect of building a successful German program according to Wehage (2007, 59) and Braunbeck (2011, 153). Similarly, the *Stammtisch*'s collaboration with the Goethe-Institut also proved essential, for it brought together all university and CEGEP faculty once a year for a conference on outreach strategies. The Goethe-Institut informed all German CEGEP students about the meeting times and locations of all university's German *Stammtisch* meetings and organized an annual open house event for all German programs in the city. Many future students who already planned on going to CU did not know about the university's German minor. The Goethe-Institut's open house provided an excellent networking occasion, a chance to share details about our revamped curriculum and future plans for the program. It was an easy and time-efficient opportunity to directly talk to prospective students and engage in conversations with fellow teachers.

CU's German *Stammtisch* grew to be the largest in the city which was the result of the coordinators' efforts to join every meeting and to extend them by going to restaurants, movies, ice skating as well as to students' non-academic events, including dance, choir, stand-up comedy and band performances. Encountering students outside the university allowed the coordinators to see them in their "everyday life" environment, learn about their interests and bond with them (and sometimes their relatives, who would as response contact the LTAs with funding options they learned about) on a deeper level. Having grown up in the target culture and being a faculty member piqued students' curiosity. The back and forth between classes during the day, *Stammtisch*, museums, movies in the evening, between serving as a role model and mentor and being an equal among equals during *Stammtisch* created an invigorating atmosphere, in which students learned about the professor's interests, hobbies and personal background. Thus, we as professors turned from a somewhat sterile facilitator into a human being with flesh and blood. While Windham (2017) hypothesizes that "cultural instruction in German courses increases perceived relevance by making explicit the practical application of intercultural competency" (88), both LTAs found that *Stammtisch* was most successful in providing an environment in which students could apply and naturally extend their cultural competency. To students, the presence of their professor illustrated the complexities involved in navigating social and cultural situations. They fulfilled the role of teacher, mentor and friend that students could turn to when nervous or anxious, while simultaneously presenting an example of someone who continuously navigates the cultural norms and standards of a foreign society. The coordinators not only stood behind their program's content, but they also lived it. The shared experiences created a tight-knit community and undoubtedly led to the success of the German program

Social media

Both Range and Bronner focused their social media activities on Facebook,[15] offering yet another means of communication that could successfully link students to the world beyond the classroom. In the very beginning, the Concordia German program Facebook site reposted selected information from the Goethe-Institut, DAAD, *Deutsche Welle*, etc. to educate students about study abroad opportunities, scholarships or the German news. In addition, we posted announcements about the German program's film nights, its book club, *Bergfest, Stammtisch*, and *Kaffeeklatsch*. In order to increase traffic to the newly established Facebook site and to streamline the process of adding new members and would-be German program students, Range made use of QR codes.[16] These became a particularly useful tool during university events that were well attended by the general student population. If students were in a rush but interested to learn more about the German program and its events, they could scan the QR code with their phones and instantly receive a link to the German program Facebook site, an invitation to be added to the listserv and a link to the German program blog. The QR codes were a tremendous success during student fairs. Upon introduction of the code at the 2014 fair, about 30 students signed up to receive more information about the German program, while more than 60 used the QR code to become part of our listserv.[17]

In addition to the German Facebook site, the German program blog, which was established to keep students updated and informed about German in addition to the cultural content taught in class, was a creative publication that initially featured information created by TAs and later on all interested students in the German program. TAs and students alike wrote short essays (sometimes less than 250 words) about cultural topics of German-speaking countries. These blog entries covered everything from history to pop culture, newly discovered foods, books and film reviews as well as German-related events in and around Montreal. In order to increase views on these sites, Range posted a variety of contests and quizzes, which offered prizes for best picture on different topics (study/travel abroad in a German-speaking country, look-alike of a German-speaking author or modern-day celebrity, etc.). Prizes included movie and theater tickets, gift cards to a local German bakery and European delicatessen stores, books, posters, cups, etc. Events and prizes were funded through private donors, such as students' parents, or the German Student Association at CU. In addition, the coordinators received small donations from the German Consulate General.

Social media use picked up rapidly and, over the years, the CGLSA created their own Instagram channel, through which students received information related to their study programs, such as deadlines, student initiatives, student association elections, etc. The Instagram channel slowly but surely replaced the German program blog and became the new platform to disperse content provided by the LTA and TAs. The increased following of the social media websites can be attributed to the fact that almost all students at CU are subscribed to the overarching student association ASFA (Arts and Sciences Federation of Associations), whose website automatically posts suggestions about joining the German section's social media channels.

In addition to using social media to disseminate information about all things German, Bronner set up a Facebook group that accompanied the TAs' sessions as virtual alternatives for students who could not attend the regular tutoring hours.[18] These groups were a novelty within CU's language programs and an opportunity for students across all language levels to ask questions and post problems, which the TAs, Bronner and fellow students could answer. The group also served as a platform to share information on scholarships, studying abroad, internships in the city of Montreal related to German and to advertise the German program's own events. Being connected online established and fostered a team spirit among students and between TAs, students and the professor due to the increased availability and convenience of the setup.

Conclusion

Given the large variety of possibilities Montreal offers for students of the German language and culture as well as the positive effects on the university's visibility and reputation, the administration's attempt to suspend admissions to the German minor in the fall of 2017 came as an utter shock. The suspension of the program caused a major uproar among colleagues, students, the German community in Montreal and beyond. The solidarity and resistance shown by various outside programs and international institutions had an enormous impact, as the administration accepted the proposal for the new German minor curriculum and decided to open the revised program in fall 2018.

Even though Concordia University has still not received a permanent German faculty position, the authors are hopeful that the German Program at CU will continue to thrive. The fact that student enrollment more than tripled over the course of five years, and continues this upward trend, shows that a whole-hearted investment in building and updating German Studies programs pays dividends. More importantly, however, if we wish for the humanities to remain relevant, we must find ways to withdraw from quantitative evaluation and instead justify the existence of our programs by rediscovering and provoking passionate interest in arts and language. More than ever, we must develop strategies that allow us to actively engage in the cultural and political dialogues that shape our reality and counteract what Francine Prose (2017) calls "the reductive simplifications in the current political and corporate discourse."

Notes

1 In the event of equal qualification, the Canadian candidate needs to be hired.
2 Among fellow Classics, Modern Languages and Linguistics colleagues, the LTA appointment was referred to as a "revolving door position" and was also renowned for its instability among other German institutions in the city.
3 The authors observed that students tend to notice their absence and erroneously draw the conclusion that their instructors are not truly invested in the program or in their success.
4 Prager and Kramer also stress the importance of building communities by "learning to use the target language within and beyond the classroom setting, i.e., through guest speakers, museum visits, relevant musical, theatrical, or sporting events; and using the language for personal enjoyment and enrichment" (42).
5 More detailed information on this topic will be provided under "Social Media."
6 This approach is similar to what Franz-Joseph Wehage suggested when he was building a small German program by implementing "courses in English that would not only count toward the general education requirements or satisfy a college writing requirement, but also attract students from other disciplines into German" (57). Both authors of this article can confirm the usefulness of such an approach, for the general education courses with German topics indeed attracted students to minor in German.
7 Bronner adopted these Rhizomatic Response Projects (RRPs) from the experimental poet and professor of media studies at Concordia University, Darren Wershler, who himself borrowed the idea from Marshal McLuhan.

8 This approach is a variant of what Jensen refers to as "peer learning" (51).
9 A full selection of preselected courses could not be provided, for departments could not guarantee to offer every individual course each semester that happens to correspond with contents related to German.
10 Past incidents with former German faculty members caused an immense loss of credibility within the higher university administration, which resulted in a refusal of support for the program for decades.
11 Enrollment was as low as nine students in some of the 300-level courses and more than tripled of the course of the next five years.
12 Enrollment at the 400 level was between 5 and 6 students and increased to over classes of 34 and more students between 2013 and 2018.
13 CEGEP is a publicly funded post-secondary education pre-university, collegiate technical college exclusive to the province of Quebec's education system.
14 CU policy prevents faculty from directly advertising at CEGEPs and high schools.
15 Neither Instagram nor Twitter were able to compete in popularity with CU students' use of Facebook in 2013.
16 A QR code is a machine-readable optical barcode or label containing information about the item to which it is attached. The QR codes Range used often contained information about the planned events by the German Club or pointed to websites and blogs.
17 A major advantage of the QR sign-up was that students landed on a website that had them fill in their personal information. This saved the coordinator valuable time compared to the traditional/physical sign-up sheet on which students' handwriting was often hard to decipher and still needed to be manually added to the listserv.
18 Tutoring sessions could also be recorded and used to prepare students for specific classes, as done by Khan in 2011, who uploaded such sessions to YouTube. Students could then choose to repeat or skip any segments as they saw fit.

Bibliography

Anton, Christine, et al. *Sag Mal: An Introduction to German Language and Culture.* Vista Higher Learning, 2014.

Baker, J. W. "The 'Classroom Flip': Using Web Course Management Tools to Become the Guide by the Side." *Selected Papers from the 11th International Conference on College Teaching and Learning*, edited by A. Chambers, Florida Community College at Jacksonville, 2000, pp. 9–17.

Barske, Tobias, et al. *Denk Mal!: Deutsch ohne Grenzen.* Vista Higher Learning, 2012.

Braunbeck, Helga. "Competition, Connection, and Collaboration in Smaller German Programs." *Die Unterrichtspraxis*, vol. 44, no. 1, 2011, pp. 146–153.

Costabile-Heming, Carol Anne. "Responding to the MLA Report: Re-Contextualizing the Study of German for the 21st Century." *The German Quarterly*, vol. 84, no. 4, 2011, pp. 403–413.

Davidheiser, James, and Gregory Wolf. "Fanning the Flames: Best Practices for Ensuring the Survival of Small German Programs." *Die Unterrichtspraxis*, vol. 42, no. 1, 2009, pp. 60–67.

Fody, Michael. "Building a 'Minor' Language Program from Scratch." *ADFL Bulletin*, vol. 8, no. 3, 1977, pp. 38–42.

Goldberg, D., et al. "Successful College and University Foreign Language Programs, 1995–99: Part 2." *ADFL Bulletin*, vol. 35, no. 2–3, 2004, pp. 27–70.

Jensen, Birgit A. "Using Flipped Learning to Facilitate Cross-Cultural Critical Thinking in the L2 Classroom." *Die Unterrichtspraxis*, vol. 52, no. 1, 2019, pp. 50–68.

Khan, Sal. "Let's use video to reinvent education." *TED: Ideas Worth Spreading*, 2011, www.ted.com/talks/salman_khan_let_s_use_video_to_reinvent_education. Accessed 6 April 2020.

Lage, M., et al. "Inverting the Classroom: A Gateway to Creating an Inclusive Learning Environment." *Journal of Economic Education*, vol. 31, no. 1, 2000, pp. 30–43.

Lord, Gillian, et al. *Language Program Direction: Theory and Practice*. Pearson, 2014.

MLA Ad Hoc Committee on Foreign Languages. "Foreign Languages and Higher Education: New Structures for a Changed World." *Profession*, 2007, pp. 234–245.

Prager, Debra N., and Daniel J. Kramer. "The Kulturpass: Strategies for Enhancing Cultural Engagement outside the German-Language Classroom." *Die Unterrichtspraxis*, vol. 47, no. 1, 2014, pp. 42–48.

Prose, Francine. "Humanities Teach Students to Think. Where Would We Be without Them?" *The Guardian*, 12 May 2017, www.theguardian.com/commentisfree/2017/may/12/humanities-students-budget-cuts-university-suny. Accessed 6 April 2020.

Rarick, Damon O. "The Student-Centered Classroom Made Real: Transforming Student Presentations in an Advanced Course on Technical German." *Die Unterrichtspraxis*, vol. 43, no. 1, 2010, pp. 61–69.

Rivers, William P., and Richard D. Brecht. "America's Languages: The Future of Language Advocacy." *Foreign Language Annals*, vol. 51, no. 1, 2018, pp. 24–34.

Wehage, Franz-Joseph. "Suggestions for a Successful German Program: The Case of Muskingum College." *Die Unterrichtspraxis*, vol. 40, no. 1, 2007, pp. 57–60.

Windham, Scott. "Culture First: Boosting Program Strength through Cultural Instruction." *Die Unterrichtspraxis*, vol. 50, no. 1, 2017, pp. 79–90.

8 Strategies for teaching 18th-century German texts in the context of program building

Jeffrey L. High, Elena Pnevmonidou and Friederike von Schwerin-High

A number of notable recent scholarly efforts exemplify activations of 18th-century concerns and debates for phenomena that shape our own and our students' realities today. Jane K. Brown's study, *Goethe's Allegories of Identity* (2014), for instance, presents Johann Wolfgang von Goethe's body of work as a direct precursor of modernist and postmodern theories and aesthetics. Steven Martinson highlights the clarifications that Goethe's *Iphigenie auf Tauris* and Gotthold Ephraim Lessing's *Nathan der Weise* are able to offer for current discussions of, and distinctions between, the transcultural and the intercultural (2016). Bernd Fischer reads Friedrich Schiller's aesthetic sphere as a prefiguration of the aesthetically permeated, technologically mediated culture of the present moment (2011). And in another recent example, Gail Hart explores the aporia attending to freedom and determinism in Schiller's poetological writings vis-à-vis ludological theorizations of popular video games (2011). The Klassik Stiftung Weimar likewise pursues effective negotiations between the classical cultural heritage and our globalized contemporary world. The Foundation's vision statement "Forschungs- und Bildungskonzept 2015" notes that increasing attention to medialization, digitization, participatory practices and the diversification and internationalization of audiences in contemporary approaches to original 18th-century cultural products "does not diminish, but rather strengthens the awareness of the inalienable intrinsic value of original works of art" (4).[1] The new lines of inquiry demonstrate continuities between current preoccupations and the discourses and debates that stood out 225 years ago. These include, in particular, human and artistic autonomy, networked connectedness, embodied experience, global awareness and aesthetic perception.

This chapter presents three case studies of pedagogical practices that articulate the relevance and resonance of 18th-century works of literature and philosophy for contemporary German Studies classes and curricula. Elena Pnevmonidou's section "The Potential of Drama Pedagogy" uses Lessing's *Nathan der Weise* as a case study that highlights the importance of drama and performance in the upper-division German-language classroom at the University of Victoria. Her pedagogical approach conceives of drama primarily as a process rooted in experiential and community learning. It focuses on the performative exploration of basic emotions to probe the psychological depth and complexity of characters, while also emphasizing micro-level textual analysis. Pnevmonidou addresses the difficulty of dealing with various levels of language proficiency in the class by having senior students codirect scenes and mentor junior students. In this way, students are able to forge strong cultural and linguistic connections to a play that may have initially seemed distant to them.

Similarly, Friederike von Schwerin-High's section "18th-Century Plays in the German Drama Survey Course" describes an upper-division course at the Claremont Colleges that aims to connect students with texts by classic German playwrights, arguing for their foundational and updatable relevance. Class work alternates between close readings of original scenes from *Emilia Galotti, Maria Stuart* and *Faust* that focus on compound words, genitive constructions and global readings that incorporate modern multimedia retellings of scenes. These micro- and macro-level discussions consider depictions of power and its abuses in relation to class, gender and the self-reflection of the aesthetic realm. Revolving around oral in-class presentations and dramatic readings, the course has recently been certified to fulfill a speaking-intensive general education requirement.

Jeffrey High's section "On the Importance of 18th-Century Literature: Recruitment, Retention and the Pursuit of Happiness" examines the critical role of 18th-century texts in program-building. Age of Schiller authors are the subject not only of upper-division German courses at California State University, Long Beach (CSULB), but also of general education and honors course offerings in English. These authors and their texts manage to occasion intensive cocurricular academic activities, participation in conferences, summer immersion experiences and the fostering of a lively scholarly community. Focusing on 18th-century German authors, and drawing on the central, complex and nuanced humanistic arguments they advance, the section makes a case for the intrinsic, indispensable as well as practical value of German Studies and humanities programs in today's changing universities.

The potential of drama pedagogy and peer-assisted learning for teaching 18th-century German literature in the L2 classroom: lessons from the student production of Gotthold Ephraim Lessing's *Nathan der Weise*

Teaching 18th-century German literature in a foreign language (L2) setting is challenging indeed. For one, there is no natural continuity between the German students encounter in language textbooks and 18th-century literary language. Unlike the German in language textbooks or in more modern texts, students do not use 18th-century German for day-to-day communication. With a text like Gotthold Ephraim Lessing's *Nathan der Weise*, this sense of linguistic estrangement is compounded by the fact that even 18th-century Germans would not likely have used the language in Lessing's *Nathan* for mundane communication. Lessing's German is a sophisticated and richly stylized literary language arranged in lyrical verse whose aesthetic complexity calls for nuanced literary analysis. Yet, as academic programs move away from the literary studies focus of traditional *Germanistik* to interdisciplinary cultural studies, students have increasingly less grounding in literary history and literary analysis. 18th-century literature confronts students with a language that they have great difficulty internalizing and relating to emotionally, socially and interculturally. The challenge of teaching 18th-century German literature in an L2 setting thus stems from the incongruence of using highly sophisticated and alienating textual material to work on what are at times basic linguistic and analytical skills.

This contribution profiles the pedagogical approach developed for teaching Lessing's *Nathan* in the context of a German drama course in the fall semester of 2017, a course that has been offered biennially since 2011 in the Department of Germanic and Slavic Studies at the University of Victoria, and that serves as the academic home of German student theater at UVic. This course was developed specifically to fill the curricular gap that emerged as the department offered increasingly fewer upper-level courses in German as well as literature courses in general. It fills this gap by creating bridges in two directions: bridging both the divide between literary history and performance, and the divide between language learning and cultural production. Thus although the course culminates in the full-length performance of a play in German, the main goal is not to achieve product-oriented drama that strives for high production value. The emphasis is instead on what in the field of drama pedagogy is referred to as "process drama" (Kao and O'Neill 1998; Schewe 2014, 12–14) that is learning and teaching by performative means. The goal is for German learners of all levels to interact in a blended linguistic setting, to develop a staging concept for a play based on literary analysis and research of the culture, theater and performance history and to have a production process that relies on the collaboration among students of diverse academic backgrounds and language competencies. Based on this experience, I will highlight three areas where drama pedagogy can support instructors and L2 learners in grappling with the challenge that is 18th-century German literature: emotive and kinesthetic learning, peer teaching and collaborative directing.

The benefit of a performative approach to teaching 18th-century literature in an L2 setting is that it adds an experiential, bodily dimension to the encounter with material that students experience as difficult, abstract and alien. Learning has long been recognized as a process in which learners bring diverse capacities to bear. Howard Gardner (1983) refers to these as "multiple intelligences," and identifies in particular linguistic, logical-mathematical, musical, spatial, bodily-kinesthetic and interpersonal intelligences. In overemphasizing the purely linguistic aspect of language, L2 teachers thus risk depriving their students of the ability to develop non-verbal and bodily communicative skills that are vital for a fuller engagement with and appropriation of a foreign language. Drama pedagogy, by contrast, enhances precisely that non-verbal and bodily dimension of learning, and there is an increasing body of evidence that a performative approach to teaching and learning is effective indeed. Erika Piazzoli (2011), for example, has found that role-play generated an "affective space" that was safe and supportive (562), produced more spontaneous communication and overall reduced "language anxiety" which is a recognized significant obstacle to foreign language learning (561; 565). Role play is also a fundamentally empathetic act as it puts one in the situation of taking and indeed living another's perspective, and drama pedagogy is accordingly seen as especially valuable in fostering intercultural learning which requires a mediation between the familiar self and an alien other (Bräuer 2002). While most drama pedagogy research focuses on L2 teaching, some research also shows the benefits of a performative approach to teaching literature. Marvin Schildmeier (2016), for instance, notes that the empathy fostered in a performative learning setting also brings about a more intense engagement with a textual passage than mere reading, making it possible in that process that "quasi als angenehmer Nebenffekt – [sich] ganz viele neue Interpetationsmöglichkeiten erschließen" (3).

My experience of teaching *Nathan* through a performative pedagogical framework confirms the findings of this drama pedagogy research. In the context of our project, drama pedagogy above all enabled the students to gain an emotive access to the text, which became the foundation for literary analysis. I began by familiarizing students with the experience of basic emotions, such as joy, fear, anger, sadness, and assigned each emotion a set of numbers from 1–12. As the students stood in a circle, I said the numbers, and the students localized the emotion on their body. This activity gave students a sense for the bodily dimension of emotions and an understanding of how quickly emotions shift. We then undertook a micro-level textual analysis of what emotions motivate individual words or word clusters within a sentence, realizing again that a single sentence can convey a multitude of emotions. We applied this analysis for example, to the opening sequence of the play, where Nathan's Christian servant Daja comes to greet him: "DAJA: Er ist es! Nathan! – Gott sei ewig Dank!"[2] (Lessing 1984, 23). Being the least sympathetic and most prejudiced, anti-Semitic character in the play, Daja also invites the most prejudiced characterization on the part of the reader who might tend to reduce the character and her actions to her cultural biases. The aim of the emotive approach was to enable students to appreciate the complexity of Daja.

After the micro-level analysis of the opening sequence, students did an activity that Susanne Even (2008) calls "empathy questions" (164–165). As they stood in the pose of Daja waiting for Nathan, I read a series of empathy questions: "Where are you standing? Are you relaxed or tense? Have you been standing here long? Do you often stand here? Are you alone? Are you often alone? Why did you come here? Where did you come from?" etc. In the subsequent discussion, students expressed surprise about how many conflicting emotions this exercise evoked in them and how complicated a character Daja is indeed. Daja is a European Christian who came to Jerusalem with her husband, who died, forcing her to earn a living by working as a servant for a

Jew. Nathan, the Jew, trusts her, the Christian, with the care of his daughter, and he trusts her not to betray his secret, that Recha is not his daughter, but an orphaned Christian girl that he adopted and raised as a Jew. Throughout the play, Daja must continually temper her prejudices, longing to return Recha to Europe, and resentment of Nathan. The play begins just as Daja almost failed in her duty of care for Recha, who nearly died in a fire, and in the opening sequence, Daja will have to report to Nathan what almost occurred in his absence. As the students stood in the waiting pose and heard the empathy questions, all this information, which seemed abstract and incidental when they initially read the play, now became viscerally relevant as they empathized with Daja. We did such micro-level textual analysis with many critical sequences in the play and enhanced the emotive with kinesthetic learning, by attaching facial expressions, gestures, postures and movements to specific, charged words or micro-sequences. Beyond serving as a mnemonic device that supported the actors' memorization of the script with "muscle memory," this approach made it easier for all the students to internalize Lessing's difficult German.

On this foundation of emotive and kinesthetic learning, working with Lessing's *Nathan* became increasingly learner-focused, as the students worked independently in small groups, co-directing scenes or doing peer-assisted language coaching. As the students collaboratively worked out the details of staging individual scenes, the codirecting also served as a more complex form of experiential literary analysis. Peer teaching in turn made possible an individualized engagement with the material as senior students took ownership of the text as experts, while the junior students built their confidence as they internalized Lessing's German and gained a more nuanced and lived understanding of their character.

The course was designed as a hybrid course, combining language and literature study with performance, and inviting German speakers of all competency levels from beginner to near native speaker. The coursework therefore needed to consist of activities and assignments that contributed to the larger collective project, the production of Lessing's play, but that were also individualized enough to be matched to and have learning outcomes appropriate for the different language competencies. For the junior students, just mastering their script and achieving a basic understanding of their character was already a significant achievement, given the level of linguistic difficulty with which they were grappling. For the more advanced speakers, the learning outcome was to do interpretative textual work based on their engagement with Lessing's sophisticated literary German. In the performance-based learning and teaching framework of the course, directing serves as a tool for literary analysis, in that the dramaturgical choices need to be based on the director's interpretation of the text. In this course, the two most advanced German speakers, who were also seniors in their German major program, collaborated as co-directors and language coaches. First, they worked together on developing an interpretation of the play. Noting how central a figure the character of Nathan is, for obvious reasons, the two codirectors decided on a staging concept that would foreground the other characters that surround Nathan, such as Daja, the Templar, Sittah and Recha. Having developed their staging concept, they then worked individually with the actors in separate sessions, helping them to develop a better understanding of their character and the script, and doing some intense language and dialect coaching work with them. This experience proved immensely gratifying, as one student, who played the character of Saladin's sister, Sittah, wrote:

> For me, it actually was very liberating when I could just let go and just let the German words spill out. They were Sittah's words and she spoke German, so in the end, the English words would have seemed less authentic. In the beginning I had the English words in my head when I spoke German, to help me try to evoke the intention behind her words, but then in the end I just referred to the German script; going back and forth to the English, just slowed down the process of "finding Sittah."

In this contribution, I wanted to draw attention to the fact that one obstacle to teaching 18th-century German literature in an L2 setting is the learners' emotional distance from the material. Drama pedagogy can help overcome this distance by enabling students to engage with it as a lived experience. In addition to enhancing the work with the foreign language, the dramatization of the foreign text also builds an intercultural interface, as it intersects the foreign language and cultural product with the students' own cultural situatedness, and learning manifests itself ultimately as the performative process of grappling with that cultural tension. The "old" 18th-century literature thus becomes not only relatable but also relevant to the learners.

18th-century plays in the German drama survey course

Major European theater traditions such as the Elizabethan Theater in England, Golden Age Drama in Spain, Commedia dell'Arte in Italy and Baroque Theater in France, all had their peak in the 16th and 17th centuries. German theater, by contrast, was a latecomer, peaking in the second half of the 18th century and partially overlapping with the time period often referred to as "The Age of Goethe." Analyzing the centrality of the theater for that cultural period, Rainer Ruppert (1995) identifies three major functions for German drama at that time: 1) it became synonymous with ethical education; 2) as an artform it offered an ersatz or compensatory public sphere for the de facto still powerless middle classes and 3) in a Habermasian sense, that alternate public sphere was able to infiltrate the actual public sphere (16–18). While these criteria clearly shaped the contemporary discourse in theoretical texts by Lessing, Goethe, Schiller and many others, my aim here is to discuss how these functions also color the topics treated *within* various plays and how undergraduate, non-native speakers of German might approach these issues.

Several years ago, the premier U.S. journal on teaching German, *Die Unterrichtspraxis*, published a survey of 18th-century advanced undergraduate German courses, conducted by Edward Larkin. In the 36 fully or partially completed questionaires that Larkin received, survey participants listed the ten texts most commonly studied in their 18th-century German literature classes with the following frequency: *Iphigenie auf Tauris* (17), *Die Leiden des jungen Werther* (17), *Faust I* (17), *Minna von Barnhelm* (10), *Die Räuber* (10), *Wilhelm Tell* (8), *Götz von Berlichinge*n (8), *Nathan der Weise* (7), *Egmont* (6) and "Was is Aufklärung" (6). What stands out in this expansive, albeit not very recent, survey of college German courses dealing with the 18th century is that among the ten most frequently studied texts, eight are dramas by Lessing, Goethe and Schiller.

In my own practice of teaching drama survey courses at Pomona College, three plays by those same three authors have turned out to be particularly productive in the undergraduate, upper-division classroom (even given the varying levels of preparation students typically bring to these kinds of classroom settings): Lessing's *Emilia Galotti* (1772), Schiller's *Maria Stuart* (1800) and Goethe's *Faust I* (1808). Several shared features enable these texts to illuminate and build on each other to provide a cohesive foundation for a diachronic drama course (that also includes plays by or excerpts from Kleist, Büchner, Hebbel, Schnitzler, Brecht, Dürrenmatt, Bachmann, Özdamar and Erpenbeck). Consistently set in a remote time and/or place, the three plays can be read as critical presentations of absolutist power dynamics, of intertwinements between gender and class, religion and ideology and (theater) aesthetics and education. As we approach these texts both through gist-oriented overviews and scene-specific, close readings, students see the mutual permeation between the aesthetic, political and pedagogical realms. Enhancing our assessment of existential, moral and political questions, these plays grapple with the agency and social standing of the main female characters, Emilia, Maria and Gretchen. Characteristically and tragically, the self-determination of these characters lies in the striking grandeur with which each of them transforms her death into an act of free will. The sublimity of these characters contrasts sharply and problematically with the surviving characters who are left to await justice, get banned or flee.[3]

While it is true that the double remove of a text written some 200 to 250 years ago and in a foreign language poses special challenges, students find many aspects of the language used in these three plays surprisingly close to modern language (Barner 1998, 24). However stylized, the characters' speech is based on natural dialogue. And since it is intended for a single, fleeting hearing rather than exclusively for reading, the dramatic language is more graspable than the linguistic register customarily found in works of prose, poetry or philosophy. The foreign-language classroom setting makes it possible to combine grammar and vocabulary exercises with an analysis of the three plays' approaches to aesthetics. Let us look at three scenes in particular, in which these three plays, as important exemplars of works of artistic expression, self-referentially reflect on the role of the arts and the politics surrounding the aesthetic realm: 1) Before we enter heaven in Goethe's "Prologue in Heaven," where God and Mephistopheles enter into their pact over Dr. Faust, the "Prelude in the Theater" presents a meta-theatrical exchange between the clown, the theater director and the poet. The conversation touches on the limits of pure art and the applicability of art to the commercial (theater director) and the entertainment sector (clown); 2) Similarly preoccupied with the politics of aesthetics, *Maria Stuart* progresses to an early scene where Mortimer (the only character in this historical play that is Schiller's own invention) explains how he, a born Protestant and Englishman, returned from Southern Europe a clandestine Catholic. What drew him to Catholicism was the powerful artistic beauty suffusing that faith; 3) Last but not least, *Emilia Galotti* begins with a scene in which the painter Conti and the Prince discuss the nature of art, its ambition toward freedom, exactitude and feeling, and the constraints put upon art by the unreliability of patronage and the vagaries of commissioned work. As students read these scenes that reflect on the nature and function of the aesthetic realm closely, they are struck by the number of compound words – or *zusammengesetzte Substantive* – so typical of German then and now:

> *Die Zusammensetzung zweier Substantive zu einem neuen Wort mit einer eigenen Bedeutung ist ein besonderes Kennzeichen der deutschen Sprache. Manchmal gerät den Schreibern (vielleicht unter dem Einfluss des Englischen) allerdings aus dem Blick, dass bei dieser Zusammensetzung nicht nur ein neuer Begriff, sondern tatsächlich ein neues Wort entsteht, das dann auch zusammengeschrieben werden muss.* (Dudenredaktion)

Similarly, students encounter many genitive constructions, where one noun is assigned to another noun to give a more detailed definition, rendered as a now uncommon attributive genitive. Attributive genitive, e.g. *der Tragödie erster Teil*, has now generally been replaced by periphrasic genitive – *der zweite Teil der Tragödie* – a difference that is important for students to notice as they become both increasingly effective speakers of contemporary German and readers of 18th-century texts. In prereading exercises during which students voice expectations and speculate on meanings, as key words during discussion, in post-reading recaps and in midterm and final exam study guides and prompts, these lists of compound words and genitive constructions help students grasp the respective scene, its semantic complexities, grammatical particularities and thematics. As findings in recent cognitive psychology research on conceptual combination tasks suggest (Kohn et al. 2011; Middleton et al. 2011), an added benefit of students' engagement with combinational activities occasioned by the decoding of genitive constructions and compounds might be the facilitation of higher-order thinking processes and creative problem solving in the foreign language. In the following examples of lists of compound words and genitive constructions, the discursive emphasis in each scene is meta-aesthetic in nature, relating to art and beauty:

Emilia Galotti *(Act 1, Scene 1)*

die Schranken unserer Kunst, das Gesicht einer Grazie, die Medusenaugen der Gräfin, der Charakter der Person, die Augen der Liebe, des Künstlers eigene Gebieterin, das Werk meiner Phantasie, der Ausspruch eines Malers, Ihr Studium der weiblichen Schönheit, das Meisterstück der Natur. [4]

Maria Stuart *(Act 4, Scene 6)*

Hass des Papsttums, der Puritaner dumpfe Predigtstuben, Kirchenfest, Gottesbild, der Säulen Pracht, Roms Weichbild, Bildnergeist, Wunderwelt, der Künste Macht, der Sinne Reiz, die Musik der Himmel, der Gestalten Fülle, Lebensteppich, des Lebens schöner Tag. [5]

Faust I, *"Prelude in the Theatre"*

der sauberen Herren Pfuscherei, Maskenfeste, Dichterhöhe, Schauspiel, Kartenspiel, Menschenrecht, des Fadens ewige Länge, aller Wesen unharmonische Menge, Frühlingsblüten, Ehrenkranz, des Menschen Kraft, Liebesabenteuer, der Jugend schönste Blüte. [6]

Given the still developing upper-division language proficiency level of the students and the limited class time, I make it a methodological habit to alternate between such lexically centered, close readings of individual scenes as described above and readings geared toward a global understanding of the text. As highly representative texts and cultural artefacts, *Faust, Maria Stuart* and *Emilia Galotti* offer the convenience – and pose the danger – of sheer endless numbers of retellings, commentaries and spoofs readily available on the Internet. To engage with one valuable example, let us briefly turn to the scholastic German publisher of classical literature, *Reclam-Universalbibliothek*. Its state-of-the-art, recently updated study guides for these three plays contain both the actual text and plenty of contextual materials that use principles of graphic design in their analytical and interpretative presentations (Leis's *Faust*; Pelster's *Maria Stuart*; Pelster's *Emilia Galotti*). Moreover, three years ago Reclam formed an official partnership with veteran theater practitioner, Michael Sommer, (of *Sommers Weltliteratur to go*), who stages hypercondensed, incisive versions of these plays. Using Playmobil figures, his ten-minute videos are now available in German and English. Sommer won the prestigious Online Grimme Award 2018 in the category of Culture and Entertainment for his efforts. For highly condensed conveyings of individual scenes, I draw on the pedagogical formats of "information gap activities" where students depend on each other to fill in missing information to complete the task of piecing together a scene, and "the flipped classroom" where a scene's content is delivered outside of the classroom and often online. I ask students to view a particular scene condensation in the form of a video clip or a graphical synopsis as part of their homework and to prepare an oral summary for presentation. Presenters and listeners assume coownership of a given scene's content and context by sharing the tasks of presenting the information clearly and level-appropriately and of listening to the presented information attentively, persistently and accountably. Other activities that have allowed this course to receive certification as fulfilling the speaking-intensive general education requirement include practicing and reciting carefully intonated readings of short scenes from the plays as well as paraphrasing and acting out several character lines in the students' own words.

As we have seen, these dramatic texts lend themselves to a wide variety of speaking, pronunciation and syntactic-semantic activities and communicative in-class tasks while also affording opportunities to connect with the classic German literary canon through discussions of aesthetic theory, gender, class and power.

On the importance of 18th-century literature: recruitment, opportunity, retention and the pursuit of happiness

The German Studies program at CSULB has been cited by directors of German programs at top research universities as one of the most prolific German programs in the U.S., and as one that has produced the greatest number of successful doctoral candidates over the past 15 years. One important reason for the relative health of the CSULB program is its cross-cultural approach to late-Enlightenment German literature and the enthusiasm of 21st-century students toward the works of Schiller, Kant and Kleist, to name but a few. The present contribution seeks to articulate the ends and means of a cultural studies program that promotes humanity before commerce through the study of 18th-century literature and thought. A number of the features of the program may serve as a model for other programs.[7]

As U.S. and European universities bow to destructive pressure to focus on narrow professional training to the detriment of a broad education toward the pursuit of happiness; as universities focus on students as future employees rather than as citizens of a human and humane republic; as universities first downsize then cut cultural studies programs that cost them little, costing us all much more in human than in financial terms; as universities switch to subject-specific ethics courses from those taught by Philosophy Departments, with no evident sincere regard for the detrimental impact of such practices on humankind; as these horrors are met with tacit approval by most, the pursuit of a happy whole is sacrificed in the service of fragments. One half-educated cohort of students is hurried through state institutions to create space for the next wave, streamlined single-major degrees in hand and, ironically, mostly lacking in the skills and wisdom that should have enabled them to pursue successful careers as but one important aspect of meaningful lives. The crass trend could hardly be more clear: the most important of all possible discourses, the moral-philosophical discussion of constitutionalism and the happiness of the individual and of humankind is to be treated as a quaint and all-but-irrelevant tradition, and commerce is the new meaning of life in what was once the enlightened holdout, Academia. As a result of this disregard for the human being and the cultivation of the mere employee, western republics face a state of socio-political danger of their own creation – an orthodoxy of ignorance regarding constitutionalism (Nietzel 2019).[8] Unfortunately, Schiller's diagnosis of the failure of his time in 1795 was never truer than it is today: "*Utility* is the great idol of our age, for which all powers are supposed to toil and to which all talents are supposed to pay homage."[9]

The following curricular and meta-curricular approach is conceived out of respect for the happiness of humanity as the end of all human activity, and, to this end, focuses on educating autonomous, whole human beings rather than mere heteronomous future employees. The approach features the following efforts toward engaging students of language in the study of 18th-century literature, all of which are informed by the goal of creating scholarly community toward an informed individual pursuit of happiness, as a contribution to the greatest happiness of the whole:

- Creating community between cultural studies professors and language students by employing literature professors who are dedicated and successful language teachers, and who teach lower-level German courses
- Organizing German faculty interaction with all German sections from first-semester German classes on up, including class visits to German language classes taught by graduate students and program events designed to address the interests of all students in the program
- Offering transitional German literature and philosophy courses taught in English open to undergraduate students of all levels of German
- German faculty teaching first-year Honors and Paideia humanities courses in English, which results in Honors and Paideia students participating in German Studies cultural activities and enrolling in German, and thus adding a humanities education to their first majors
- Active faculty mentoring and participation in all German Studies Student Association activities
- Mentoring of students who serve as lead organizers of events, and who almost exclusively replace faculty in serving as hosts of and moderators for visiting artists and scholars
- Supervising student-run German Studies conferences and running professional skills workshops to this end, which results in student acquisition of organizational, hosting and moderating skills
- Mentoring students in the creation of abstracts and composition of scholarly papers, which results in the acquisition of scholarly writing, presentation and public-speaking skills

- Teaching at, soliciting scholarship funding for and encouraging students to attend summer immersion programs with a cultural studies emphasis, which allows students to more quickly proceed to upper-level courses taught in German, and to declare and complete double majors
- Faculty coteaching of content courses with qualified M.A. candidates, which provides both training and experience toward the promotion of qualified candidates in their pursuit of fellowships, applications to doctoral programs and securing employment
- Coauthoring conference papers, articles, encyclopedia entries and book reviews for publication with current and former students, which promotes the career advancement of both current students – who in turn mentor CSULB undergraduate students – and former students, who in turn mentor their own as professors

In addition to courses on German culture from its beginnings to the present – any period of which could be the focus of a given program – central laboratories for these approaches at CSULB since 2002 have been 18th-century literature courses that emphasize cross-cultural and untimely connections; for example, teaching the philosophy of the German Enlightenment along with those of the Dutch War of Liberation, the U.S. War of Independence and the French Revolution; comparing Shakespeare's *Richard III*, *Hamlet* and Disney's *The Lion King* to Schiller's *The Robbers*, or teaching Schiller's *Don Carlos* parallel to Verdi's *Don Carlo* and George Lucas' *Star Wars*. Such activities, which largely inform courses with traditional subjects, such as *Reason, Revolution and Reaction* or simply *Heinrich von Kleist*, facilitate student understandings of the relevance of past periods and authors for their own lives and social and political surroundings, to date never more so than in the 2020 discussions of the crumbling constitutionalism of western republics.

An important aspect of the education and training of CSULB German Studies students regards student-run German Studies events and conferences – 15 major events in Fall 2019, in addition to weekly student-run *Stammtisch* (informal gathering of the German Studies students) and *Sprechstunde* (targeted conversation activities often designed to prepare students for program events such as lectures or trips to the LA Opera) – which results in student investment in the health of the program and the acquisition of organizational, scholarly and public-speaking skills. At the highest level, these events are international conferences, including: "Who is this Schiller Now?" (2009), "Kleistian (pre-)Occupations" (2011), "Wanted? Georg Büchner" (2013), "Inspiration Bonaparte?" (2014) and "Writing Revolution" (2019), topics that run parallel to program curriculum. Students are involved in the planning and execution of the conferences from the earliest phases, serving on a variety of committees (grant-writing, paper selection, catering, promotion, transportation, etc.) and ultimately hosting and presenting at the conferences. Students plan and run the German Embassy Campus Weeks events (scavenger hunts, lectures, films) and volunteer at local events including the German Currents Film Festival in Hollywood, as well as at cultural events at the Thomas Mann House and the Villa Aurora, where they have volunteered at the German Pre-Oscar Party and hosted the final day of their 2018 "German Art in SoCal" conference. Although these events are largely run by M.A.s and seniors, lower-level German language, Honors and in Fall 2019 Paideia students have participated in significant numbers, and, due to the accomplishments of the community of students they experience, they are thus more likely to subsequently participate in immersion schools, study abroad, event planning and enroll in multiple senior-level literature courses.

Since dominant and destructive "get a job" discourses – both university internal (administrators and surprisingly advisors) and external (parents of students, politicians and business interests) – self-evidently dominate, as seen in national policy, enrollment and media trends, the role of faculty in exposing the fallacy driving this collusion and aggressively countering the proponents of "the myth of the underemployed, unhappy humanities graduate" with reason is crucial (Jaschik 2018). Retention of incoming students is the first guarantee that there will be future human beings to whom one can teach the principles of freedom and happiness through 18th-century literature. And, yes, these people will have jobs as part of their lives, according to the available external evidence (Fitzgerald 2018) and according to our experience: former students work, for example, as professors, teachers, lawyers, event organizers, marketing and corporate executives.

Mentoring, community and opportunity are all important motivating factors leading to increased student retention and broader participation in immersion schools and study abroad, which results in upper-level enrollment. Thus, in response to a nationwide and international environment hostile to enlightenment, the CSULB German program is necessarily "home-grown" to a significant extent:

- Of the five undergraduates in the Spring 2019 Senior/M.A.-level course on Schiller, taught in German, all five had first-semester German at CSULB, all five had taken a German literature course taught in English in their first two years, all five completed a German B.A., four completed double B.A.s, and three came from Honors Program freshman German Studies seminars (Schiller, Kleist) taught in English
- Of the eight M.A. candidates in the same course, six had first-semester German at CSULB, six had taken a German literature course taught in English at CSULB during their first two years of study, six completed German B.A.s at CSULB, five completed double B.A.s and one came from an Honors Program freshman German Studies seminar taught in English
- Of the 13 combined students, nine participated in one summer immersion school and five participated in two or more

- Of the 13 combined students, seven participated in study abroad programs, four participated in internships in German-speaking countries and three served as Fulbright English TAs

The most significant statistic above is the number of students who had their first semester of German at CSULB and progressed via literature courses taught in English to senior-level seminars taught in German and to the M.A. program. Indeed, of the 19 M.A.s from CSULB who went on to doctoral programs in the humanities between 2011 and 2019 at, among other institutions, Cincinnati, Davis, Harvard, Johns Hopkins, Vanderbilt, Washington and Washington University in St. Louis, seven took first-semester German at CSULB and completed both B.A.s and M.A.s at CSULB. To an important extent, as a result of the steady progression of students from language to cultural studies courses, CSULB has graduated an average of 5.0 M.A.s a year for the past decade – 50 M.A.s from spring 2010 to spring 2019, with six M.A.s graduating in 2020.

A second important insight to be gleaned from the data is the utter refutation of the benefits of keeping students on campus in the mercenary pursuit of enrollment, which does not necessarily go hand-in-hand with retention in the long view. Indeed, contrary to a widespread belief I have encountered in 20 consecutive years of teaching at summer schools, namely, that encouraging study at summer schools and abroad leads to decreased upper-level enrollment at the home institution – participation in study abroad and in summer immersion programs, such as the *Deutsche Sommerschule am Pazifik*, actually increases upper-level enrollment both in semesters preceding immersion school enrollment and in subsequent semesters. This, in turn, means that not encouraging participation in off-campus study results – on the least important level – in less enrollment in upper-level courses, and – on the most important level – in both lesser numbers of educated global citizens and in less-educated citizens, as well as in a perpetuation of an orthodoxy of ignorance dangerous to the freedom and happiness of all.

As western republics wobble, it has become self-evident that their higher education systems are guilty of complicity in their own destabilization by creating populations unaware of the significance of the discourses that brought these republics into existence. The importance of knowledge acquired best from Late Enlightenment thought is crucial to the welfare of the individual and to the democratic state, and toward the requisite understanding of the meaning of the individual pursuit of happiness in service of the happiness of the whole. This knowledge is the most effective foil to the short-sighted administrative, commercial and political stratagems described above, and, yes, it produces marketable skills. CSULB German Studies students pursuing both lives and careers in art history, biology, business, comparative literature, engineering, English, event organization, film, history, law, marketing, museum curation, music, philosophy, political science and theater, among others, go on to attractive positions and top Ph.D programs as a result of their German Studies and humanities acumen. To this, as one recent CSULB graduate stated, they do so on their own terms: "I am incapable of passing over the words '*Freiheit*' [freedom] or '*Glückseligkeit*' [happiness] without critical engagement." This student, and students like her, are the rational moral agents and autonomous citizens without whom the republic cannot stand, and far less than this, but nonetheless, they are the employees whom employers seek and increasingly cannot find, employees with the humanities skills to not only justify their hiring, but to make likely their advancement to leadership positions: "oral communication, critical thinking, ethical judgment, working effectively in teams, working independently, self-motivation, written communication, and real-world application of skills and knowledge" (Hart Research Associates 2018, 3). This "real world" need not be – as many politicians, university administrators and parents would have students believe – just a job to be followed by death – but the life-long individual and civic pursuit of progress toward what Schiller called the "*Menschenrepublik*" (NA 22: 141), the guiding principle of a human and humane world that is in grave danger of being abandoned by those most responsible for its promotion: university leaders.

Notes

1 "...das Bewusstsein für den unveräußerlichen Eigenwert eines Originals nicht schwächen, sondern stärken"
2 DAJA: It's him! Nathan! – Thank God you're finally back!
3 For particularly probing illuminations of this topic see Berman (1988); Kontje (1992); Locki; Maurer (2005).
4 the barriers of our art, the face of one of the Graces, the Medusa eyes of the Countess, the character of the person, the eyes of love, the painter's own mistress, the work of my imagination, the declaration of an artist, your sketch of feminine beauty, the masterpiece of nature.
5 the hatred of the papacy, the Puritans' dull preaching rooms, church festival, the image of God, the pillars' splendor, Rome's outline, creator-spirit, wonder-world, the arts' power, the appeal of the senses, the music of the heavens, the figures' abundance, life-carpet, life's beautiful day.
6 the clean gentlemen's bungling, masked festivals, poet-height, show-play (drama), card-game, human-right, the thread's eternal length, all beings' inharmonious crowd, spring flowers, wreath of honor, the power of humans, love-adventure, youth's most beautiful blossom.
7 My sincere thanks to Luke Beller, Elaine Chen, Josephine Claus, Glen Gray, Natalie Martz, Courtney Yamagiwa (CSULB), and Rebecca Stewart (Harvard University), for their support in creating this section.
8 Nietzel concludes: "We don't need more engineers who know nothing about the Civil War, police officers who believe Churchill was a fictional character, or nurses who have never been moved by a great novel."
9 "*Der Nutzen ist das große Idol der Zeit, dem alle Kräfte frohnen und alle Talente huldigen sollen.*" (Schiller, Schillers Werke, vol. 20, 311).

Bibliography

Barner, Wilfried, editor. *Lessing: Epoche, Werk, Wirkung: Ein Arbeitsbuch für den literaturgeschichtlichen Unterricht.* Beck, 1998.

Berman, Marshall. *All That Is Solid Melts into Air: The Experience of Modernity.* Penguin, 1988.

Bräuer, Gerd. *Body and Language: Intercultural Learning through Drama.* Ablex, 2002.

Brown, Jane K. *Goethe's Allegories of Identity.* University of Pennsylvania Press, 2014.

Dudenredaktion. "Schreibung von zusammengesetzten Substantiven." Duden online, www.duden.de/sprachwissen/sprachratgeber/Zusammengesetzte-Substantive. Accessed 18 June 2020.

Even, Susanne. "Moving in(to) Imaginary Worlds: Drama Pedagogy for Foreign Language Teaching and Learning." *Die Unterrichtspraxis*, vol. 41, no. 2, 2008, pp. 161–170.

Fischer, Bernd. "Zur kulturpolitischen Dynamik des ästhetischen Spiels in Schillers Briefen *Ueber die ästhetische Erziehung des Menschen*." *Who Is This Schiller Now: Essays on His Reception and Significance*, edited by Jeffrey Highet al., Camden House, 2011, pp. 133–146.

Fitzgerald, Jonathan D. "Everyone knows English majors can't get jobs. Except the employers who hire them." *The Boston Globe*, 13 Nov. 2018. www.bostonglobe.com/magazine/2018/11/13/everyone-knows-english-majors-can-get-jobs-except-emp loyers-who-hire-them/STfhSEbHW9TtoJmv8bPitL/story.html. Accessed 7 June 2020.

Gardner, Howard. *Frames of Mind: The Theory of Multiple Intelligences.* Basic Books, 1983.

Hart, Gail. "Save the Prinz: Schiller's *Geisterseher* and the Lure of Entertainment." *Goethe Yearbook*, vol. 18, 2011, pp. 245–258.

Hart Research Associates. "Fulfilling the American Dream: Liberal Education and the Future of Work. Surveys of Business Executives and Hiring Managers." Association of American Colleges & Universities, July 2018, www.aacu.org/research/2018-future-of-work. Accessed 7 June 2020.

Jaschik, Scott. "Shocker: Humanities Grads Gainfully Employed and Happy." *Inside Higher Ed*, 7 Feb. 2018, www.insidehighered.com/news/2018/02/07/study-finds-humanities-majors-land-jobs-and-are-happy-them. Accessed 7 June 2020.

Kao, Shin-Mei, and Cecily O'Neill. *Words into Worlds: Learning a Second Language through Process Drama.* Ablex, 1998.

Klassik Stiftung Weimar. "Forschungs- und Bildungskonzept 2015." October 2015, www.klassik-stiftung.de/assets/Dokumente/Bildung/Klassik_Stiftung_Weimar_-Forschungs-_und_Bildungskonzept_2015_01-1.pdf. Accessed 7 June 2020.

Kohn, Nicholas W., et al. "Conceptual Combinations and Subsequent Creativity." *Creativity Research Journal*, vol. 23, no. 3, 2011, pp. 203–210.

Kontje, Todd. "Staging the Sublime: Schiller's 'Maria Stuart' as Ironic Tragedy." *Modern Language Studies*, vol. 22, no. 2, 1992, pp. 88–101.

Larkin, Edward T. "Assessing the Age of Goethe in the Undergraduate Curriculum: A Report." *Die Unterrichtspraxis*, vol. 24, no. 1, 1991, pp. 49–55.

Leis, Mario. *Johann Wolfgang Goethe: Faust I.* Reclam, 2017.

Lessing, Gotthold Ephraim. *Nathan der Weise*, edited by Christoph E. Schweitzer, Suhrkamp/Insel, 1984.

Lokke, Kari. "Schiller's 'Maria Stuart': The Historical Sublime and the Aesthetics of Gender." *Monatshefte*, vol. 82, no. 2, 1990, pp. 123–141.

Martinson, Steven. "Transcultural Literary Interpretation: Theoretical Reflections with Examples from the Works of Gotthold Ephraim Lessing and Johann Wolfgang Goethe." *Humanities*, vol. 5, no. 3, 2016, pp. 51–63.

Maurer, Karl-Heinz. "Verführung durch Mitleid: G. E. Lessings *Emilia Galotti* als Selbstaufhebung der Tragödie." *The German Quarterly*, vol. 78, no. 2, 2005, pp. 172–191.

Middleton, Erica L, et al. "How Do we Process Novel Conceptual Combinations in Context?" *Quarterly Journal of Experimental Psychology*, vol. 64, no. 4, 2011, pp. 807–822.

Nietzel, Michael T. "Whither the Humanities: The Ten-Year Trend in College Majors." *Forbes*, 7 Jan. 2019, www.forbes.com/sites/michaeltnietzel/2019/01/07/whither-the-humanities-the-ten-year-trend-in-college-majors/#6a6c95b464ad. Accessed 7 June 2020.

Pelster, Theodor. *Lektüreschlüssel XL. Friedrich Schiller: Maria Stuart*. Reclam, 2017.

Pelster, Theodor. *Lektüreschlüssel XL. Gotthold Ephraim Lessing: Emilia Galotti*. Reclam, 2017.

Piazzoli, Erika. "Process Drama: The Use of Affective Space to Reduce Language Anxiety in the Additional Language Learning Classroom." *Research in Drama Education*, vol. 16, no. 4, 2011, pp. 557–573.

Ruppert, Rainer. *Labor der Seele und der Emotionen: Funktionen des Theaters im 18. und frühen 19. Jahrhundert*. Edition Sigma, 1995.

Schewe, Manfred. "Taking Stock and Looking Ahead: Drama Pedagogy as a Gateway to a Performative Teaching and Learning Culture." *Scenario*, vol. 7, no. 1, 2014, pp. 5–23.

Schildmeier, Marvin. "Von Empathie, Fantasie und guten Handschuhen: Erfahrungen mit Drama und Theater am University College Cork." *Scenario*, vol. 10, no. 2, 2016, pp. 73–82.

Schiller, Friedrich. "Schillers Werke. Nationalausgabe." *Im Auftrag des Goethe- und Schiller-Archivs, des Schiller-Nationalmuseums und der Deutschen Akademie*, edited by Julius Petersen und Gerhard Fricke, Verlag Herrman Böhlaus Nachfolger, 1943ff.

Sommer, Michael. *Reclam präsentiert: Sommers Weltliteratur to go*. sommers-weltliteratur.de/projekt. Accessed 7 June 2020.

9 Technology-enhanced learning approaches to curriculum development
Architecture meets the humanities

Gabriele Maier

Introduction

Low student enrollment is a big problem for many language departments in the U.S., but it can be extremely challenging for small language programs, since they tend to be more prone to severe financial cuts and even complete elimination. As many of my colleagues have already remarked in their respective chapters in this anthology, according to a recent MLA report in 2018, "[c]olleges closed more than 650 foreign-language programs in a recent three-year period [2013–2016]" – among them 86 German programs – and chances are that those numbers will be higher in 2020 when the MLA is scheduled to conduct its next survey (Johnson 2019). Trying to increase student numbers is not an easy task, especially without a college-wide language requirement that helps fill classrooms at the elementary or intermediate level. Attempts to remedy this malaise are multifold and include offering courses in English to attract students without any language background (with the hope of piquing their interest in language classes), courses with a STEM focus or a relevant topic for the job market (e.g., Business German or French for Engineering), extracurricular activities (*Stammtisch*, film series, karaoke nights, etc.), study abroad opportunities, mentorship programs between beginners and more advanced language students, teaching assistant opportunities for undergraduate students, or partnerships with external organizations such as the Goethe-Institut, chambers of commerce or even public schools. Not all novel activities are successful since it depends on one's institution and student body whether innovative ideas gain traction and cater to students' interests.

Especially at technology-oriented institutions, like Carnegie Mellon University (CMU) in Pittsburgh, which historically lacks a strong appreciation for the humanities, even the most original ideas can result in failure when students are unable to see the value in adding yet another item to their weekly schedules. Over the last several years, professors in the Dietrich College of the Humanities and Social Sciences at CMU have made an effort to launch new initiatives – the most recent being the Humanities@CMU Initiative in the fall of 2019 – that more aggressively promote the humanities, make their presence on campus known, encourage community outreach, help educators refine their teaching methodologies and create innovative classes that cross over various disciplines. Since technology plays a decisive role in shaping CMU's identity, technology-enhanced learning has been at the core of many recent initiatives, as well as interdisciplinary research and teaching endeavors that promise to attract students from various academic fields and to raise their awareness of the humanities.

Carnegie Mellon University is a private institution in Western Pennsylvania, primarily known for its world-class programs in the School of Computer Science, College of Engineering and its School of Drama. Each year CMU attracts students from "almost every country" of the world (Carnegie Mellon University's Global Presence) and is ranked "in the top 5 for national universities with the highest percentage of international undergraduates" (Undergraduate International Students). In the fall of 2018, CMU admitted 6,285 international students, both undergraduates and graduates, "with students from outside of the United States making up 22 percent of the degree-seeking undergraduate student body" (Student Enrollment 2018). Given its global student body, CMU takes pride in its countless connections to international institutions and scholars, its branch campuses around the world (e.g., Qatar, Rwanda and Australia) and the jobs across the globe students obtain after graduation. Ironically, it comes as a surprise that the study of foreign languages, a true marker of global citizenry, is not heavily promoted but seen as an unwelcome stepchild that is not part of the core curriculum of a CMU student. As a consequence, the Department of Modern Languages (ML), like so many other foreign languages departments in the U.S., is plagued by low enrollment, and few students declare majors and minors in the foreign languages ML offers, be it in Arabic, Chinese, French, German, Italian, Japanese, Russian or Spanish. Even though CMU does not have a language requirement, data shows that 48% of all students take at least one foreign language class during their time at CMU, and many continue to register for more courses. Yet, it is not enough to fill up courses, especially at the advanced level, and provide ML with a continuous stream of new students every year. Thus, many faculty members have been scrambling to find innovative ways to attract more students and have recently been aided in their efforts by college-wide initiatives that include workshops, round table discussions and a number of grants to foster the creation of new courses with an emphasis on technology and collaborative teaching.

Over the last few years, Dietrich College has tried hard to make it easier for faculty members to become program innovators. Together with the Eberly Center for Teaching Excellence and Educational Innovation, Dietrich College has made a concerted effort to support innovative teaching in its multiple facets. It has offered generous financial support for faculty members to conceptualize, design and execute new classes. Several years ago, Grand Challenge seminars for all first-year students were launched that focus on "real complex global problems like climate change, food insecurity or racism" (Grand Challenge Seminars). These seminars are interdisciplinary and cotaught by faculty from multiple fields. So far, over a dozen seminars have been conducted and student feedback has been mostly positive. Equally helpful have been week-long workshops at the end of every spring semester that introduce instructors and graduate students to technology-enhanced learning and digital humanities. Both workshops feature a number of guest speakers from the Pittsburgh area that showcase their research as well as their educational work in the classroom and provide innovative ways to combine technology with the humanities. Last but not least, funding opportunities in the form of seed grants exist that aim to aid in the pursuit of learning research or in designing and testing innovative educational practices. The above workshops, along with a seed grant of $15,000, made it possible to conceptualize and teach the class Digital Vienna 1900, which will be the focus of this chapter. The pilot course combined literary studies with art history, urban planning and technology, and featured collaborative teaching between me, from Modern Languages, and Francesca Torello, faculty member of the School of Architecture. In the remainder of this chapter, I intend to delineate the rationale for this innovative course, depict our theoretical framework, describe the course content and finally assess whether we were successful in the creation of a new class that heavily relied on interdisciplinary teaching and technology-enhanced learning.

Reconceptualizing Vienna at the turn of the 20th century

Teaching Vienna at the last turn of the century is not a new idea by any means. Due to the richness of Viennese culture around 1900 and the impact the cultural debate of this era had on the development of a modern sensibility, "fin-de-siècle Vienna" has become an important academic course in many disciplines, be it in German Studies, literary studies, history and art and architectural history. Since this era's scientific discoveries, philosophical and literary movements, and stunning innovations in the realm of urban planning and architecture still have a significant influence today and connect to the fields of literature, art, philosophy, history, politics, architecture, psychology and music, the course, Vienna 1900, is popular among students. The possibilities are endless and so are the texts that can be used to demonstrate what Vienna in 1900 was like.

Since Vienna 1900 ideally encompasses numerous different fields, it can be challenging for one instructor to be an expert in all subject areas. As William Newell (1994) states: "An interdisciplinary topic takes more than one person's interest, even expertise, because an interdisciplinary course requires multiple perspectives" (37). Vienna 1900 is a class that lends itself well to collaborative teaching where experts from different fields come together to share their knowledge with the class, aiming for a "genuinely interdisciplinary integration of different approaches" (Klein and Doty 1994, 2). Hence, I teamed up with my colleague, Torello, who has a strong background in art history and urban planning, in the fall of 2015 to conceptualize a class that would do just that:

rely on our different knowledge and educational backgrounds to showcase architecture, the arts, the humanities and the many connections between those diverse disciplines. In addition, we relied on guest speakers to cover topics we both felt ill-equipped to teach, such as the significance of 12-tone music and the waltz. We also planned a trip to our local art museum where a curator prepared an array of Viennese artifacts from the period in question and visited Pittsburgh Opera to watch Richard Strauss' *Salome*.

Approaching Vienna 1900 from different angles of expertise was a first and crucial step towards revitalizing the class but it was not enough to give the class new life. Torello and I had taught Vienna 1900 multiple times in our respective disciplines; Torello, with a heavy focus on urban planning, art history and architecture; I, with a strong emphasis on history, philosophy, literature and psychoanalysis. Yet, in our previous classes, we had employed more traditional teaching methodologies, such as lectures, paper writing or in-class PowerPoint presentations, following in the footsteps of countless colleagues of ours who had taught Vienna 1900 over the years as a staple of their curriculum. While our classes were successful, they were teacher-centric and did not draw on the expertise of the student body. Overall, the classes felt repetitive and writing-intensive and did not take into account the visual, auditory and tactile aspects of learning. Our goal for our team-taught class was to move away from "lecture and direct instruction" which according to Thom Markham (2011) should be "long forgotten remnants of a prior age" (38) and toward a constructivist approach to teaching and learning that entailed the use of technology – specifically, the creation of a digital interface – to encourage students to take learning into their own hands and benefit from each other's academic specializations. Even though we knew that constructivist learning approaches "can also present great new challenges for instructors and learners" (Blessinger and Carfora 2014, 7), we wanted to restore agency to our students, provide them with the tools to conduct "authentic explorations of knowledge and understandings" (Kraglund-Gauthier 2014, 198) and help them "actively construct their understanding by working with and using ideas" (318), as Krajcik and Blumenfeld (2005) charge. In short, we wanted to learn as much from our students as they would learn from us; we wanted to empower them to pursue their individual interests.

Theoretical foundations and course design

Digital Vienna 1900 was taught in English to attract students from various disciplines and to make collaboration between Torello and myself possible. Our class met twice a week, on Tuesdays and Thursdays, for 80 minutes per session. Both of us were present at every class and cotaught Tuesday's session for the first half of the semester while, Talia Perry, a practicing architect and former student of the School of Architecture, was in charge of our Thursday sessions, which were dedicated to 3D modeling. After about six to seven weeks, when students were familiar with Rhino, the modeling software, and

Perry's instructions had come to an end and we shifted to two cotaught classes per week. Digital Vienna 1900 was housed in Modern Languages but was cross-listed with the Department of English, the Department of History, the School of Architecture and the Center for the Arts in Society, whose mission of bringing the fine arts and the humanities together mirrored the objectives of our class. Enrollment was good for a brand-new course: our student body consisted of ten students – two freshmen, two sophomores, one junior and five seniors – who came from such diverse fields as modern languages, English, drama, architecture, physics and design which significantly contributed to the interdisciplinarity of our class. A few students had some rudimentary knowledge of the German language, but no one was able to read German texts in the original. Students took our class as a general elective and were not privy to 3D modeling or Austrian history and culture before they signed up for Digital Vienna 1900.

Our teaching methodology and pedagogical framework were inspired by a project-based learning (PBL) as well as inquiry-based learning approach (IBL) to "allow[] students to learn by doing and applying ideas" (Krajcik and Blumenfeld 2005, 317). Rooted in theories of John Dewey and inspired by the constructivist educational movement, students' active construction of knowledge lies at the heart of these approaches "in a socially participatory way," be it with their peers, their instructors or community members (Blessinger and Carfora 2014, 12). In both learning approaches, which we saw as complementary to one another, "[s]tudents drive their own learning through inquiry, as well as work collaboratively to research and create projects that reflect their knowledge," as Stephanie Bell (2010) delineates in her article "Project-Based Learning for the 21st Century: Skills for the Future" (39). As a student-centric learning method, both approaches presuppose that "teachers shift from expert providers of knowledge to facilitators of learning" (Jean Lee et al. 2014, 21). Thus, the role of the teacher is "not to provide answers, but rather to help direct their students to find the answers themselves (e.g., by suggesting useful paths of enquiry)" (Franc and Morton 2014, 84; see also Kraglund-Gauthier 2014; Blessinger and Carfora 2014). Even though, as Maryellen Weimer suggests, the shift in power might result in "confusion or resistance at the outset" among the students, it will, in the end, "improve the learning experience, motivation and classroom atmosphere" (qtd. in Tschoepe 2014, 176). Hence, in both approaches the process of learning is as important as the final product, a big change from more traditional teaching approaches, and the emphasis on soft skills is a crucial part of that process. As Vogler et al. (2018) note, it is "the ability to collaborate with others, communicate clearly, lead effectively and solve problems and challenges" (459) that constitutes the core of all learning objectives and is of equal significance for students as hard skills "because these are the skills that individuals need and use on an ongoing basis throughout life" (Wurdinger and Qureshi 2015, 286). It is those so-called "life skills," "specifically problem solving, creativity, responsibility, communication, and self-direction" (Wurdinger and Qureshi

2015, 286) that play a crucial role and that are usually not taken into consideration when evaluating students' performance. Intrigued by the potential of PBL and IBL to fundamentally change our old ways of teaching and to provide students with more agency in their learning process, we began to implement critical elements of both approaches into our syllabus which formed the basis for our actual course in the fall of 2016.

According to the Galileo Educational Network (2015), at the heart of inquiry-based learning lies the "study into a worthy question, issue, problem or idea. It is the authentic, real work that ... those working in the disciplines actually undertake to create or build knowledge." The same holds true for PBL which postulates that students "engage in real-world activities that are similar to the activities adult professionals engage in" (Krajcik and Blumenfeld 2005, 317). Due to its real-world focus, PBL has been mainly applied in STEM fields (Bell 2010; Wurdinger and Qureshi 2015; Thomas) and most research has been conducted on "project-based science" (Blessinger and Carfora 2014, 34). Yet, despite its heavy focus on the sciences, both IBL and PBL can be applied "to any subject area" as "[p]rojects are widely used in social studies, arts, and English classes" (Krajcik and Blumenfeld 2005, 329) "where the nature and types of questions and problems can vary greatly" (Blessinger and Carfora 2014, 15). Following Blessinger and Carfora's suggestion, we decided to make the exploration of spaces our point of departure. We wanted our students to examine public spaces as well as interiors as they originally were when the intellectuals and architects of the time first saw them (e.g., famous Viennese cafés or the exhibition spaces where art collections could be viewed). As our primary spaces, we chose the coffeehouse, the exhibition hall, the music venue and the university – public spaces that showcased traditional as well as modern architectural styles while, at the same time, being crucial meeting points where intellectual exchanges took place, making those spaces one of the "actors" of these intellectual networks. Our goal was two-fold: to have students study the architectural significance of the aforementioned buildings, while, at the same time, explore the intellectual networks found in those spaces, such as *Jung Wien* (Young Vienna) and *Wiener Kreis* (Vienna Circle). Within the framework of the assignment, students were free to conduct research on those subject areas they were most interested in and to come up with innovative ways of linking ideas, people and spaces with one another. Despite the fact that our project did not try to respond to an authentic problem, we established the connection to the real world in a different manner by having our students participate in the creation of a map that was to become a public resource with the intention of educating people about Vienna 1900.

Through their projects we wanted students to "become better researchers, problem solvers, and higher-order thinkers" (Bell 2010, 42) and intended to achieve this by emphasizing three crucial aspects of PBL/IBL: structured student-collaboration, the use of new technology and the implementation of scaffolded assignments throughout the entire course.

Structured student collaboration: To cultivate structured student collaboration and to increase students' agency in their research process, we put students into interdisciplinary groups that combined different fields of study and levels of expertise. As Thom Markham states: "PBL is inherently a collaborative process, both for students and teachers" (39). Our goal was for students to share their respective knowledge with one another and for more advanced students to help less experienced students with their projects. We created four groups, with two groups of two and two groups of three participants. All four groups stayed together over the course of the semester (Krajcik and Blumenfeld 2005, 325) and embarked on a number of research activities as well as the creation of 3D models of buildings as they appeared in Vienna at the turn of the 20th century, e.g., Café Museum and the Secession Building. Designated times for research were built into our teaching schedule. Whereas on Tuesdays, we discussed assigned texts on various topics related to the history and culture of Vienna as a class (see section on Course Structure and Materials), on Thursdays, students worked in groups at the computer lab in the School of Architecture where they either practiced 3D modelling with the help of Perry or engaged in research activities. Students researched the architecture of their respective buildings to understand the differences between traditional and modern building philosophies, read architectural theory to appreciate the broader intellectual context and investigated important writers and artists to evaluate the role they played in the intellectual debate and their place in the "social networks" of the city. Torello and I provided students with guidelines for each class period and were always available for advice and research support. Yet, first and foremost, we wanted our students to decide on their own which course their research activities should take and what it was they were most interested in researching in their groups.

Use of technology: In order to address the complex context of the city and enable students to work with the materials in an interactive way, we employed digital tools that helped us reach our goals. "Technology tools can help transform the classroom into an environment in which learners actively construct knowledge," Krajcik and Blumenfeld charge (325) and highlight the possibility that technology can foster higher-order learning. Under our guidance, students started to create an interactive map of 19th-century Vienna with the intention to navigate the city and to visualize literary and historical data. In a subsequent step, we planned to incorporate 3D models progressively into the map, allowing students to explore public spaces as well as interiors and their connections to the people who frequented them. The inspiration for this part of our project was *What Jane Saw*, where a retrospective of paintings by Sir Joshua Reynolds is reproduced in a digital room as it was when writer, Jane Austen, saw it in 1813. We devised exercises that directed the students to do hands-on work on modeling these spaces of disciplinary exchange. In addition to hiring Perry to familiarize our students with the modeling software, Rhino, we also employed three teaching assistants from the School of Architecture who provided one-on-one tutoring for our students when they needed additional help. What we intended to do was to start building the map in our pilot class and then use it as a learning tool in the future that could be expanded upon by other instructors and their students and – in the end – become an educational tool for the general public, as stated previously.

Scaffolding: In order to help students with the task at hand, we employed the technique of scaffolding throughout the entire semester. As Reiser and Tabak (2005) delineate, "Scaffolding the process refers to helping learners with strategic choices and executing processes to achieve solutions. ... Scaffolding can transform tasks so that learners can succeed by engaging in simpler tasks that are still valuable for learning" (48). We tried to make the investigation into the meaning of spaces more manageable so that students wouldn't feel overwhelmed and had clear guidelines as to how to structure their research. Following Bell's postulate that "[s]caffolded instruction ensures success," we made a concerted effort to "use organizers that aid[ed] students in bridging the gaps that exists in knowledge and skill" (Bell 2010, 41) so that they could "extend their competencies" (Lu et al. 2005, 305). Thus, over the entire course of the semester students slowly collected information, organized it in their groups and wrote short research summaries that all constituted important pieces for their final project for the end of the semester. We broke up the big project into smaller pieces that were clearly marked on the syllabus and that instructed students to hand in their work-in-progress frequently to receive feedback. By making excessive use of scaffolding we tried to avoid "significant frustration" (Lee et al. 2014, 20) among the students that can arise if students feel that the teacher, now facilitator, does not provide enough guidance throughout their learning process. The different tasks students had to fulfill were: a) the modeling of a 3D space; b) the collection of artifacts; c) the mapping of a network and d) the presentation of their final product which will be described in more detail as follows:

a) Modeling of a 3D space: From the very outset our class was taught with a focus on the significance of spaces at its core; spaces constituted the key component where all explorations departed from and returned to. Spaces became our anchor points which brought our readings and research activities together and made interdisciplinary investigations possible. The inquiry into the meaning of spaces replaced the "chewy (original, detailed, focused, challenging, intellectually engaging, and – most of all – researchable) question" (Watts 2014, 135) so prevalent in inquiry-based and project-based learning, as described previously. In order to make a space come alive, students were asked to create a digital model that would fit within the categories of buildings marked on our syllabus: the coffeehouse, the exhibition hall, the music venue, the university, and the selected buildings were Café Museum, the Secession Building, the Vienna Opera House and the Kunsthistorische Museum. Since modeling a building such as the Kunsthistorische Museum would have been a rather overwhelming task, we allowed students to choose specific spaces within their selected building as their primary focus. All modelling was done as a group and received a group grade at the end of the semester. Reconstructing parts of a building was to help students visualize the space and understand specific architectural features in more detail. We saw modeling as a means toward more in-depth research, as a vehicle for further investigations into the network of people who frequented the particular space, their discussions and intellectual exchange and the various artifacts connected to the building.

b) Collection of artifacts: We asked students to collect three artifacts per group member of various kinds (visual, auditory, linguistic) that pertained to their chosen building and write a short description (250–300 words per material) of each that contained a short bibliography of at least three sources for each artifact. By researching selected artifacts, such as a billiard table and the coffee drink *Kleiner Brauner* for Café Museum or the sculpture "Theseus defeats the centaur" for the Kunsthistorische Museum, students simultaneously gathered information about the specific time their artifacts were created, the people who created them and what significance they harbored within the context of their specific building. Since each student did their individual research – even though working together during designated times in class was encouraged – students were able to choose the items they were most interested in and convey their knowledge to their classmates, thereby also educating us as instructors.

c) Mapping of a network: Another crucial component of our class was the mapping of a network that pertained to the space students were reconstructing as a 3D model. This network map had to include three people per group member, which meant that in a group of three members, the network consisted of nine people. In addition to the mere process of mapping, students had to write a short profile of each character that included relevant details about their life, such as education, profession, important accomplishments, etc. Furthermore, each profile had to contain a short section that delineated the connection of the respective figure to other people in the network and distinguish connections based on family ties, marriages, common environments and intellectual connections (e.g., reading each other's books). We encouraged students to use, in part, their collection of materials to demonstrate connections in creative ways. Thus, in the group that focused on Café Museum, Oskar Kokoschka, Peter Altenberg and Ludwig Wittgenstein were discussed with regard to their connection to Adolf Loos, the architect of Café Museum. In the case of the Secession Building, Gustav Klimt, Sigmund Freud and Arthur Schnitzler were part of a larger network that focused on their significance for the younger Viennese generations to embrace modern times. Grades were given individually for the respective profile of a network member and also as a group for the visualization of the network itself.

d) Final presentation: Following Newell's advice that "it is natural in an interdisciplinary course to ask the students to pull the course together in a concluding assignment" (49), all assignments culminated in the final product, a 20–25 minute, in-class presentation that combined all elements researched and modeled over the course of the semester: the description and analysis of various artifacts, the creation of a network of people and their individual biographies as well as the 3D model of a building (or parts thereof) that showcased the crucial space where artists and intellectuals gathered. The presentations in class were accompanied by a four-page summary of all the above that demonstrated the ability of our students to put their research into a coherent narrative. While the final presentation and write-up were only worth 10% each and considered one assignment among many others, both were instrumental for us in gauging how well students were able to establish essential connections between the respective pieces of their research activities. Furthermore, it was a way for us to assess our interdisciplinary teaching endeavor and evaluate the success (or failure) of our PBL and IBL approaches.

Monitoring students' learning process throughout the semester

While the scaffolding of student projects seemed an important feature regarding PBL and IBL, we also tried to focus specifically on the learning process of our students and how they arrived at a particular product. As Blumenfeld et al. (1996) point out, "students may not be aware that they need help nor seek it when needed. They may not know how to ask questions that identify their problem" (38). Thus, apart from assignments that received a grade and helped us gauge how far students had progressed, we also created mandatory tasks for our students that helped us understand the struggles and challenges they were facing along the way. Students were supposed to give a number of informal presentations, write weblog entries and provide us with anonymous course evaluations at mid-point and at the end of the semester.

Informal presentations: In addition to the final presentation which received a group grade, students gave a number of informal presentations that were intended to offer clear check-in points regarding students' research as well as possible questions and concerns students might still harbor about their projects. As Linda Watts (2014) argues, "work-in-progress presentations enable class members to share sources, strategies, and advice with their peers" (141). In addition to brief ad hoc reports students delivered almost every class time that were not graded (Newell 1994, 48), we required a number of longer and more substantial group presentations where students showcased their findings, be it their artifacts, their networks of people or their 3D models. During those presentations, students explained their research process, delineated successes and struggles and showcased their work-in-progress. Even though class presentations were ungraded, they were still quite formal in nature and required students to think through their findings before they stepped in front of their peers. Overall, it was not so much the product we were interested in but the care and attention with which students approached their projects and the strategies they had tried out to reach a certain goal. We wanted our students to explore a problem from different angles, to be creative and innovative and to rather experience failure while investigating a new path than to not try at all. Since presentations preceded the submission of all major assignments, it was a great opportunity for students to receive feedback from their peers that could be used to revise their projects and to integrate new ideas and suggestions that were generated during class discussions. Hence, when it was time for the final presentation that encompassed research components from the entire semester, students were well-versed in the act of presenting and had received enough detailed feedback so that they felt quite confident with regard to their final product.

Weekly blog entries: Since self-directed research was difficult to monitor, we decided to keep track of our students' research activities via weekly blog entries so that we could lend a helping hand and assess how well students progressed. Over the course of the semester, we used Tumblr as our weblog. Students were required to post entries every week, with blog entries differing depending on the specific place within the rotation students were in. Each week students rotated within their group and posted a different blog entry, according to a schedule we distributed at the beginning of the semester. There were three possible blog entries that students were to do: 1) a short response to reading assignments in class (and how those readings helped advance their own projects); 2) completed research summaries that explained the different steps the group had undertaken to gather certain materials (be it in the form of articles, photos, audio pieces, etc.) and how that particular material helped advance their project and 3) a discussion of open research questions and strategies that should be employed to make progress and set an agenda for the next week. Even though blog entries were rather short, between 350–400 words, they also functioned as a "reflective practice" (Watts 2014, 143) which helped students refocus and find new ways to move forward. Students received detailed feedback from us on a regular basis. Especially, with regard to open research questions, we provided students with advice and suggestions on which additional books, articles or websites to consult to move their research forward. Completed blog entries received individual grades and full points if they were done according to the guidelines provided by us. Since interdisciplinary collaboration was a key component of the class, blog entries also helped us observe student behavior within their respective teams, evaluate whether collaboration in groups indeed led to enhanced learning and determine whether students benefited from the interdisciplinary approach in their written assignments.

Student evaluations: Last but not least, we relied on student evaluation forms that we devised with the help of Eberly Center consultants to gauge whether our class was successful. Since our class was a pilot course that had received grant funding, we worked closely with the Eberly Center and received advice and feedback throughout the semester. Before the course started, we spent multiple sessions with an Eberly Center consultant designing our syllabus, numerous class activities and the map of Vienna 1900.

146 *Gabriele Maier*

In addition, Eberly Center consultants helped us create midterm as well as end-of-the-semester evaluation forms and conducted an in-class focus group with our students. During that focus group consultants interviewed students about: 1) students' progress with regard to their research projects; 2) their perceptions of how the course was going for them and 3) suggestions for improvement of the course. According to the feedback we received we were able to modify certain features of the class and refine our teaching approach to cater to students' needs.

Course structure and materials

At the beginning of our course we asked students to complete a mind map to help us understand what they knew about or associated with Vienna at the turn of the last century. The results were rather sobering – apart from a few miscellaneous facts about Viennese culture, students were unfamiliar with the time period. A couple of students had heard of the term Austro-Hungarian Empire, knew that Austria used to be a monarchy, had a vague idea that Sigmund Freud might have been Austrian or had accidentally come across writers such as Arthur Schnitzler and Stefan Zweig in previous courses. Even though Gustav Klimt and Art Nouveau were mentioned a few times, no one was aware of the rich Viennese art and cultural scene. It became clear from class discussions that most students had signed up for Digital Vienna 1900 because they were intrigued by the interdisciplinarity of the course as well as the creation of 3D models. Given the limited knowledge students displayed, we decided to focus heavily on historical and cultural background readings to provide students with the details they needed before they could dive into 3D modelling and their self-directed group research endeavors.

Our materials were derived from scholarly books, articles, novels and short story collections and were put into constant dialogue with one another. We greatly relied on Carl Schorske's *Fin-de-Siècle Vienna: Politics and Culture*, Peter Vergo's *Art in Vienna 1898–1918* and Leslie Topp's *Architecture and Truth in Fin-de-Siècle Vienna* which provided students with a solid overview of Vienna 1900 that combined history, politics and the arts. Other theoretical texts that we used were Wolfgang Maderthaner and Lutz Musner's *Unruly Masses. The Other Side of Fin-de-Siècle Vienna*, Allan Janik and Stephen Toulmin's *Wittgenstein's Vienna*, Harold B. Segel's *The Vienna Coffeehouse Wits 1890–1938* and Elizabeth Clegg's *Art, Design, and Architecture in Central Europe 1890–1920*, just to name a few. We also assigned numerous primary texts such as excerpts from Stefan Zweig's *The World of Yesterday*, Arthur Schnitzler's "Lieutnant Gustl," Robert Musil's *Young Torless*, Otto Wagner's "The Development of a Great City," Adolf Loos' *On Architecture* and excerpts from Sigmund Freud's *Civilization and Its Discontents*. At first glance, our reading list seemed to replicate the ones utilized by more traditional courses on Vienna 1900, but it was the pairing of our texts with one another that offered new exciting perspectives and generated lively class discussions. For example, during our unit on the University of Vienna, we combined the Viennese educational system with Gustav Klimt's university paintings, and excerpts from Sigmund Freud's *Civilization and Its Discontents*. Moving across disciplines while still being securely anchored in one particular space (e.g., the University of Vienna) allowed students to make connections between key intellectual figures, their accomplishments and the spatial entity that would have been impossible in previous classes of ours that focused on only one discipline at a time.

Class time was structured around group work – both during our weekly project-based learning units and while discussing assigned readings – to facilitate collaboration among the students and to present them with the opportunity to express their thoughts in an intimate setting. Since student participation was low at first, we moved to a teaching model that had students start out in groups (not necessarily in their assigned groups for the semester) at the beginning of each lesson to discuss class readings as well as their own research. In their groups, students answered study questions, shared the content of their blog entries, talked about their respective research activities and asked their peers for advice. We allocated 20–25 minutes to discussions about reading assignments – an entire hour when student groups conducted self-directed research – and then moved to presentation mode, where students reported their results to the entire class and informed us of remaining questions their groups still had. Listening to other students' presentations and their questions gave some of the quieter students more confidence to share their opinions with the class and ask for guidance when it came to research-related difficulties or struggles with their 3D models. Group work also fostered close bonds between the students which was crucial regarding positive learning outcomes

Another aspect that featured prominently in our class and contributed to student learning were talks by selected guest speakers and visits to cultural institutions, such as the Carnegie Museum of Art and Pittsburgh Opera. In early November of 2016, Pittsburgh Opera presented Richard Strauss' *Salome* which coincided nicely with our session on the Vienna Opera House and two guest lectures by our colleague Franco Sciannameo from the School of Music. Not only was Sciannameo able to prepare our students for the opera in a way that neither Torello nor I could have done but he also briefed them on their impressions and thoughts after their visit and described the historical significance of operas and operettas in Vienna 1900, the importance of Johann Strauss and the waltz for Viennese society and the onset of modern music in the form of Gustav Mahler, Arnold Schönberg and Alban Berg. Our section on the Vienna Opera House received enthusiastic feedback, and so did our evening at the opera. Similarly, students were delighted to visit Carnegie Museum of Art where a curator gave a lecture on paintings, drawings and furniture by the Secession movement and the Viennese Workshops. Students were able to examine archived materials that were usually hidden from public view, talk about their own projects and ask specific questions that pertained to their research activities. Seeing those artifacts in person, a student remarked afterwards, made Vienna 1900 come alive and highlighted the impact the Viennese Workshops in particular had, and still have, on our current sense of aesthetics and the designs we value. Relying on the expertise of colleagues and outside sources was crucial in helping students learn and in generating enthusiasm for the subject at hand.

Student evaluations at midpoint

In addition to the many assignments students completed that helped us gauge whether our teaching was successful, we conducted midterm evaluations and a subsequent focus group led by Eberly Center consultants to gather suggestions for improvement, as well as end-of-the-semester evaluations, both in writing and online. Overall, the feedback we received from our midterm evaluations was quite positive. Students appreciated the choice and breadth of our texts and felt that class discussions were informative and helpful. The selection of "primary sources of the time period" was praised, whether it was "writings, short stories, music, or paintings to analyze and understand the artists of the time period." Students loved the "interdisciplinary aspect of the course – from history to art" and found the "amalgamation of architecture and history" quite informative. They also approved of our assignments, be it the weekly blog entries, the "check-in points throughout the semester about projects," our "push for self-driven research, with supporting resources" and the freedom of project-based learning. Interestingly enough, students did not complain about group work. We did not encounter a single comment about "social loafing," which Lee and Lim (2012) describe as "the phenomenon of people exerting less effort to achieve a goal when they work in a group than when they work alone" (214) and is often a point of criticism when it comes to project-based learning. Yet, besides a few positive comments regarding our project-based learning approach, it was project-based learning in and of itself that students did not feel comfortable with and asked for significant changes regarding our pedagogical methodology.

What students were most critical of was the self-directed research part of our class, and, in particular, the creation of 3D models. Students thought that the modeling component was too stressful, felt "very confused about some aspects of the software," found the "Rhino tutorial a little too fast" and requested "more guidelines to help begin their research." Overall, students felt that the course was divided into two parts: "[T]he research/modeling project and the readings and discussions" seemed "disjointed and oftentimes ... like separate classes. I feel that if they were more interconnected the class would flow more fluidly." Another student wrote: "I love the idea of exploring the use of space and their artifact/network collection, but they are not connecting in the way I want them to." As students became increasingly more focused on their own buildings and spent a lot of their self-directed research-time in class exploring those spaces, they were rather frustrated with the fact that most of the readings we had assigned did not feature their chosen buildings. It became apparent that we as instructors had failed to convey to our students that course readings were merely supposed to provide the historical and cultural framework, a point of reference that was meant to serve as the backdrop for students' own research projects.

Since project-based learning was at the core of our class, we tried to address the criticism with the help of our Eberly Center consultants. We were already aware of the fact that students can "struggle with the unfamiliarity of the PBL environment, which poses challenges for implementation" (Lee et al. 2014, 22) since students tend to be "used to sitting in class and being told what to do" (Lee et al. 2014, 25). "[R]edefining students' expectations in unfamiliar ways" (Lee et al. 2014, 25) left students unsure how to navigate the tasks before them. Thus, we made a concerted effort to emphasize again and again in what ways our readings in class were connected to the 3D models students were working on and how the information provided by those texts offered an essential framework for the research each group was conducting. In addition, we designed separate handouts and class activities that were meant to connect readings and 3D models and to get discussions started (Newell 1994, 49) and hired another teaching assistant during self-guided research periods to support students in their investigations. We also gave students the opportunity to present their research more often during class time in order to discuss their successes and remaining struggles with their classmates and come up with viable solutions. Overall, we wanted to give project-based learning and 3D modeling another try and were hopeful that students would see the value in what they were creating, which would become most apparent in their final projects.

Final projects and student evaluations at the end of the semester

While evaluations at midpoint provided us with a window into students' personal thoughts about our class, we also heavily relied on numerous assignments to assess how students were responding to specific tasks throughout the semester. In particular, the final presentation was of great interest to us since it brought together all previous assignments and gave students a chance to elaborate on their research process one last time. Overall, final presentations were a big success. Students had prepared slides that showcased, among other things, rotating 3D models and their places on the map of Vienna 1900. While not all 3D models were complete buildings, they all demonstrated an impressive attention to detail in the form of architectural features. Even though students had repeatedly complained about their inability to create 3D models, their presentations told an entirely different story. Not only had the buildings themselves been generated but also furniture, paintings and even silverware were part of the models which attested to the fun students must have had with them. In their presentations, students moved smoothly from 3D model to selected artifacts to their network of people and effortlessly fitted them all into a greater narrative about Vienna 1900. Not a single presentation was a disappointment, neither during the actual presentation nor during the ensuing question-and-answer period, and our grades reflected our enthusiasm. It didn't come as a surprise that students felt very pleased with their final projects. Asked on our end-of-the-semester evaluation form whether students were satisfied with their work, answers ranged from "quite" and "mostly" to more elaborate responses such as "[t]his class was a new experience for me, and I feel I not only learned new content, but also new learning and research skills;" "I am satisfied with my exploration of networks and attempted modeling;" "I am! I think my group covered a lot of research and learned things that we didn't know before." The final project was well received by students and seemed to indicate that the adjustments we made to the course over the second half of the semester were somewhat successful.

The success of our various improvements also became apparent with regard to the accomplishment of our learning objectives: a) to recognize the individual roles that historically significant actors played in the intellectual debates and social networks and b) to analyze how networks of actors can impact intellectual, artistic and cultural developments, which were met with unanimous consent in our final evaluation. "You were very successful in explaining the connections between these people," a student stated. "This makes me think about how much influence they may have had on each other's creative tendencies." Another remarked: "Very successful. Good and logical organization of topics and weeks." One student even explicitly mentioned the role the 3D model played in this: "It was transmitted successfully, and our 3D model was paramount in these considerations." Answers mirrored the excellent final projects that students had completed. Furthermore, students reiterated their contentment with the selection of informative texts, engaging class discussions, the intriguing interdisciplinary aspect of the class, the interesting guest lectures and the new research skills that were acquired. Yet, criticism of the disconnect between modeling, readings and assignments persisted, as did concerns over the lack of guidance when it came to research and 3D modeling.

Limitations and directions to be taken in the future

Despite our joint efforts to remedy the alleged disconnect between our teaching and students' research, our end-of-the-semester evaluations were reminiscent of the ones at midpoint. Again, students did not acknowledge a connection between the course content and the 3D modeling and commented accordingly: "I struggled to find the connections with the 3D model;" "I think space as a catalyst for intellectual exchange is interesting, and I understand it better now, but not really through the 3D modeling – more through imaging and networking" and "I still don't understand how space – especially modeling the space – connected to the exchange and innovation. The space did not have a tangible connection which made it very difficult to discuss/

understand." Even though we as instructors had made every effort to emphasize frequently what purpose modeling served within the bigger scheme of our class, we had obviously not succeeded, which was a rather frustrating realization given the excellent final projects students proudly presented. Since the general tenor was still quite critical of a core feature of our newly devised class, we sat down to revisit the available data from evaluations and focus groups one more time in order to understand what exactly went wrong.

In particular, the data collected from the focus group proved extremely helpful at second glance, as it highlighted an aspect we had not taken seriously enough until then: students' lack of confidence due to the interdisciplinarity of our class. While combining our individual knowledge to create a multifaceted course had been stimulating and inspiring for us, it felt overwhelming for our students who were uncomfortable talking about subject areas, be it music, literature, architecture or psychology that differed significantly from their majors and minors. According to our students their perceived lack of knowledge posed a crucial obstacle with regard to their engagement in deeper discussions. What students were looking for was "a reading ... about the role of each discipline – for example, as a particular theory or cluster of concepts – used in the course" (Newell 1994, 47) before they felt confident enough to voice their opinion in class. Even our idea of putting students into teams and giving them enough flexibility to pick and choose their own projects turned out to be detrimental to students' learning experience. Instead of drawing on each other's expertise, students felt equally lost in their groups and unsure of how to approach the research component without step-by-step guidance from their professors. And since class readings did not always address their chosen research topics, the disconnect between what we as instructors expected and what students felt they desperately needed became more and more apparent. We gradually realized that Newell was indeed right when he postulated that "even the best-designed interdisciplinary courses face the problem of making the logic of their structure apparent to students" (44). We had not succeeded in providing our students with basic information on how to navigate an interdisciplinary classroom and had failed to assure students that feeling lost while doing research was a natural and necessary part of the process. In addition, we did not make it clear enough that PBL and IBL meant that finding connections between 3D models and discussions in class was not the responsibility of the instructors but up to the students themselves to combine class materials with their own findings to construct a plausible narrative.

Given the challenges the interdisciplinarity of our course brought with it, we determined to implement four significant changes in our next iteration of the class: We decided 1) to make explicit from the very beginning what our pedagogical framework entailed, how we had conceptualized the class and why we were asking students to perform certain tasks; 2) to introduce students to the respective methodologies of the various disciplines; 3) to add a more substantial component of self-assessment throughout the semester and 4) to place less emphasis on the creation of 3D models.

1. **Delineating our learning approaches in more detail**: Since we still believe in the benefits a project-based/inquiry-based learning approach could bring about, we do not want to change our pedagogical framework in our next iteration of the course but would like to give it another try. Yet, we decided to change fundamentally the way students are introduced to our learning approaches. Instead of expecting our students to simply accept our teaching methodology, we need to explain and discuss our approaches with them from the very beginning and make them aware of the possible pitfalls and challenges our approaches entail.

2. **Introducing each academic discipline**: Instead of spending a substantial amount of each week modeling a building (see #4), we intend to focus on the requested methodologies used in different subject areas and provide students with more background readings to help them understand an academic field in more detail. As Caviglia-Harris and Hatley (2004) charge: "One of the most important aspects of the design of a team-taught class is the planning of transitions between course components" (398). Instead of moving seamlessly from one subject area to the next, we intend to implement a separate unit at the very beginning of our class where students will read and discuss different fields, discover how they operate and have a chance to compare and contrast those different methodologies.

3. **Adding self-assessment**: Even though we devised blog entries for students to reflect on their research activities and plan for the week ahead, solely focusing on research may not be enough. Implementing weekly journals whose entries are longer and leave more room for complex thought seems a better idea than the weblogs. As Barron et al. (1998) point out, "self-assessment helps students develop the ability to monitor their own understanding and to find resources to deepen it when necessary" (284). By giving students the space to reflect on their research and the methodologies used in class we might gain better insights into the way our class is going and into the needs our students may have.

4. **Creation of 3D models**: In hindsight, we also wonder whether we placed too much emphasis on technology and the creation of 3D models. Despite the excitement students displayed at the beginning of the semester, spending many hours on modeling seemed to have a detrimental effect on students' enthusiasm and did not contribute to their learning experience the way we had hoped for. Even at a place like CMU, where the use of technology is ubiquitous, the amount of exposure to technology students can tolerate is limited. Even though we intended to use technology as a means to an end, it turned out to become the end itself. While 3D modeling still seems an important feature of the class, limiting the modeling to a smaller space, such as a room or feature of a building,

might yield better results. Overall, we intend to create a map ourselves with 3D models that features an interactive component. Students will still be asked to research networks and artifacts and integrate them on the map, but the exploration of spaces via texts and individual research, not the modeling of those spaces, will be the main feature of the class.

Overall, we felt that, all things considered, our class went well, and we enjoyed trying out a different teaching approach despite a number of hiccups. The available research suggests that the fact that our course faced a number of problems seems to be a normal occurrence, since it takes multiple iterations to arrive at a satisfactory result: "The second time provides a much better sense of the problems involved. The standard rule of thumb is that the third time though is the best." (Newell 1994, 47). We still believe in interdisciplinary teaching – which according to Seabury and Barrett (2000) is "particularly well suited to adult learners" (15) – in PBL/IBL and in the benefits of using technology to enhance students' learning experience. Yet, moving from one subject area to another while crossing various disciplines posed challenges we had not anticipated (Caviglia-Harris and Hatley 2004, 398) and were rather unprepared to remedy. The fact that our students felt lost in class indicated that students had not been exposed to interdisciplinary teaching before and were unfamiliar with our approach – a common occurrence according to Vogel et al. (464) – and the same held true for PBL and IBL. Helping instructors navigate those difficulties would be something teaching centers like the Eberly Center could do in the future, since "[f]aculty need further support to make collaborative interdisciplinary work a regular part of their professional lives" (Seabury et al. 20; see also Markham 2011, 40/41).

In the end, we are left with the fundamental question as to whether our newly devised class managed to recruit students for modern languages. The answer is not a straightforward one given the high number of seniors – five out of our ten students had one semester left to graduate – that were part of the class. From the five remaining students, one freshman decided to major in French and Francophone Studies, while another student, who majored in dramaturgy, expressed an interest in German but did not have room in her schedule to commit to a language class. As a result, there is definitely potential to attract students through the use of technology, project-based/inquiry-based and interdisciplinary teaching, but universities and their teaching centers might have to provide more in-depth resources for faculty members to make those classes successful.

Bibliography

Barchas, Janine. *What Jane Saw*. The University of Texas at Austin, www.whatjanesaw.org/. Accessed 22 April 2020.

Barron, Brigid J. S., et al. "Doing with Understanding: Lessons from Research on Problem- and Project-Based Learning." *The Journal of the Learning Sciences*, vol. 7, no. 3/4, 1998, pp. 271–311.

Bell, Stephanie. "Project-Based Learning for the 21st Century: Skills for the Future." *The Clearing House*, vol. 83, no. 2, 2010, pp. 39–43.

Blessinger, Patrick, and John M. Carfora. "Innovative Approaches in Teaching and Learning: An Introduction to Inquiry-Based Learning for the Arts, Humanities, and Social Sciences." *Inquiry-Based Learning for the Arts, Humanities and Social Sciences: A Conceptual and Practical Resource for Educators*, edited by John M. Carfora and Patrick Blessinger, Emerald Publishing Limited, 2014, pp. 3–25.

Blumenfeld, Phyllis C., et al. "Learning with Peers: From Small Group Cooperation to Collaborative Communities." *Educational Researcher*, vol. 25, no. 8. 1996, pp. 37–40.

Caviglia-Harris, Jill L., and James Hatley. "Interdisciplinary Teaching. Analyzing Consensus and Conflict in Environmental Studies." *International Journal of Sustainability in Higher Education*, vol. 5, no. 4, 2004, pp. 395–403.

Carnegie Mellon University's Global Presence. Carnegie Mellon University, www.cmu.edu/global/. Accessed 19 April 2020.

Franc, Catherine, and Annie Morton. "Inquiry-Based Learning for Language Learning: The Case of French Advanced Level at the University of Manchester (UK)." *Inquiry-Based Learning for the Arts, Humanities and Social Sciences: A Conceptual and Practical Resource for Educators*, edited by John M. Carfora and Patrick Blessinger, Emerald Publishing Limited, 2014, pp. 77–103.

Grand Challenge Seminars. Dietrich College of Humanities and Social Sciences, www.cmu.edu/dietrich/students/undergraduate/programs/grand-challenge/. Accessed 29 April 2020.

Johnson, Steven. "Colleges Lose a 'Stunning' 651 Foreign-Language Programs in 3 Years." *The Chronicle of Higher Education*, 22 January 2019, twww.chronicle.com/article/Colleges- Lose-a-Stunning-/245526. Accessed 19 April 2020.

Klein, Julie Thompson, and William G. Doty. ""Editors' Note." Interdisciplinary Studies Today." *New Directions for Teaching and Learning*, vol. 58, 1994, pp. 1–6.

Kraglund-Gauthier, Wendy L. "Using Inquiry-Based Learning to Identify Issues and Develop Pedagogical Awareness of Teaching with Technology: A Self-Study from a Pre-Service Teacher Education Class." *Inquiry-Based Learning for the Arts, Humanities and Social Sciences: A Conceptual and Practical Resource for Educators*, edited by John M. Carfora and Patrick Blessinger, Emerald Publishing Limited, 2014, pp. 197–217.

Krajcik, Joseph S., and Phyllis C. Blumenfeld. "Project-Based Learning." *The Cambridge Handbook of the Learning Sciences*, edited by Keith Sawyer, Cambridge UP, 2005, pp. 317–344.

Lee, Hye-Jung, and Cheolil Lim. "Peer Evaluation in Blended Team Project-Based Learning: What Do Students Find Important?" *Journal of Educational Technology & Society*, vol. 15, no. 4, 2012, pp. 214–224.

Lee, Jean S., et al. "Taking a Leap of Faith: Redefining Teaching and Learning in Higher Education Through Project-Based Learning." *Interdisciplinary Journal of Problem-Based Learning*, vol. 8, no. 2, 2014, pp. 19–34.

Lu, Jingyan, et al. "Problem-Based Learning." *The Cambridge Handbook of the Learning Sciences*, edited by Keith Sawyer, Cambridge UP, 2005, pp. 298–318.

Markham, Thom. "Project Based Learning: A Bridge Just Far Enough." *Teacher Librarian*, vol. 39, no. 2, 2011, pp. 38–42.

Newell, William H. "Designing Interdisciplinary Courses." *New Directions for Teaching and Learning*, vol. 58, 1994, pp. 35–51.

Reiser, Brian J., and Iris Tabak. "Scaffolding." *The Cambridge Handbook of the Learning Sciences*, edited by Keith Sawyer, Cambridge UP, 2005, pp. 44–62.

Seabury, Marcia Bundy, and Karen A. Barrett. "Creating and Maintaining Team-Taught Interdisciplinary General Education." *New Directions for Adult and Continuing Education*, vol. 87, 2000, pp. 15–24.

Student Enrollment. Carnegie Mellon University Institutional Research and Analysis, 17 September 2018, www.cmu.edu/ira/Enrollment/pdf/fall-2018-pdfs/university-facts-2018-student-enrollment-by-citizenship-race-sex.pdf. Accessed 23 April 2020.

Thomas, John W. "*A Review of Research on Project-Based Learning.*" www.bobpearlman.org/BestPractices/PBL_Research.pdf. Accessed 16 April 2020.

Tschoepe, Aylin Yildirim. "Changing Landscapes of Education: Teaching Architecture through Inquiry-Based Approaches." *Inquiry-Based Learning for the Arts, Humanities and Social Sciences: A Conceptual and Practical Resource for Educators*, edited by John M. Carfora and Patrick Blessinger, Emerald Publishing Limited, 2014, pp. 169–195.

Undergraduate International Students. Carnegie Mellon University Undergraduate Admission, admission.enrollment.cmu.edu/pages/undergraduate-international-students. Accessed 23 April 2020.

Vogler, Jane S., et al. "The Hard Work of Soft Skills: Augmenting the Project-Based Learning Experience with Interdisciplinary Teamwork." *Inter Sci*, vol. 46, 2018, pp. 457–488.

Watts, Linda S. "Historical Detectives at Work: A Casebook Approach to Guided-Inquiry for Undergraduate Learning." *Inquiry-Based Learning for the Arts, Humanities and Social Sciences: A Conceptual and Practical Resource for Educators*, edited by John M. Carfora and Patrick Blessinger, Emerald Publishing Limited, 2014, pp. 127–146.

"What is Inquiry?" Galileo Educational Network, 2 December 2015, galileo.org/blog/what-is-inquiry/. Accessed 16 April 2020.

Wurdinger, Scott and Mariam Qureshi. "Enhancing College Students' Life Skills through Project Based Learning." *Innovative Higher Education*, vol. 40, 2015, pp. 279–286.

10 *Freundschaft, Motivationstraining* und *Märchen*

Learning by living life in the GDR

Andrea Meyertholen

For today's foreign language (FL) instructors, the stakes are high to "do it all." With budgets shrinking and enrollments declining (Looney and Lusin 2019), FL programs are under pressure to legitimize their value to students, parents and their own institutions. The tyranny of enrollment metrics which dictate high recruiting and retention rates can provoke anxiety about whether courses are "too challenging" or "entertaining enough." At the same time, the growing focus on measuring, documenting and reporting student progress asks us to develop assessment tools and implement methods of evaluating qualitative learning outcomes with quantitative data to prove academic rigor and improve teaching efficacy (Sandrock 2010). As instructors, we face the inauspicious task of making ourselves and our courses relevant, fun, attractive and useful without compromising pedagogical integrity or diluting linguistic content. The following presents a paradigmatic example of how I approach the challenge of "doing it all." Drawing from a drama-pedagogical framework, I integrate drama-based activities with grammar instruction and writing assignments to foster communication, collaboration and critical thinking about culture in the target language (L2). Student-centered and communicative in spirit, this strategy continues to be effective and is enthusiastically received.

Preliminary reflections and contextual considerations

Like many of our peer institutions, the Department of German Studies at the University of Kansas in Lawrence confronts enrollment, recruitment and assessment concerns by emphasizing non-linguistic aspects of language learning: cultural awareness, politico-economic significance and transferrable skills such as perspective-taking (assuming the viewpoint of someone else's experience), critical thinking or effective communication, all of which are vital for any major or path in life. This strategy addresses the "usefulness" of German in a world where everyone allegedly speaks English, while also responding to degree- and university-level assessment demands which are largely unconcerned with language proficiency. Targeting instead cultural awareness, the learning outcomes for our assessment requirements reflect the

Five-C's (Communication, Cultures, Connections, Comparisons and Communities) promoted by ACTFL's *World-Readiness Standards for Learning Languages* (The National Standards Collaborative Board 2015). Courses must: 1) sensitize students to a non-US culture and its value systems (C1). Since factual knowledge cannot guarantee effective cross-cultural communication or flexible responsiveness to cultural difference, students must also 2) engage in a critical process of self-reflection to analyze how their cultural background (C1) informs and limits their behaviors, assumptions and worldviews. While the concentration on the non-linguistic advantages of FLs makes strategic sense for program-building and assessment purposes (Byrnes 2002; Windham 2017), it also makes for good pedagogical practice.

The position that "[l]anguage is a complex multifunctional phenomenon that links an individual to other individuals, to communities, and to national cultures" (235), as stated in the MLA report in 2007, has, since the 1990s, been fertile ground for scholarship asserting the centrality of interculturalism to FL education (FLE) and developing intercultural competence among FL students (Kramsch, Context and Culture 1993; Byram 1997; Byram and Zarate 1997; Schulz and Tschirner 2008; Witte and Harden 2015; Giorgis 2018). Indeed, the Latin roots for "foreign" – from "door" (*fores*) and "outside" (*foris*) – indicate how FL functions as our metaphorical door to the world that helps us not only define ourselves but *know* ourselves through the study of another language, its speakers and its cultural milieu. As Claire Kramsch summarizes: "We only learn who we are through the mirror of others, and, in turn, we only understand others by understanding ourselves as Others" (The Multilingual Subject 2009, 18). For students to regard their familiar habitus with foreign eyes places them in the perspective of the "Other" to experience it from the inside-out and to regard their culture from the outside-in. Through self-reflexive perspective-taking, FL students activate their capacity to think critically and empathically, ideally, according to Kramsch, "discovering that each of these cultures is much less monolithic than was originally perceived" (Context and Culture 234) and breaking down reductivist black-white categories that encumber intercultural understanding.

Promoting intercultural competence and prioritizing culture in FLE has elicited disagreement about how to address it in the classroom and whether instruction in the first language (L1) or target language (L2) is most effective. Several studies, unsurprisingly and understandably, indicate a preference for L1 among instructors and students that, theoretically, allows for more nuanced discussions and sensitivity to complexities (Tang 2002; Brooks-Lewis 2009; Edstrom 2009). Although addressing cultural issues in L1 can be a useful shortcut, it does not necessarily result in enhanced cultural understanding or avoidance of stereotypes (Fichtner 2015). Besides losing valuable L2-contact hours, separating "culture" from language instruction undermines the essential interlinkage of the two and risks conveying the impression to students that devoting time to one comes at the expense of the other (Chavez 2002, 136). My intention in the classroom is to capitalize on cultural awareness and preserve what makes the German classroom unique: the German language. To that end, I have found an effective strategy in drama pedagogy.

Advantages of drama pedagogy in FLE

Drama pedagogy adopts philosophies and practices from the theater and redeploys them in the classroom to facilitate students' communicative, imaginative and oftentimes physical participation in the learning process. Though not restricted to FLE, it has received increasing intention in the past decades by L2 instructors looking to contextualize grammar instruction, enhance student participation and deepen students' interaction with literature and culture (Haggstrom 1992; Even, Drama Grammatik 2003; Schewe and Shaw 1993; Schewe 2016, "Drama und Theater 2007;" Even and Schewe 2016). The expanding corpus of scholarship exploring drama and FLE is complemented by the continued presence of the academic journal *Scenario* and numerous workshops, conferences and online resources (Belliveau and Kim 2013). Despite a heightened methodological profile, drama pedagogy in practice remains underutilized (Matthias 2007; Even, "Moving in(To) Imaginary Worlds" 2008; Dinapoli 2009).

I, too, was initially skeptical and limited my repertoire to the decontextualized dialogues and role-plays offered by introductory L2 textbooks that are frequently used among most FL instructors. Seeing its techniques brought to life in workshops and teaching demonstrations, coupled with successful experimentation in my own classes, soon emboldened me to move beyond the standard scripted scenarios and one-dimensional stock characters and explore the possibilities of the "process-oriented educational drama" that, according to Kao and O'Neill (1998), "aim[s] to go beyond short-term teacher dominated exercises. Instead the drama is extended over time and it is built up from ideas, negotiations, and responses of all the participants in order to foster social, intellectual, and linguistic development" (x). Similar to theater plays, students and teachers put themselves into the context of a longer and larger story in which complex characters have likes, dislikes, emotional baggage and motivations driving their actions. Rather than merely going through the motions of the scripted context, students adopt the personae of the characters in order to create deeper context and character development through their own imaginative additions or spontaneous reactions to the unanticipated additions of others. Even describes how "learners are beholden to the worlds they have co-constructed; they are committed to the characteristics of the personae and places they have collaboratively invented, and they have to take the consequences for their own actions within these worlds" ("Moving in(To) Imaginary Worlds" 162). Fictional people and places are fleshed out through activities where students must act and react from the perspective of another persona, using pre-existing knowledge to improvise with spontaneous speech. Learning becomes performative, literally and figuratively.

Over the years, I have devised various iterations of (interviews, podium discussions, altered scene re-enactments, talk shows, etc.) to place students in contextually situated action and interaction where they usually assume perspectives of other personae. I design and deploy activities judiciously and consider how to reveal the relevance to students' lives. Depending on topic and proficiency level, I identify my learning objectives in advance and ensure both their integration into the activity and articulation to the class. Some activities need only impromptu planning, while others necessitate more preparation, because they unfold over days or weeks. Lower-level courses may focus on vocabulary, phrases, pronunciation and/or ease of speech, which are also admirable goals for more advanced classes. In the latter, I aim for novel, level-appropriate ways to unpack literary texts, probe various viewpoints surrounding current events or hone higher-level conversational skills. Prime linguistic advantages lie with the use of L2 in contextually situated social interactions which often unfold through spontaneous utterances and in-the-moment decisions, as they would "in real life" outside the classroom. Thinking quickly, creative problem-solving, collaboration, empathic communication and the capacity for non-dualistic thought are only a few of the secondary skills which I have witnessed improve as students gain confidence as individuals and L2 speakers. While I am continually impressed by my students' inventiveness and intelligence, the most unexpected and professionally satisfying aspect of drama pedagogy for me is observing the increased vocal presence of shyer students, who tend to thrive under the aegis of being someone else (Even, "Moving in(To) Imaginary Worlds"). I generally observe an increased willingness to take risks in a supportive environment that is fostered through cooperative activities, often with humorous outcomes (Koerner 2012; Marini-Maio and Ryan 2011). Adaptable to all levels and classroom types, drama pedagogy rarely requires technological support, only the imaginative power of students and teacher.

Yet, I do not restrict drama pedagogical techniques to imaginary or literary world-building but have found them equally well-suited for courses that explore historical realities. Designed to foster critical thinking and further cultural knowledge, these courses are subject to university-level assessment for intercultural competency. Student work undergoes yearly review to evaluate the extent to which it demonstrates the acquisition of C2 knowledge and the ability to self-reflect on C1. Since drama pedagogy by design transports students into the perspectives of other people, it engages them in precisely the type of perspective-taking that is vital for intercultural competency. Drama pedagogy also presents me with the opportunity to cultivate culture while still using the target language.

In the remainder of this article I intend to describe a module from an intermediate-level course where drama pedagogy was put into practice through classroom activities, grammar instruction and writing projects that transported students into the cultural and historical "Other" of former East Germany.

Course description: high intermediate German II

High Intermediate German II is the second course of a fifth- and sixth-semester sequence offered every fall and spring, respectively. Required of all majors and minors, it functions as a "bridge" transitioning students from lower-level language-intensive courses into advanced-level topic courses. Coursework focuses on developing oral and written German skills through more extensive treatment of key issues that are important for understanding sociocultural debates and institutional structures affecting German-speaking countries today. To maximize discussion time of its various literary, visual and cinematic texts, the sequence assumes that students complete grammar-related content independently outside of class. As this expectation does not usually align with students' practical needs or desires, I provide basic in-class reviews of grammar and integrate its practical application into the current topic of discussion, generally as warm-up activities. Classes meet three times a week for 50 minutes and range from 12 to 18 students of A2–B2 proficiency, they require regular attendance and active participation in German. Major components of the final grade include: three tests, two 300-word formal essays (each with a second, corrected draft), informal journaling, an oral presentation and grammar homework. A 500-word essay as final exam demonstrates level L2 proficiency and intercultural competency.

The course consists of three modules lasting 5–6 weeks each: 1) Reunified Berlin ; 2) Forms of *Vergangenheitsbewältigung* and 3) The "Other" Germany, or the German Democratic Republic (GDR). The final module generally spans the final six weeks of the semester when students complete the second essay and third test, begin their final essay and review passive, subjunctive I and adjective endings.

Module 3: the socialist lives of "others"

Due to the fact that students grow younger with each year that I teach, I do not assume a lot of prior knowledge about the GDR (1949–1989). Aside from knowing *that* it existed, students typically enter with a remarkably consistent basic inventory of associations: GDR = East Germany = the "bad" Germany = communism = USSR = dictatorship = Berlin Wall = oppression = spying/ *Stasi*. As this equation shows, perceptions are overwhelmingly negative and slightly erroneous, tending toward oversimplified, binary categories with the implicit understanding that West Germany equals capitalism and winners. I find that most students have not seen *Goodbye Lenin!* (2003); thus, any vague notions of *Ostalgie* are usually *Trabis* and *Ampelmännchen* encountered on prior trips to Berlin. At the end of the module and during its course, students frequently express surprise that life in the GDR "wasn't all bad:" that its former citizens could have nostalgia for its redeeming values, that it had redeeming values at all and moreover, that their 21st-century selves actually share many of these values (typically the theoretical ideals of equality, equal access and equal opportunity characteristically espoused by socialist ideologies). Of course, students still have much to criticize, as they should considering the pervasiveness of state-orchestrated surveillance, oppressive measures and the double standard that women, despite having a more progressive presence in society, were still systemically beholden to traditional gender roles. Reflecting on everyday life in the GDR, students in the most recent iteration "couldn't imagine" living in a society without certain freedoms, a basic level of trust or more control over educational and vocational paths.

Yet that they "couldn't imagine" life in the GDR indicates that they *were* imagining themselves there and inhabiting perspectives other than their own. In naming both negative and positive qualities, and even identifying overlap with their own worldviews, students were demonstrating their growing awareness of nuance, tolerance of cognitive dissonance and the willingness to reflect on their own worldviews. Students could talk about the GDR not as a monolithically bad beacon of communism, but as a society with advantages and disadvantages whose specter continues to haunt the politics and policies of contemporary German culture. I aim to facilitate their progression from black-white thinking to shades of grey in level-appropriate German, while being aware of the fact that I must quantitatively assess their growth at the end of the semester.

To convey the realities of life in a socialist state to a generation raised on technology and capitalism, I apply drama pedagogical techniques to transport my students into an East German classroom where they are expected to behave appropriately in the immersive environment as we learn about the country's politics and culture. We continue to explore different products and perspectives through film, first venturing to the dark side with *Das Leben der Anderen* (2006) before ending the semester with the relentlessly optimistic DEFA-*Märchenfilm Drei Haselnüsse für Aschenbrödel* (1973). Outlined below is the most recent iteration along with sample activities and assignments.

Teaching East Germany with drama-based techniques

Weekly Outline and Explanation

Week 1: Setting the Stage

Students assimilate basic factual knowledge about the GDR and the Federal Republic of Germany (FRG) through photographs and explanatory texts.[1] Students are responsible for learning a selection of key dates (1945; 1949; 1953; 1961; 1989; 1990), historical figures and vocabulary pertinent to formative events (*Luftbrücke; Wirtschaftswunde; Mauerfall*). Passive voice is reviewed through sentences that encompass historical events, dates and unit vocabulary.

Week 2: Back in the GDR

I assume the persona of an ideal party member and my students become members-in-training. After undergoing a boot-camp-style *Motivationstraining* (see below), we learn about central features of the FRG (*der kapitalistische Klassenfeind*) and GDR (*unser sozialistisches Vaterland*). Students receive a list of concepts and work together to assign them to the appropriate country: *privater Besitz/VEB, soziale Marktwirtschaft/Planwirtschaft, viele Parteien/SED*, etc. An overview of the Ministry for State Security (*Stasi*) closes the week.

Week 3: Das Leben der Anderen *(DLdA, 2006)*

Told from the perspective of an initially committed *Stasi* agent, the film wallows in the "dark side" of the GDR: surveillance, oppression, mistrust and abuse of power. Its cinematic tropes are accessible and engaging to students, while its characters – none of whom are purely "good" or "bad" – offer many opportunities for drama pedagogy (see below). Out-of-class screening (English subtitles) maximizes in-class discussion time. If not already on a popular streaming platform, many institutions digitize movies for uploading onto course sites to facilitate repeat viewing. Subjunctive I is reviewed.

Week 4: Pop culture in the GDR and the Brothers Grimm's "Cinderella" ("Aschenputtel").

To balance the "dark side" of *DLdA*, students learn about the GDR's "bunte Seite" through cult objects of *Ostalgie*: music, products, fashion and fairy tale films (*Märchenfilme*) produced by the state-controlled film studio (DEFA). Students learn about the post-war status of the Grimm fairy tales, including their brief banning. After reviewing conventional fairy-tale tropes and vocabulary, students read the 1812 Grimm version of "Cinderella" ("*Aschenputtel*"). Adjectival endings are reviewed.

Week 5: DEFA and Drei Haselnüsse für Aschenbrödel *(3HfA, 1973)*

Students read an English-language article about DEFA-*Märchenfilme*,[2] before watching the East German adaptation of Cinderella in 20–30 minute-increments (German subtitles). The film lends itself to interpretations involving gender and class: the plucky, pants-wearing heroine subverts traditional gender roles, the monarchy provides comic relief and the stepfamily exudes bourgeois excess. Through journal entries (see below) and comparative analysis, students discover how fairy tales are contingent upon their contextual milieu and function as socializing agents.

Week 6: Scaffolding for final essay

Students receive the assignment for their final essay, to be completed independently after classes end. The remaining lesson time is devoted to scaffolding activities (see below) to help students choose topics, develop thesis statements and organize arguments. Instructor and peer feedback are provided.

Sample activities, assignments and assessment

Motivationstraining

Day One. Class begins with a YouTube video containing music and images of the period. Currently, I prefer to play the national anthem "Auferstanden aus Ruinen" (subtitled in English) over a montage of historical footage. I have previously used patriotic party songs or the like from the *Junge Pioniere*. In those cases, I chose music subtitled in German with simple, repetitive choruses and encouraged students to sing along (which they have always done so far). Regardless of the song, at the end of the music I open a custom-designed PowerPoint filled with images and language of the GDR strategically choreographed to accompany the "lecture" that follows. I immediately assume the persona of a stereotypically overzealous believer in the GDR and its socialist ideology, greeting the class with "*Freundschaft!*" the accompanying gesture and the encouragement that they respond in kind.

Always in character, I inform them of the time (1970s), place (GDR classroom) and occasion: I have begun to question their commitment to our socialist mission and therefore *Motivationstraining* is necessary to ensure their future as upstanding GDR-*Genossen*. Text and images on the PowerPoint slides reinforce verbal input. Using socialist lingo and words widespread in GDR-culture, I explain to my students tongue-in-cheek how their socialist fatherland provides them with protection (*antifaschistischer Schutzwall*), guaranteed housing (*Plattenbauwohnung im modernen Stil*), cars (wait for a *Trabi*), typical GDR-products (long lines at the local *Kaufhalle*), guaranteed work (*Helden der Arbeit*), etc. They also receive guaranteed education ... albeit party members (*SED*), participants of youth organizations (*FDJ*) and non-churchgoers are preferred. And above all – no *Westfernsehen*!

Though playing with stereotypes, this irreverence and my total commitment to the role have so far unfailingly engaged students, who after some initial confusion catch on quickly and readily play – or sing – along. Aside from their enthusiastic participation, I regularly receive unsolicited positive feedback directly after this lesson. The ironic delivery alerts students to the parodic nature of the lesson, as well as the banalities and absurdities of everyday life in a socialist country. The weeks that follow tease out these introductory impressions as we examine them in greater depth and from multiple angles. In the ensuing lesson, for example (mentioned above), students compare the essential features of capitalist and socialist systems in order to weigh the advantages and disadvantages of each. Critiquing the limitations of capitalist systems from their "Other" point of view, students identify potential difficulties for those transitioning from a socialist state to a capitalist economy. These difficulties, as students discover, coincide with many challenges and cultural conflicts contemporary Germany continues to confront.

Informal Journaling

To complement formal writing assignments, students keep a journal for informal writing in which they respond to questions related to the course content with at least seven sentences. Entries are assigned as homework and are graded according to effort and quality of thought, not grammatical correctness. Journaling has proven enormously successful as a tool synchronized with other class activities and major assignments to help students: 1) articulate ideas for discussions of the following day; 2) accomplish preparatory steps for formal assignments and 3) practice vocabulary, grammar or stylistics. Besides having freedom to experiment with writing structures without worrying about grades, students exhibit greater confidence and eagerness to share their ideas and respond to classmates in spoken German.

- **DLdA:** Before the initial viewing of the film, students are assigned one of the four main characters whose persona they assume (in a class of 16 four students are assigned to each character). In four separate journal entries, students consider the situation of "their" person regarding: 1) character development and turning points; 2) personality, motivation, behavior and 3) whether their informal/official complicity with the *Stasi* can be understood or excused. Lastly, students 4) formulate two questions to pose to each of the other three main characters if given the chance (six questions in total). These four entries encompass four class periods and are combined with both a class podium discussion (see below) and their second essay.[3]
- **3HfA:** Students write three entries that are in sync with the English-language article, film viewing and class discussion. Entries must contain three-four adjective endings or stylistic phrases (*Meiner Meinung nach, Einerseits/Andererseits*, etc.). In recent prompts, students: 1) considered what social norms their favorite childhood movies conveyed (gender roles, marriage, good/bad behavior); 2) reflected on the role of the monarchy in *3HfA* and 3) predicted a "Happily Socialist Ever After" ending for the film.

Podium Discussion DLd4

The effective and entertaining "podium discussion" format is ideal for approaching controversial and complex topics from various perspectives while using L2. I use this format to stimulate student discussions regarding why citizens would act in implicit or explicit compliance with a totalitarian regime. Students can better engage with this abstract and difficult question as they identify and sympathize with the film's main characters and also gain a clearer understanding of daily life in the GDR. I frame the discussion as a debate among the four main characters to simplify the topic enough for intermediate L2 learners. Now all students have the opportunity to question each other about, or demand accountability for, motivations, behavior and actions.

Students break into four groups according to their assigned character (each group collectively represents one person). Using their fourth journal entry, students pose preformulated questions and devise extemporaneous replies as their characters. Although students collaboratively embody one character, they answer individually but have the support of fellow group members whose own dramatic improvisations may supplement or redirect the conversation. Students are encouraged to ask follow-up questions and propose hypothetical alternatives as they act and react to spontaneously unfolding events. After 20–30 minutes of student debate, I reserve at least ten minutes for an out-of-character wrap-up discussion where we reflect upon the lives of "Others," and talk about our personal reactions to the characters' actions now that we have walked in their shoes for a while. I encourage students to look for shades of gray and justify their opinions by taking more than one perspective into account. To supplement or replace the podium discussion, several drama-pedagogical exercises detailed by Even ("Moving in(To) Imaginary Worlds") are beneficial for collaboratively constructing character perspectives such as "hot-seating" (168) or critically examining specific scenes through embodied play-acting as in "still images" (167). In the former, one student (or a partnership) assumes the persona of a main character and answers questions from the class based upon their knowledge from the movie. In the latter, students recreate a still shot from the movie which can then be manipulated in various ways: the class might call out instructions to alter the scene or the actors might change their constellation and prompt the class to consider a new outcome of events.

Integrated Grammar Instruction

Below are a few ideas for thematically related in-class activities to anchor grammar structures to real communicative tasks. For outside practice, I compose or adapt handouts which integrate grammar structures with themes or characters:

- **Passive (Review of historical content, week 1).** Students work in pairs or groups to describe photographs of historical events (the Berlin airlift, the *Montagdemos*, 9 November, 1989) with the help of unit vocabulary and information about the two German states. All sentences must be in the

passive voice. While photographs can be displayed on PowerPoint slides or disseminated as handouts, I often tape them to classroom walls to simulate the interactive experience of walking around in a museum. Students incorporate dates in their passive sentences and arrange them chronologically.
- **Subjective I/Indirect Speech (*DLdA*, week 3).** As modeled in scenes from the movie, students assume their roles of party members-in-training to "inform" on the suspicious statements of peers, neighbors or film characters. They report instances of overheard direct speech by translating it into the subjective I ("indirect speech"). Instructors can pre-formulate instances of direct speech themselves or enlist students to do so.
- **Adjective Endings (*3HfA*, week 5).** My personal favorite is *Aschenbrödel*-Mad Libs. Students break into groups and have 3 minutes to write a list of fifteen adjectives of their own choosing that they number from 1 through 15. Subsequently, students receive a cheesy love letter written by the "Prince" (i.e., me) to his beloved *Aschenbrödel*—albeit with missing adjectives. Students insert each of their adjectives into the numbered blanks (in order!) along with appropriate adjective endings. During dramatic readings of each letter, we control for grammatical correctness by checking adjective endings as a class.

Final essay and concluding reflections

The extent to which my pedagogical objectives are achieved is assessed through a formal essay of 500 words that functions as a final exam for the course. As such, mastery of cultural knowledge, linguistic proficiency and the capacity for critical thought factor into the final grade for which I use a four-category rubric adapted from the Goethe-Institut's standards for B2-writing proficiency. Categories 1 and 2 encompass cultural knowledge and critical thinking skills, while 3 and 4 address proficiency: 1) content (development of ideas, fulfillment of task); 2) organization and cohesion; 3) range (vocabulary, grammar) and 4) accuracy (syntax, orthography, morphology, punctuation). Student work undergoes an additional round of evaluation based on a separate rubric that measures intercultural competency for university-level assessment. This rubric consists of three categories: 1) self-awareness of C2 vis-à-vis C1; 2) analysis of C2 and 3) application of cultural knowledge. This second assessment is independent of the assignment grade and has no impact.

These final two assessments not only define my objectives for the semester, they also provide feedback about the achievements of my students: Have they learned new cultural content? Can they apply it to novel situations? How well have they mastered new grammatical structures? From this evidence and personal experience, I critically examine the course and my teaching. I look for opportunities to enhance the overall quality of education and creatively address unexpected challenges. With respect to this module, drama-pedagogical techniques consistently prove effective for developing critical thinking, cultural sensitivity and self-reflection. However, the fruits of this labor are most evident in classroom discussions and activities. As I discovered, students do not necessarily or intuitively transpose these skills into well-organized essays that formally demonstrate the competencies they have already informally displayed in the classroom. The final essay is particularly problematic. It is due a week after classes end, students are largely left to their own devices during a stressful period and tend to "forget" the strides taken during the semester. Although student work consistently meets expectations for all assessment categories, each iteration has revealed points of weakness which I target through further scaffolding techniques. The most recent iteration produced the most sophisticated critical thinking skills I have yet encountered in any of my classes: a collective leap in quality that I attribute to improvements made in response to lessons learned over the course of several iterations.

Lesson #1

Perfect the prompt. To ensure that students had the opportunity to demonstrate the required skills, I formulated assignment instructions that specifically invoked the competencies and cultural knowledge at stake in both rubrics (see above). Specificity was key; the more explicitly the assignment sheet laid out what students needed to provide, the more consistently they delivered those results to me. They also had better guidance about how to proceed independently. For the final essay, students now compare the Brothers Grimm's "Aschenputtel" with DEFA's *Aschenbrödel* and explain how the latter's treatment of love, class or gender reflects the historical realities of its (socialist) cultural context. The current prompt provides a detailed outline that structures the essay into paragraphs, including a conclusion in which students must devise a new adaptation of the Cinderella story which reflects our modern-day culture and its social structures. This allows students to demonstrate their newly gained knowledge about one culture and apply it to the novel context of another.

Lesson #2

Tailor assignments and activities to the task at hand. To help students develop opinions and model critical thinking skills, all journal entries and in-class activities revolved around love, class and gender—the aspects specified in the prompt. I distributed a list of 40–60 adjectives and divided the class into four groups: *Aschenputtel, Aschenbrödel, Prinz* (movie) and *Stiefmutter* (movie). Each group created a list on the whiteboard by writing down all adjectives descriptive of their assigned character. Analyzing these four lists of characters and their descriptive adjectives, we compared, contrasted and drew conclusions about "desirable" and "undesirable" characteristics of women, men and social classes. Equally successful was the "Panel-of-Experts" approach. Here, each group acted as an authority of an assigned topic (love, class or gender) and led a class discussion on their given topic by presenting a hypothesis about what moral or message the film promoted. Finally, I staged a family reunion in a talk-show format where students were assigned roles from the two families depicted in the film (*Prinz, Stiefmutter, Aschenbrödel*, etc.) to hash out unaired grievances. Those not "on stage" attended as audience members armed with provocative questions to pose to the students "on stage" in character. I moderated as host. This flexible format can be staged to last fifteen to twenty minutes and restaged to allow students to switch roles. I allowed students a day to prepare by assigning them the task of formulating three to four questions as a homework assignment.

Lesson #3

Flip the classroom when possible. Students viewed *DLdA* on their own to maximize in-class discussion time and were required to bring their journal responses in which they assumed the position of an assigned character to class. With the extra time for *DLdA*, students met with their character groups to exchange observations and ideas, while I circulated to monitor the use of L2. With respect to *3HfA*, I combined informal journaling with in-class viewing. Each day students wrote a journal entry based on a prompt which prepared them for watching 20–30 minutes of the film in class. For example, before watching many scenes involving the prince's family, students considered how a movie meant to instill socialist values and level class differences would handle issues of monarchy and upward mobility, issues which are integral to the Cinderella tale. These journal prompts alerted students to subtler aspects embedded in the film and helped move them beyond passive consumption to active and critical viewing. I took care to scaffold aspects of the final essay into the journal prompts so that students would have already completed much of the critical thinking legwork required for its completion.

Lesson #4

Scaffold, scaffold, scaffold. For all formal writing assignments, I scaffolded the preparatory stages of essay development into the class periods preceding the due date as homework assignments. First, we read the prompt together and addressed questions. Then students had a week to choose a topic and complete the following assignments: 1) gather pertinent vocabulary and stylistic phrases; 2) write a thesis statement and 3) organize 3–4 textual examples in an outline. In the final two class meetings, students worked in groups to compare results and solicit feedback before volunteering to share as a group.

As the course continues to evolve, each iteration yields stronger results and affords new occasions to explore creative approaches to tackling challenging topics and cultivating the critical competencies involved in FLE. This module is a perennial favorite, not only because students discover the low-budget marvels of East German cinematic special effects or the rhinestone-studded wonders of David Hasselhoff singing on the Berlin Wall. The drama-pedagogical strategies described above bring a past era and bygone country back to life and allow students to explore its perspectives and problems from the inside-out without sacrificing L2-acquisition. Students learn how to recognize the limitations of their own cultural viewpoint to gain insight into the "Other's" perspective. Drama pedagogy offers unique opportunities to create motivational and positive educational experiences where students return from their German-language journeys with skills and knowledge that will serve them well whatever their future may bring.

Notes

1 The textbook *Anders gedacht* (Motyl-Mudretzkyj/ Späinghaus, 2014) contains a level-appropriate overview.
2 For historical overviews with provocative handling of gender, I recommend Benita Blessing's article "Happily socialist ever after?" (2010) or an excerpt from Qinna Shen's *The Politics of Magic* (2015).
3 Students basically synthesize their responses to the first three entries as informed by class discussion to produce their second essay.

Bibliography

Belliveau, George, and Won Kim. "Drama in L2 Learning: A Research Synthesis." *Scenario*, vol. 7, no. 2, 2013, pp. 7–27.
Blessing, Benita. "Happily Socialist Ever After? East German Children's Films and the Education of a Fairy Tale Land." *Oxford Review of Education*, vol. 36, no. 2, 2010, pp. 233–248.
Brooks-Lewis, Kimberly Anne. "Adult Learners' Perceptions of the Incorporation of Their L1 in Foreign Language Teaching and Learning." *Applied Linguistics*, vol. 30, no. 2, 2009, pp. 216–235.
Byram, Michael. *Teaching and Assessing Intercultural Communicative Competence.* Multilingual Matters, 1997.
Byram, Michael, and Geneviève Zarate, editors. *The Social and Intercultural Dimension of Language Learning and Teaching.* Council of Europe, 1997.
Byrnes, Heidi. "The Cultural Turn in Foreign Language Departments: Challenge and Opportunity." *Profession*, vol. 1, 2002, pp. 114–129.
Chavez, Monika. "We Say 'Culture' and Students Ask 'What?': University Students' Definitions of Foreign Language Culture." *Die Unterrichtspraxis*, vol. 35, no. 2, 2002, pp.129–140.
Das Leben der Anderen. Directed by Florian Henckel von Donnersmarck. Sony Pictures Classics, 2006.
"Deutsch-deutsche Geschichte (Überblick)." *Anders gedacht*, edited by Irene Motyl-Mudretzkyj and Michaela Späinghaus, 3rd ed., Cengage, 2014, pp. 309–311.
Dinapoli, Russell. "Using Dramatic Role-Play to Develop Emotional Aptitude." *International Journal of English Studies*, vol. 9, no. 2, 2009, pp. 97–110.
Drei Haselnüsse für Aschenbrödel / Tři oříšky pro Popelku. Directed by Václav Vorlíček. Deutsche Film AG (East Germany) and Barrandov Studios (Czechoslovakia), 1973.

Edstrom, Anne M. "Teacher Reflection as a Strategy for Evaluating L1/L2 Use in the Classroom." *Babylonia*, vol. 17, no. 1, 2009, pp. 12–15.

Even, Susanne. *Drama Grammatik. Dramapädagogische Ansätze für den Grammatikunterricht Deutsch als Fremdsprache*. Iudicium, 2003.

Even, Susanne. "Moving in (To) Imaginary Worlds: Drama Pedagogy for Foreign Language Teaching and Learning." *Die Unterrichtspraxis*, vol. 41, no. 2, 2008, pp.161–170.

Even, Susanne, and Manfred Schewe, editors. *Performatives Lehren, Lernen, Forschen / Performative Teaching, Learning, Research*. Schibri-Verlag, 2016.

Fichtner, Friederike. "Learning Culture in the Target Language: The Students' Perspectives." *Die Unterrichtspraxis*, vol. 48, no. 2, 2015, pp. 229–243.

Giorgis, Paola. *Meeting Foreignness: Foreign Languages and Foreign Language Education as Critical and Intercultural Experiences*. Rowman & Littlefield, 2018.

Good Bye, Lenin!. Directed by Wolfgang Becker. X Verleih AG, 2003.

Haggstrom, Margaret. "A Performative Approach to the Study of Theater: Bridging the Gap between Language and Literature Courses." *The French Review*, vol. 66, no. 1, 1992, pp. 7–19.

Kao, Shin-Mei, and Cecily O'Neill. *Words into Worlds. Learning a Second Language through Process Drama*. Ablex, 1998.

Koerner, Morgan. "German Literature and Culture under Revue: Learner Autonomy and Creativity through Theme-based Theater Practicum." *Die Unterrichtspraxis*, vol. 45, no. 1, 2012, pp. 28–39.

Kramsch Claire. *Context and Culture in Language Teaching*. Oxford UP, 1993.

Kramsch Claire. *The Multilingual Subject*. Oxford UP, 2009.

Looney, Dennis, and Natalia Lusin. *Enrollments in Languages Other Than English in United States Institutions of Higher Education, Summer 2016 and Fall 2016: Final Report*. MLA, 2019, www.mla.org/content/download/110154/2406932/2016-Enrollments-Final-Report.pdf. Accessed 4 April 2020.

Marini-Maio, Nicoletta, and Coleen Ryan, editors. *Dramatic Interactions. Teaching the Foreign Language, Literature, and Culture through Theater*. Cambridge Scholars Publishing, 2011.

Matthias, Bettina. "Show, Don't Tell: Improvisational Theatre and the Beginning Foreign Language Curriculum." *Scenario*, vol. 1, no. 1, 2007, pp. 56–69.

MLA Ad Hoc Committee on Foreign Languages. "Foreign Languages and Higher Education: New Structures for a Changed World." *Profession*, 2007, pp. 234–245.

The National Standards Collaborative Board. *World-Readiness Standards for Learning Languages*. 4th ed., American Council on the Teaching of Foreign Languages, 2014.

Sandrock, Paul. *The Keys to Assessing Language Performance: A Teacher's Manual for Measuring Student Progress*. American Council on the Teaching of Foreign Languages, 2010.

Schewe, Manfred. "Drama und Theater in der Fremd- und Zweitsprachenlehre: Blick zurück nach vorn." *Scenario*, vol. 1, no. 1, 2007, pp. 1–13.

Schewe, Manfred. "Taking Stock and Looking Ahead: Drama Pedagogy as a Gateway to a Performative Teaching and Learning Culture." *Scenario*, vol. 7, no. 1, 2013, pp. 5–23.

Schewe, Manfred, and Peter Shaw. *Towards Drama as a Method in the Foreign Language Classroom*. Peter Lang, 1993.

Schulz, Renate A., and Erwin P. Tschirner, editors. *Communicating Across Borders: Developing Intercultural Competence in German as a Foreign Language.* Iudicium, 2008.
Shen, Qinna. *The Politics of Magic: DEFA Fairy-Tale Films.* Wayne State UP, 2015.
Tang, Jinlan. "Using L1 in the English Classroom." *English Teaching Forum*, vol. 40, no. 1, 2002, pp. 36–42.
Windham, Scott. "Culture First: Boosting Program Strength Through Cultural Instruction." *Die Unterrichtspraxis*, vol. 50, no. 1, 2017, pp. 79–90.
Witte, Arnd, and Theo Harden, editors. *Foreign Language Learning as Intercultural Experience. The Subjective Dimension.* Peter Lang, 2015.

11 Branching out with STEM in the German classroom

Melissa Etzler and Michelle Stigter-Hayden

The rising interest in STEM in the German curriculum

The fact that undergraduate German Language and Studies programs are currently in a precarious position is undeniable. A recent report from the Modern Language Association reveals that the numbers of students enrolled in German courses decreased 16.3% between 2009 and 2016, and German is not alone in this decline. In the same period, French enrollment decreased by 19.3% and Spanish 18.1% (Flaherty 2018; Looney and Lusin 2019). Low enrollment in languages increasingly demonstrates students' tendencies to shift away from interdisciplinarity, despite the frequent encouragement by universities, and to focus solely on their primary field of study at the expense of gaining a well-rounded, diverse education that would prepare students for those "soft skills" so desired in the workplace (Leckrone 2020). As Anke Finger and Niko Tracksdorf (2019) claim, the dwindling number of students enrolled in languages "directly affects the 'client base' of students who may never have needed the humanities more for both their civic engagement and career building, especially in combination with subjects that have traditionally been separated from language and culture programs" (203). In reaction to this downward turn and to reach those students "separated from language programs," German programs need to experiment with innovative means of aligning courses with student interest, while simultaneously working on retention and expansion. One means of appealing to a larger number of students is offering courses in German that demonstrate an alliance with their primary or secondary majors in the STEM (science, technology, engineering and math) fields. According to the most recent data offered by Emsi, a labor market analytics firm, on the career tracks of graduates of four-year colleges across six academic programs (languages and philosophy, the social sciences, business, communications, engineering and IT), 54% went into business roles, 25% went into STEM jobs and 21% went into soft skill jobs. Given these statistics, the question arises: to what extent should the rising number of students in STEM fields affect German Studies programs?

Throughout the United States, German Studies has become increasingly interdisciplinary as it has coordinated its course offerings and specialization tracks in accordance with the primary majors of its students, e.g., there are currently many German and engineering dual degree programs[1] or business German concentrations. Today, most universities offer Business German within their standard rotation as either a skills/bridge course or a more advanced upper-division class. Despite the fact that 25% of majors will specialize in one of the STEM fields, rarely do universities have a concentration in STEM-German, the University of Massachusetts being one of the few that offers this option.[2] Even if it is not viable to create a specific concentration, the large number of students in STEM suggests that at least one upper-division course in STEM in addition to occasional integration of STEM topics throughout students' first two years of language study would be valuable for student retention and expansion, and also as a portfolio-building and professionalization strategy.

Particularly within the past few years, the American Association of Teachers of German (AATG) and the Goethe-Institut have encouraged and supported an integration of STEM subjects into the L2 classroom. In 2019, the Goethe-Institut sponsored the Sustainability Summit at Loyola University Chicago and the PASCH German STEM Workshop in Washington. Between 2015 and 2018, the AATG *MINT-Fortbildungskurs* in Leipzig was offered; and the authors of this chapter, Michelle Stigter and Melissa Etzler participated in the program in 2017 and 2018, respectively. The goal of the program was to demonstrate that instructors of German, thus non-experts in the STEM fields, could easily incorporate these subjects within their L2 classrooms by keeping the ubiquitous nature of STEM in mind. The phrase *MINT im Alltag* was employed daily in the course as a reminder that everyone was capable of discussing STEM topics in their German classes since these are global issues with which students in the U.S. and German-speaking countries grapple constantly. A few of the topics discussed in the course which were accompanied by local outings in Leipzig included: weather and climate change, various methods of public transportation, radio broadcasting and transmissions, etc. The benefits of integrating these STEM topics into the German classroom were strongly emphasized since such exposure can better prepare students for their future careers or internships abroad. Due to the emphasis placed on everyday STEM topics in the AATG *MINT-Fortbildungsseminar*, the participants learned that it is valuable to expose students to STEM topics throughout their college careers as this helps them attain a global competence while simultaneously practicing the five "C" goal areas as illustrated in the *World-Readiness Standards for Learning Languages* (2015).

The pedagogical benefits for STEM-integration

Engaging U.S. students in discussions on STEM topics especially encourages a reflection on the goal area "Comparisons" (World-Readiness Standards for Learning Languages). Because learners often "do not recognize and understand the cultural roots of many of the behaviors and beliefs in their own society until they see how these are manifested in another culture," it is important to address such universal topics in order for students to compare and contrast cultural beliefs and values (World-Readiness Standards 89). In addition to honing the ability to cross-compare between cultures, studies in STEM topics enable "intercultural competence," defined by Traci O'Brien (2020) as "the results of any learning that fosters global citizenship" (82). Because in the humanities instructors expect their students to ultimately actively engage in the global community, it is essential that they have the opportunity in the L2 to discuss universal topics. This will help them to become aware of global issues that extend beyond the scope of the type of texts typically utilized in the L2 classroom: literature, film and/or the "culture" sections appearing at the end of many language-learning textbooks.

Another benefit for teachers interested in including STEM-based lesson plans in the German-language classroom is that STEM often requires a task-based approach. While it originated from communicative language teaching (CLT), task-based approaches focus more squarely on the improved efficacy of language learning when hands-on experience is involved. As one of the guiding principles of language learning, "performance-based tasks may elicit a response from students at a higher level of proficiency than proficiency-based tasks due to the nature of rehearsed questions and responses as opposed to unique and personal, organically-produced language" (ACTFL). Later in this chapter, Michelle Stigter will describe a few of the in-class STEM-inspired experiments conducted by her students, all of which derived from the methodology behind the task-based approach. Because the STEM-related materials utilized in the L2 classroom were originally intended for a native German-speaking audience, the instructor is also engaged in an authenticity-centered approach. As Frieda Mishan (2004) explains in her book *Designing Authenticity into Language Learning Materials*: "[t]he central premises of the authenticity-centered approach are the use of authentic texts for language learning and the preserving of this authenticity throughout the procedures in which they are implicated" (ix). The combination of hands-on experimentation and the use of authentic materials is beneficial for students because experimentation is conducive to honing communicative skills (one must spontaneously explain or react to the process at hand) and expanding one's vocabulary. Thus, preparing our students now by introducing STEM in the manner of general cultural education in German adds to the diversity of their curriculum and provides them with a pragmatic skill set – the ability to discuss interdisciplinary topics in English and German and compare and contrast worldviews on scientific, environmental and sociological subjects.

Incorporating STEM in German, an overview of texts

While the level of interest in students for STEM subjects is clear, instructors of German language and culture may be hesitant to incorporate lessons on subjects in which they have not been trained or do not feel well versed. Yet, there are numerous ways to include STEM despite an instructor's potential lack of expertise since students already tend to encounter a plethora of topics in STEM on a daily basis. Regardless of whether or not students major or minor in a STEM field, many will have an inherent interest in learning more about topics relevant in both German-speaking countries and the U.S. and how the opinions regarding such topics vary by country. For instance, many students are curious to learn more about the latest developments in renewable energy, climate change, recycling programs and AI/robotics. Once the topics of focus have been decided, the instructor can determine how technical or scientific the language and thematic components of the unit should be – depending on their own comfort level.

Another reason why many German teachers shy away from incorporating STEM-based lesson plans into their courses is the lack of knowledge regarding suitable teaching materials. Particularly textbooks intended for students from German-speaking countries at the high school (*Gymnasium*) level are of special interest since the language used in those publications is compatible with that of U.S. students in their second or third year of German instructions at the university level. Furthermore, these textbooks typically: a) include a multitude of images so even if there is unfamiliar vocabulary, the context is still comprehensible and b) the material covered overlaps with the topics addressed in foundational courses in the U.S., such as biology, physics, chemistry and math. While these topics are familiar to college-level students in the U.S., students of German are simultaneously introduced to authentic materials that are used by "native speakers in culturally authentic contexts of use" and thereby assist in deepening the students' cultural awareness (Kramsch 2000, 72). Thus, using authentic German textbooks to activate U.S. students' preexisting knowledge on STEM topics empowers students since they can focus on vocabulary acquisition and intercultural comparisons of already familiar material.

Last but not least, to ensure students attain a level of competency in the L2 that will enable them to converse with a group of their peers in a German-speaking country, it is important that the learning materials are contemporary, culturally relevant and thought-provoking. Such materials also grant instructors the opportunity to include "the 3 c's" outlined by Freda Mishan: culture, currency and challenge. Mishan explains: "*Culture*, in that authentic texts incorporate and represent the culture/s of speakers of the target language; *currency*, in that authentic texts offer topics and language in current use as well as those relevant to the learners; *challenge*, in that authentic texts are intrinsically more challenging yet can be used at all proficiency levels" (44). Although U.S. students will be familiar with the topics introduced in German-language textbooks related to STEM, much of the vocabulary will be new and challenging. Thus, students' language acquisition progresses in a way that is, as Stephen Krashen (1981) states, a "little beyond [their] current level of competence" as outlined in his input hypothesis or "i + 1" (103). Introducing students to STEM-related materials also prepares them for real-world discussions on contemporary issues (*currency*) such as climate change or technological advancements. In the following paragraphs, I, Melissa Etzler, will provide an overview of texts that are challenging, yet prepare students for authentic and topical discussions on universal STEM-related issues.

One of the textbooks given to the participants of the AATG *MINT-Fortbildungskurs*, which offers an impressive range of guided activities and is adaptable across multiple levels of German instruction, is Josef Leisen's *Handbuch Sprachförderung im Fach. Sprachsensibler Fachunterricht in der Praxis* (2019). This text includes 40 different units (*Methoden-Werkzeuge*), which can be used in class or as homework assignments, followed by various activities that are student-centered and focus on everything from writing, speaking and reading to hands-on, in-class experimentation modules. Every activity in Leisen's *Handbuch* is explained in a systematic manner, clarifies the pedagogical goals and includes tips for variations of the activities. For instructors who happen to have an entire class of STEM-field students, this text will be ideal. For instructors who would prefer to provide their students with an introduction to STEM topics and vocabulary, however, the text will prove more challenging since some of the concepts will be new to students of the humanities. Since the final reading, writing and speaking activities provided by the book are the most technical, I will focus on the applicability of the first 40 units of the text.

One strength of the first 40 units of the *Handbuch* is the variety of topics together with the vocabulary that is both geared toward general knowledge and more specialized terms. In a German-language classroom of mixed majors, instructors will likely be hesitant to teach a lesson focusing solely on *Das Periodensystem, Der Druckmesser, Cytologie, Zellteilung bei der Pflanzenzelle*, or *Holz und seine Dichte*. Yet, within the first 40 units there are also activities focusing on general knowledge, the vocabulary of which is arguably useful for all students. If one considers the breadth of vocabulary necessary to read articles in *Der Spiegel* that focus on scientific or technological developments for instance, an introduction to this type of vocabulary in the language classroom will be of long-term value for students.

Each unit of the *Handbuch* is typically two pages long, featuring a page of pedagogical tips for instructors followed by an in-class activity, and focused on one STEM-inspired theme. The topics range from mathematics to physics to mechanics and emphasize honing speaking or writing skills at various levels. To offer two brief examples: 1) the unit on *Sprachhilfen für Rechenarten* provides students with the necessary vocabulary to be able to verbalize mathematical problems such as 6 + 2 = 8 (30–31). This unit can easily be integrated into the introductory German classroom at the same time students learn numbers. This advances students' capabilities from simply counting in sequence to practicing numbers in a realistic way involving addition, division, subtraction and multiplication; 2) While the unit on mathematics is conducive to an in-class speaking activity, the unit on *Das Sonnensystem* hones students writing skills (58–59). This section features a series of tables with information such as simple questions ("*Wie viele Monde hat der Jupiter?*") or basic facts ("*Der Saturn hat Ringe*"). Students are responsible for integrating this material into a cohesive narrative in the form of a newspaper article. These types of practical and modifiable exercises can be used at all levels for vocabulary building, speaking or writing practice.

Perhaps the most beneficial activities within the *Handbuch* are the strategies presented in the conclusion of the first 40 units since these can be included in STEM and literature/culture courses alike. These units offer guided instructions for managing a wide variety of in-class exercises. For example, in *Stille Post* students translate information selected by the instructor into various modalities (80–1). If the students are presented with a graph, for example, they must convert this information into a table and then into a written text/narrative. In the activity *Kartentisch*, students are placed into groups, i.e., four students per group, with five groups in total (88–89). Each group is given a series of cards with sentences written on them that have been taken from a key text (for example, *Der Spiegel* on recent trends in environmental protection). Students read the sentences and then place them, linearly, on a table according to the order of relevance. As a follow-up, the groups walk from table to table, examine each other's results and then defend their decisions. In *Expertenkongress*, groups of students (four per group) are given a brief article that they need to be able to verbally summarize within a limited amount of time (94–95). After the allotted time is over, all but one student stands up from their table and they redistribute themselves so that there is one "expert" on each topic at the new tables. They then have a set amount of time to summarize their article for the others at the table. The others take notes and, as a follow-up, several individuals vocally share what they learned with the class. Activities such as these are widely applicable since they require the instructor to provide only the primary material that can then be taught in a multitude of ways. If an instructor prefers not to rely on a textbook, nearly any scientific article from the *Wissenschaft* section of *Der Spiegel* can be introduced via these strategies from the *Handbuch*. One could spend any 50-min class utilizing one of the suggested activities and could use the previous class scaffolding the information (through brief introductory lectures on the topic, mind maps, vocabulary exercises, interviews, etc.) so the students are prepared on the activity day. Due to the wide-ranging strategies and various themes offered in the *Handbuch,* it is highly recommended for any instructor wanting to branch out into STEM topics in class or is simply looking for new student-centered activities.

For a few additional textbook options, I will mention three other STEM-related textbooks originally intended for students in *Gymnasium* that are also appropriate for more advanced students at the university. The book *Erlebnis Naturwissenschaft. Materialien für den projektorientierten Unterricht: Energie* (2006), published by Schroedel (www.westermann.de), offers focused lessons via short readings that are accompanied by graphs, mind maps, tables and charts. The topic, which will be of interest to all students, is focused on the different types of energy available: solar, wind and fossil fuels. The descriptions of the various forms of creating energy are coupled with the ways one can make their home more energy efficient. The level of the readings in *Energie* are quite advanced and only recommended at the upper-division. Additionally, because the book is quite technical, its purpose is to inform rather than inspire immediate discussion or in-class activities. Thus, while *Energie* offers moments that do encourage discussion or in-class experimentation, the learning skills most activated are reading comprehension and vocabulary acquisition. Another text, which is quite similar to *Energie* in its structure and purpose, is *Nano Scout. Spannende Welt der Mikroelektronik*. *Nano Scout* introduces issues such as global warming, environmental protection and how technology can best be implemented to protect our world. The readings in *Nano Scout* are challenging even for students in their fourth year, but the images and graphs that accompany the texts make it manageable if scaffolded instruction is provided. Although the readings are advanced, since *Energie* and *Nano Scout* deal with contemporary global issues and provide technical descriptions in an accessible way, both will generate discussion in the classroom and provide valuable moments for cross-cultural comparisons.

I will conclude this textbook overview by mentioning two book series intended for children that include a STEM focus, are applicable at all levels of instruction and worked well in the STEM course at Butler University. First, the "Benny Blu" series (www.bennyblu.de) has titles such as *Erfindung. Die Welt verändern* (which covers everything from the invention of the wheel to the Internet and includes a wide variety of simple experiments intended to be conducted in class) or *Wetter. Regen, Wolken, Sonnenschein* (sections of this book can be included when students are introduced to vocabulary on the weather and the seasons). Second, the "Bauer Hubert" series (www.bauerhubert.de) features titles such as *Bauer Hubert und das Geheimnis der Stromkuh* (on how manure is converted to electricity) and *Bauer Hubert im Reich der magischen Pflanzen* (covering the role plants play in producing energy through photosynthesis). Such books are entertaining to students and, because the language level is quite accessible, students feel empowered when reading them. Students also become more in-tune with cultural differences by way of such texts. They can be asked to consider which books from their childhood immediately come to mind and then reflect on why these texts had or lacked a STEM focus. Finally, students can discuss what this difference says about the priority of introducing STEM topics at a young age and how/why this varies across cultures (one can, of course, also mention such informative television series as *Die Sendung mit der Maus*). While this is a necessarily abridged overview, each of these texts can serve as a springboard into STEM.

Butler University and the course

Butler University is a private Liberal Arts college in Indianapolis that enrolls roughly 1,200 incoming freshmen per year. The German program comprises one tenure-track faculty member; one lecturer whose responsibilities are divided between teaching in German, the Core curriculum (required courses aimed at educating students in a variety of disciplines) and running the Modern Language Center; and one lecturer whose responsibilities include instructions in German and the First Year Seminar (Core). In a typical semester, the German program offers one course of elementary German, two sections of second-year instruction and two upper division classes. Students whose major is in the College of Liberal Arts and Sciences are required to complete two years of language instruction or two courses at the upper-division if, as freshmen, they happen to place into the third year of a foreign language. Butler University currently has two primary majors, five secondary majors and 26 minors. This is a representative and average number of students in German and we have seen little variation within the past five years. In accordance with the data offered by Emsi, about 25% of our students of German are also in STEM fields. Because we regularly offer a course in Business German to appeal to the roughly 25% of our students in Business, we decided to integrate STEM-themed classes into our program, which led to the development of Michelle Stigter's upper-division course, Land of Science and Innovation.

German 319: land of science and innovation

The significance of motivating students

There are many motivations for teaching a STEM-centered course within the context of a German program. Tapping into students' intrinsic motivation is a key to engaging students and recruiting them to become life-long German speakers, majors and minors. "Numerous studies have confirmed that, relative to extrinsic motivation, intrinsic motivation leads to better conceptual learning, greater creativity, more cognitive flexibility, and enhanced well-being" ("Intrinsic Motivation"). Intrinsic motivation launches students beyond the frequent mundanity of standard language acquisition into areas that are more challenging, both intellectually and creatively. Students in a STEM-focused course also develop language skills appropriate for STEM-related professional purposes. They develop new linguistic registers that make the STEM workplace more accessible for them, and they understand some of the fundamental hallmarks of those workplaces within the German context.

In developing the STEM course, it was crucial to keep in mind that intrinsic motivation needed to be instigated in every student while simultaneously preparing our students majoring in the STEM-fields for the workplace. In order to accommodate interests, students played a significant role in choosing the content of the course. Based on the idea that "for an individual to be intrinsically motivated for an activity, that individual must find the activity interesting" ("Intrinsic Motivation"), the course content was determined in collaboration with the students enrolled in the course. The first day of class was an opportunity for students to share their interests, select from prepared subtopics and suggest additional thematic units. While this meant that there were some last-minute changes to the teaching materials, this allowed students a voice in a class that was designed to attract and retain students from across the university. These changes were also easier to accommodate since we were not bound to a specific textbook. Instead authentic resources in simple German such as *Sendung mit der Maus* [3] as well as the *Bauer Hubert* and *Benny Blu* books[4] were used when possible to scaffold an introduction to a new topic. Once students were familiar with the concepts, I used a variety of texts and videos from German internet sources as instructional materials, as well as several of the books listed in the previous section of this chapter.

Having a say regarding the content of the course empowered students who were taking the course out of necessity – it was the only upper-level German content course available, and due to a large number of courses in our rotation, it has thus far only been offered once since its genesis in 2017. Many of those students were less interested in learning STEM-related information in German and more interested in completing their major/minor requirements. Those students' marginal interest in STEM created a space for us to consider the intersections of science and current events such as environmental protection, ethics in the pharma industry, and the impact of individual choices in progressing towards a common good. It also allowed students in specialized science programs such as pharmacy to suggest topics I had not thought about, e.g., animal experimentation.

The expanding themes and more advanced proficiency enabled students to be engaged at all levels of Bloom's taxonomy in German (see Figure 11.1).

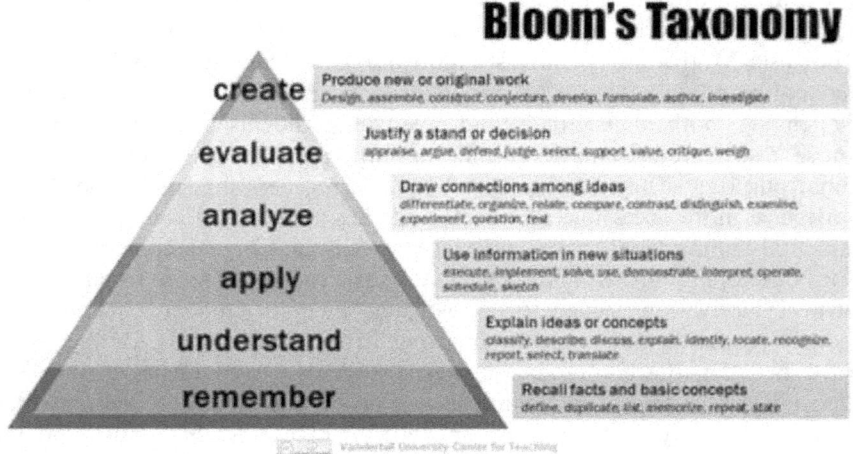

Figure 11.1

Through its assignments and structure, this course targeted "applying," "analyzing," "evaluating" and "creating" within the framework, while refining students' knowledge of STEM-related vocabulary and concepts. The work was spread across various language modalities based on those outlined in the NCSSFL-ACTFL Can-do Statements published in 2014:

Modality	Assignment
Interpersonal Communication (remember, understand, apply, analyze, evaluate, create)	In-class discussions Experiment group work
Presentational Speaking (remember, understand, apply, analyze, evaluate, create)	Presentation project
Presentational Writing (remember, understand, apply, analyze, evaluate, create)	Weekly summaries of *Spektrum der Wissenschaften* Experiment reports *Lebenslauf*
Interpretive Listening (remember, understand, apply, analyze, evaluate)	Pre- and in-class videos In-class conversations Experiment instructions and group work
Interpretive Reading (remember, understand, analyze, evaluate)	Pre- and in-class readings Weekly article reading from *Spektrum der Wissenschaft* Internship search Experiment instructions
Intercultural Communication (remember, understand, apply, analyze, evaluate)	Evaluate, compare and contrast related to topics and discussions

As summarized in the chart, several different formative and summative assessment types enabled students to learn and use their new scientific lexicon in German. Every week students were invited to pursue their own interests by choosing any article from *Spektrum der Wissenschaft* [5] and summarizing it. This exposed students to more complex, scientific language that they were intrinsically motivated to understand since it was an article of their choice.

Motivation also played a role by design in two other assignments: presentations and internship research. For their presentations, students were required to pick a STEM-related advancement or professional. They then researched that person or idea, created a visual guide about their chosen subject and presented it to the class. Once again harnessing their curiosity and intrinsic motivation, students pursued their own interests within the parameters of the course. This allowed a student who was highly motivated to explore the technical side of the VW diesel scandal, while another student majoring in business could investigate the ethical dilemma of the diesel scandal. Students could also pursue topics that spoke to their non-academic interests and beliefs such as recycling, energy efficiency or the environmental impact of pesticides and herbicides.

After an entire semester of studying STEM-related topics and thinking about the intersections of their own interests, students were required to create a *Lebenslauf* which highlighted their STEM skills and targeted a specific internship or job that appealed to them. Integrating career-readiness skills into the curriculum of a course that is partially based on language instruction for professional purposes was a natural choice. It reinforced the concept of developing vocabulary registers for specific purposes and areas of interest. In addition, it was an opportunity to discuss the idea of tailoring a résumé for a particular opportunity and gave students a chance to consider the substantive differences between a German *Lebenslauf* and a U.S. résumé.

STEM Experiments in the Classroom

While completing different types of assignments enabled students to reach higher levels of Bloom's Taxonomy, the hands-on experiments conducted by students were the most meaningful and differentiated the class from a typical advanced-level content course. Once we investigated a topic and studied the relevant concepts and vocabulary in a thematic unit, we conducted an experiment from beginning to end. This meant that students wrote a scientific report that entailed a detailed description of the experiment, a hypothesis, data, findings and a conclusion. This genre of writing was significantly different from their previous experiences in German and needed proper scaffolding including a review of relevant grammar concepts. After examining a model experiment report in German, students received a blank report form they could use to organize their information while conducting their experiments. After they noted the key elements and data, they then composed the information into a *wissenschaftliches Protokoll*.

The purpose of the experiments was not to make revolutionary new discoveries – it was to create opportunities for new German knowledge to be acquired by language students in a new area. With that in mind, I facilitated experiments that were highly engaging and safe to conduct in a standard classroom, outdoors or the language center. As a pedagogy specialist, I am not a STEM-orientated teacher or even a quantitatively minded person; thus, it was my responsibility to ensure we stayed within the limitations of my personal comfort and safety zones with the experiments. Several other factors were also considered when selecting experiments as the task-based learning experience for a topic: intellectual accessibility, readily available materials, viability of the experiment and estimating how interesting the students would find the experiment. In short, the experiments needed to meet the following criteria in order to be conducted as part of the course:

- Simple: the experiment could not be so challenging or complex that it was difficult to follow linguistically or intellectually. The goal was language in action, not discovering a new type of combustion engine.
- Availability: the materials needed to be readily available and inexpensive. There was not a lab fee for the course, so material costs needed to be as close to free as possible. Many of the materials such as food waste and 1-liter bottles were sourced by students.
- Viability: As part of the experiments, students needed to make observations and record data. It was imperative that students could conduct the experiment with a very high chance of achieving the desired outcome.
- Interest: These experiments needed to appeal to both halves of the course – those STEM-minded students, as well as students with waning interest in the topic. Choosing experiments that had relevance to issues facing students and/or society (such as the environment or natural medicine), provoked curiosity and fostered intercultural communicative competence that kept students highly engaged.
- Accessible: The topics and experiments needed to be understandable by me so that I could guide the class though the units, including conducting the individual experiments.

With these guidelines in place, experiments were chosen for units when appropriate. The three most memorable experiments were: 1) determining if wood was dry enough to burn in accordance with German environmental protection laws; 2) creating a miniature biogas plant from food waste and 3) brewing a holistic cough remedy.

1 Wood experiment: While wood is a renewable resource, burning wood can contribute significantly to air pollution, including the release of toxins and other fine particulate matter into the atmosphere. The release of those harmful substances is dramatically reduced in Germany through environmental protection regulations related to chimney maintenance and filtering, as well as the requirement that only seasoned wood with a moisture content of less than 18% be burned. In this unit, the focus was on how German regulations to protect the environment impact the country's citizens. While there are expensive instruments to measure the moisture content, there is also a simple soap test that can be conducted to determine whether the xylems still contain liquid.[6] After collecting a pile of wood from the university's facilities department, the class conducted its own moisture content testing. This simple experiment gave students their first opportunity to put their German scientific vocabulary to use and write their first lab report. This experiment was highly engaging for students, and it even was trending on Twitter for a few days.

2 Biogas experiment: Our attempt to create a miniature biogas plant in a bottle was a multi-session experiment with continuous opportunities for hypothesizing, observing and discussion. This was different from the other experiments in the course because we began and concluded the thematic unit with the experiment serving as the red thread throughout our discussions of renewable energy sources, farming's impact on the environment and composting.[7] Because students provided their own food waste, the class was able to make important observations regarding how different foods impacted the biogas production process. For example, those who included citrus peels in their biogas bottles saw significantly lower biogas output than students who did not. This experiment also provided the class with the opportunity to navigate different linguistic registers – while the food waste used was part of a common conversational register of foods, the concepts of the biogas plant and scientific method were only discussed using a scientific academic register. Students need practice with appropriate registers in their native languages as well as in German, and this experiment helped many to understand the difference between the two.

3 Holistic cough remedy experiment: Since I chose not to engage in any experiments related to our final topic of animal experimentation and instead focused the unit on ethics and laboratory animal rights in Germany, our final experiment for the semester involved German ideas of homeopathy and home remedies. This experiment was more of a cooking session, requiring students to brew a batch of onion tea with honey, a typical remedy for coughs.[8] While students were not required to try their brews on sick students and make observations, they had to reflect on how the relationship to homeopathy and medicine can be different in Germany compared to the United States. This deep dive into intercultural communicative competence enriched their understandings of themselves, our collective culture and German culture regarding medicine.

Thus, at the heart of all of the units and experiments during this semester-long course revolving around STEM in German was the concept of intercultural communicative competence. The introduction to the "NCSSFL Interculturality Can-Do Statements" summarizes:

> The need for language competence in a global society touches every sector of life. From career preparation in an international workforce to citizen diplomacy and national defense to one's role in a social or virtual community, communication across cultures is key. Learners today must have the language proficiency to communicate with global audiences, the insight into the cultural perspectives that shape those audiences, and the ability to behave appropriately in a variety of cultural contexts.

The thematic units, including the experiments, covered throughout the semester enabled students to reflect on their own relationships with concepts, as well as the cultural aspects embedded in each of the topics. At the advanced level, students expressed themselves with higher linguistic proficiency, enabling the class to focus less on grammar and structures and more on thoughts and ideas. We were able to tap into students' intrinsic motivation as we discussed ideas like renewable energy and how it relates to their individual lives. Regardless of whether or not the student is STEM-inclined, all of us are impacted by the resources we all share as citizens of planet earth.

Conclusion: concerns and drawbacks regarding STEM-themed courses

While teaching a STEM-themed advanced German course draws the attention of scientific and analytically minded students and gives instructors another access point to help students develop intercultural communicative competence, it is important to be mindful of some of the drawbacks of developing a course with STEM focus. As mentioned previously, not all students are enamored by STEM topics, but in many small programs, the STEM course may be the only German course offered during a semester. This may either cause reluctant learners to enroll in the course or some students may choose to skip enrolling in German that semester. When we surveyed our students, approximately half had a genuine interest in STEM, and the other half would rather have had a different option that semester. It is important to note that the majority of majors and minors expect to register for advanced German literature and culture courses, but there is not an expectation that they will need to take a STEM course in German.

Catering to the push for more STEM focused coursework also sends students, faculty and administrators an unintended message: it reinforces the idea that STEM is much more important and should take precedence over the humanities-based courses typically taught in German programs. This feeds into the ideas expressed by people such as Governor Bevin of Kentucky who postulated with regard to French: "There will be more incentives to electrical engineers than French literature majors, there just will, all the people in the world who want to study French literature can do so; they're just not going to be subsidized by the taxpayers like engineers will be, for example" (Cohen, 2016). Whether discussing French, German, English or another field in the humanities, the sentiment in such messaging is the same: STEM is critical, whereas the humanities are a waste of time and money. What politicians fail to recognize is that as a society we need the critical thinking and imagination fostered by the humanities to challenge the status quo and spark innovation. John Horgan (2018) from the Center for Science Writings at Stevens Institute of Technology summarizes:

> But it is precisely because science is so powerful that we need the humanities now more than ever. In your science, mathematics and engineering classes, you're given facts, answers, knowledge, truth. Your professors say, "This is how things are." They give you certainty ... The humanities are subversive. They undermine the claims of all authorities, whether political, religious or scientific ... the humanities remind us that we have an enormous capacity for deluding ourselves.

Rather than acquiescing to the short-sighted demand for more STEM and less humanities, it is our hope that we as German scholars approach German as an interdisciplinary field where a multiplicity of thoughts, perspectives and ideas can be explored without exclusivity. Learning languages is highly relevant in the age of Google Translate, and expanding our curriculum to include subjects of interest such as STEM-related fields encourages students to continue to develop their skills in topics they are intrinsically motivated to study, whether professionally or personally. Learning the STEM-relevant language and cultures of the German-speaking world will foster mutual understanding and respect, stimulating cultural shifts that embrace change and difference.

Notes

1 See for example the University of Rhode Island's International Engineering Program which offers a B.A. in German coupled with a B.S. in one of eight engineering disciplines: https://web.uri.edu/engineering/academics/iep/curriculum/.
2 The University of Massachusetts, Amherst offers iSTEP (International Science, Technology and Engineering Programs) that includes scientific and technical German language instruction at all levels, coordinated study abroad programs and internship and research opportunities in Germany. https://www.umass.edu/german/iSTEP.
3 *Sendung mit der Maus* can be found at https://www.wdrmaus.de/.
4 More information about the *Bauer Hubert* project, including the books, can be found at https://www.bauerhubert.de/. *Benny Blu* books and available topics can be found at http://www.bennyblu.de/.
5 For further information about the *Spektrum der Wissenschaft* magazine, visit https://www.spektrum.de/
6 A resource for this experiment can be found at: (https://www.tipps.adurofire.de/wissen-und-ratgeber/brennholz/so-testen-sie-ob-ihr-kaminholz-trocken-ist/)
7 For more information about the biogas experiment, please visit this resource: https://www.bsr.de/assets/downloads/BSR_Biogas_Experiment_2016.pdf
8 The following resources were used for this experiment: https://www.youtube.com/watch?v=bKsBc3QW6ac and https://heilkraeuter.de/.

Bibliography

Busch-Lauer, Ines. "MINT-*Kompetenz im studienbegleitenden DAF-Unterricht – das Praxisbeispiel Westsächsische Hochschule Zwickau (WHZ).*" *Deutsch als zweite Bildungssprache in MINT-Fächern*, edited by Erwin Tschirner et al., Schriften des Herder-Instituts, Stauffenberg, 2017, pp. 167–181.
Cohen, Patricia. "A Rising Call to Promote STEM Education and Cut Liberal Arts Funding." *The New York Times*, 21 February 2016, www.nytimes.com/2016/02/22/business/a-rising-call-to-promote-stem-education-and-cut-liberal-arts-funding.html. Accessed 1 June 2020.
"Communicative Tasks for Language Learning." American Council on the Teaching of Foreign Languages, www.actfl.org/guiding-principles/communicative-tasks. Accessed 1 June 2020.

Erlebnis Naturwissenschaft. Materialien für den projektorientierten Unterricht: Energie. *Bildungshaus Schulbuchverlage*, Westermann Schroedel, 2006.

Experiment zur Biogaserzeugung. *Handreichung für Lehrkräfte mit Anleitung und Protokollbogen. Ab Klassenstufe 5.* Umwelt aktiv gestalten. Berliner Stadtreinigung. www.bsr.de/assets/downloads/BSR_Biogas_Experiment_2016.pdf. Accessed 1 June 2020.

Fain, Paul. "Philosophy Degrees and Sales Jobs." *Inside Higher Ed*, 2 August 2019, www.insidehighered.com/news/2019/08/02/new-data-track-graduates-six-popular-majors-through-their-first-three-jobs#.XUQmcbq8LGk.gmail. Accessed 1 June 2020.

Finger, Anke, and Niko Tracksdorf. "Go Global, Build Networks, Create Nodes: Integrating the Humanities and the Professions." *Die Unterrichtspraxis*. vol. 52, no. 2, 2019, pp. 203–212.

Flaherty, Colleen. *"L'œuf ou la Poule?" Inside Higher Ed*, 19 March 2018, www.insidehighered.com/news/2018/03/19/mla-data-enrollments-show-foreign-language-study-decline. Accessed 1 June 2020.

Horgan, John. "Why STEM Students Need Humanities Courses." *Scientific American*, 16 August 2018. blogs.scientificamerican.com/cross-check/why-stem-students-need-humanities-courses/. Accessed 1 June 2020.

"Intrinsic motivation." *The Concise Corsini Encyclopedia of Psychology and Behavioral Science*, edited by W. E. Craighead and C. B. Nemeroff, 3rd ed., Wiley, 2004.

Kramsch, Claire, et al. "Authenticity and Authorship in the Computer-Mediated Acquisition of L2 Literacy." *Language Learning and Technology*, vol. 4, no. 2, 2000, pp. 72–95.

Krashen, Stephen D. *Second Language Acquisition and Second Language Learning*. Pergamon, 1981.

Laverick, Erin. "Project-Based Learning." *English Language Teacher Development (ELTD) Series*. TESOL Press, 2018.

Leckrone, Bennett. "When It Comes to Future Earnings, Liberal-Arts Grads Might Get the Last Laugh." *The Chronicle of Higher Education*, 14 January 2020, www.chronicle.com/article/When-It-Comes-to-Future/247842. Accessed 1 June 2020.

Leisen, Josef. *Handbuch Sprachförderung im Fach. Sprachsensibler Fachunterricht in der Praxis*. Ernst Klett Sprachen, 2019.

Looney, Dennis, and Natalie Lusin. "Enrollments in Languages Other Than English in United States Institutions of Higher Education, Summer 2016 and Fall 2016: Final Report." MLA, 2019, www.mla.org/content/download/110154/2406932/2016-Enrollments-Final-Report.pdf. Accessed 1 June 2020.

Mishan, Frieda. *Designing Authenticity into Language Learning Materials*. Intellect Books, 2004.

NCSSFL-ACTFL Can-Do Statements. American Council on the Teaching of Foreign Languages, 2014. www.actfl.org/publications/guidelines-and-manuals/ncssfl-actfl-can-do-statements. Accessed 1 June 2020.

NCSSFL Interculturality Can-Do Statements. American Council on the Teaching of Foreign Languages, 2017. www.dodea.edu/Curriculum/foreignLanguage/upload/NCSSFL-KY-SC-Intercultural-Can-Do-Statements.pdf. Accessed 1 June 2020.

O'Brien, Tracy S. "Beyond Cash Value: Promoting Real-World Competence in the Global Turn." *Die Unterrichtspraxis*, vol. 53, no. 1, 2020, pp. 82–98.

Schroth-Wiechert, Sigrun. *Deutsch als Fremdsprache in den Ingenieurwissenschaften. Formulierungshilfen für schriftliche Arbeiten in Studium und Beruf*. Cornelsen, 2011.

Seifert, Ingolf, and Henry Wojcik. *Nano Scout. Spannende Welt der Mikroelektronik.* Cool Silicon, www.cool-silicon.de/das-spitzencluster/spitzencluster-wettbewerb/spitzenclusterprojekte/nanoscout/. Accessed 1 June 2020.

Shrum, Judith L., and Eileen W. Glisan. *Teacher's Handbook: Contextualized Language Instruction.* 4th ed., Heinle Cengage Learning, 2010.

World-Readiness Standards for Learning Languages. National Standards in Foreign Language Education Project (NSFLEP), 2015.

12 The *Deutsche Sommerschule am Pazifik*
A model and asset to small German programs

Carrie Collenberg-González

In his article "Attracting and Retaining Students in Small Undergraduate German Programs," James C. Davidheiser responds to the significant decline of German enrollments in U.S. colleges and universities in the 1990s to address the most vulnerable group of programs: small undergraduate German programs, which are defined as "schools with an enrollment under 5,000 and three or fewer faculty members in German" (60). Davidheiser's article lists twelve ways to attract students to German and fifteen ways to retain students. His strategies for attracting students rely on methods of outreach (website, brochures, working with high schools and inviting community members) and program building (establishing a minor, scholarships and events). His strategies for retaining students focus on community building (German club, *Stammtisch*, German house, honorary societies and bulletin boards) and opportunities (study abroad, short term German programs, internships, intensive weekends, advanced courses, January term, relevant speakers and proficiency interviews) in order to create an outstanding program that offers many "choices and ways for students to be successful in learning German" (65). At the end of his article, he also mentions the effectiveness of German plays and the acknowledgement and accommodation of various learning styles. Davidheiser's examples have proven effective in attracting and retaining students in the German program at Portland State University and at the *Deutsche Sommerschule am Pazifik*, which is the focus of this chapter.

The methods of outreach, program building, community building and opportunities outlined by Davidheiser in 1999 are still relevant today, over 20 years later, and are not to blame for the trending decreases in foreign language enrollments in the United States and even at Portland State University (Jaschik 2018; see also Looney and Lusin 2016). To effectively increase or at least stabilize enrollments, we need paradigm shifts at departmental, institutional and national levels that prioritize the humanities and value critical thinking and intercultural exchange over profit and technocratic reason. Instead of a perfect four-year plan for students to graduate on time, we need to reform the economic systems that demand they pay for education and enter the working world as degree-holding adults, saddled with crippling debt. More than ever, we need the humanities because we need great solutions to national and global crises, and for that, we need great thinkers. These great thinkers of the future are in our classes, and it is imperative that we keep them in mind in our desperate and impassioned attempts to build, rehabilitate, sustain or grow our small German programs and reframe the humanities in general. This chapter addresses the *Deutsche Sommerschule am Pazifik* (DSaP) – the intensive five-week immersion summer school at Portland State University. It begins with an overview of the German program at Portland State University and some of the ways in which Davidheiser's strategies are implemented. It then discusses the enduring legacy of the DSaP and its relationship to language acquisition, academic coursework and community. Finally, it addresses the benefits and risks of summer immersion programs, and how they can serve students from other institutions.

Admittedly, the German program at Portland State University is neither "small" by Davidheiser's definition nor compared to many German programs across the country that are struggling to create degrees or even offer upper-division classes. Portland State University is a public, urban university located in downtown Portland, Oregon – a city with a population near 600,000 and a metropolitan area population of 2.4 million. Portland State University has an enrollment of approximately 26,000 students and, like many institutions in the state of Oregon, uses the quarter system. The German section is housed within the Department of World Languages and Literatures, which includes 18 languages and is the largest department within the College of Liberal Arts and Sciences, which is the largest college in the institution. In the German section, approximately 40 students minor and 20 students major in German. In Spring 2020, 17 students graduated with a degree in German; of these degrees, eight were Bachelor's degrees, eight were minors and one was a Master's. According to a 2019 report in the *Chronicle of Higher Education*, Portland State University ranked 15th in the nation in terms of graduating German Bachelor's degrees. Despite these numbers, the German program (and all world language programs) at Portland State University are engaged in a perpetual state of vigilance to convey the significance of teaching foreign languages amidst rapidly increasing budgetary constraints.

Our courses accommodate the students by providing articulated and consistent offerings that help them make progress toward their degree. We offer approximately ten courses per term: three sections of first-year German, three sections of second-year German, two third-year language and content classes and two fourth/fifth-year content classes, one of which is usually offered in English. Many of our students in the first- and second-year language classes are completing the university language requirement to fulfil the requirements of a B.A. As such, while the lower-division classes are usually full (25 students), the upper-division classes are smaller, with between ten and 25 students. The topics of the content courses rotate on a two- to three-year cycle with courses focused on specific periods, genres, theme or individual authors. The program is supported by two tenure-track professors, one non-tenure track professor and between two and four adjunct instructors of German or graduate teaching assistants.[1] All three full-time professors are certified to proctor Goethe-Zertifikat B1, B2 and C1 exams, which are offered at the end of the spring term in the third-year sequence and at the end of the *Deutsche Sommerschule am Pazifik*.

The language-learning community at university, state, national and international levels also serves our students. Cultivating a strong sense of community is essential at such a large, decentralized institution like Portland State University and gives students a sense of purpose. At the institutional level, a German club, a bi-monthly *Stammtisch* and various events throughout the year keep students engaged. Students keep in touch through email or social media and meet at the language lounge (where they can get free soup and tea), at local restaurants or sometimes in faculty backyards for picnics and outdoor movie nights. Our faculty members are on many committees that support student learning and advocacy. At the state level, our faculty holds elected positions in the Oregon Association of Teachers of German and attend COFLT (Confederation in Oregon for Language Teaching) events. We are also active at the national level, with regular presentations at ACTFL (American Council for the Teaching of Foreign Languages), GSA (German Studies Association) and WiG (Women in German); and we often bring our students with us to these conferences and help them present their own research. At the international level, we encourage our students to go abroad with our well-established exchange programs through IE3 Global, and we frequently attend professional development workshops in Germany and Switzerland. Our active involvement in local, national and international organizations informs our teaching and how we convey the significance of learning German today.

We attribute much of the success (i.e., survival) of our program to the consistent implementation of community-building strategies like the ones Davidheiser outlines in his article. But perhaps the most significant community-building aspect we have is the *Deutsche Sommerschule am Pazifik* – a five-week intensive summer immersion program. After being immersed in German for five weeks, our students leave the school and return to their upper-division classes with renewed confidence in their ability and stronger relationships with their peers, the field, and with other students, and faculty from regional and national communities. The *Deutsche Sommerschule am Pazifik* serves as a helpful model for how to attract and retain students and can help small German programs supplement their curriculum and retain their own students.

This chapter focuses on how the *Deutsche Sommerschule am Pazifik* sustains small German programs by representing a successful one, by sending out cadres of students who understand how important it is to learn German and who are prepared and inspired to continue their studies. To do so, it elaborates on key features that facilitate both rapid language acquisition and academic training and illustrates how these benefit students and teachers alike. In addition, it highlights debates regarding the cultural and financial implications for students in U.S. immersion schools versus study abroad as well as student credit hours and progress toward degrees. Finally, it will address the challenge to reconcile our obligation as educators and administrators of small undergraduate programs to provide the best and most efficient programs with the increasingly desperate budget and enrollment conditions that threaten our vision of the humanities and our livelihood.

The *Deutsche Sommerschule am Pazifik*

The *Deutsche Sommerschule am Pazifik* was founded in 1958 by H. F. Peters and remains, along with the Middlebury Language Schools and the *Deutsche Sommerschule von New Mexico in Taos Ski Valley,* one of three German summer immersion programs in the United States for post-secondary students. The trajectory of these immersion schools over the past 40 years follows a similar downward slope as many German programs which have lost enrollment or been cut altogether. In 1979, there were eight German immersion summer programs in the United States (Heckmann-French and Diekman Bond 1979).[2] Although others were founded after that report was published, all of them, except the three mentioned above, have since had to shut their doors. In many cases, the programs closed with the retirement of the dedicated faculty member who had carried the heavy administrative load of running the school. Fewer overall foreign language students as well as competitive study abroad programs also contributed to the declining enrollments that threatened summer immersion programs and made them difficult to sustain. In addition, reduced funding demanded that schools cut their expenses and increase their tuition. Caught up in the fray, the established knowledge of the benefits of summer immersion programs and their magic seems to have paled or been forgotten entirely.

Although this article focuses on the *Deutsche Sommerschule am Pazifik*, all three remaining schools share this "magic" as well as a certain lineage. In his unpublished essay written on the occasion of the 30th anniversary of the *Deutsche Sommerschule am Pazifik,* founding director H. F. Peters describes the significance of the so-called "Middlebury model" in his conception of the school in the late 1950s (2). Peter's son, George, founded the *Deutsche Sommerschule von New Mexico* along with Peter Pabisch in 1976 and used the model of the *Deutsche Sommerschule am Pazifik.* Most significantly, however, all three of these schools are bound together in a type of "magic." George Peters and Peter Pabisch describe this "magic" after the German weekend they organized in 1976 that led to the foundation of the *Deutsche Sommerschule von New Mexico*: "In a written evaluation of one of the weekends, a high school teacher referred to the 'magic spell' which seemed to unite participants from their arrival to departure. We have felt this spell, too. It is the spirit of companionship and involvement springing from genuine enthusiasm for what is German. It is the spirit of play in the best sense of the word" (110). Having grown up in Portland with his father who founded and directed the *Deutsche Sommerschule am Pazifik* for over 30 years, George Peters knew very well what this magic was all about. And Vassar professors Lilian Stroebe and Marian Whitney also knew it in 1914 when they founded "*de[n] etwas andere[n] Zauberberg*" (a different kind of magic mountain), the German school and very first language school at Middlebury College (Larson 2012, 21; Freeman 1975). Call it group identity, shared trauma, play or simply magic – it reigns sovereign at summer schools and is fundamental to the experience. Add the concept of immersion and, on top of that, German to this already transformative phenomenon and it is simply cathartic. Students at Portland State University who attend the *Deutsche Sommerschule am Pazifik* bring this magic, along with their advanced proficiency, into their fall classes, which in turn inspires students who have yet to attend the *Sommerschule* to consider doing so.

The demanding schedule and high expectations at the *Sommerschule* provide an environment that allows students to thrive. Once they arrive, they swear to speak only German and even sign an oath that hangs in the main hall throughout the five-week program. Each summer, approximately 40 students from all over the United States attend the school and live together with faculty in a dorm on the beautiful, secluded and wooded campus of Lewis and Clark College. They enroll in three four-credit classes: one three-hour morning language class (articulated); and two afternoon upper-division content courses. The classes are taught by a team of six visiting professors, two of which also serve as the resident directors (*Hauseltern*). Students and faculty take all meals together and spend the evenings working on projects and homework in the common room. One of the most beloved classes is the theater workshop that prepares students to perform a play and generally draws an audience of 80 to 100 people from the community. Our days off are planned group excursions to sites like the Pacific Ocean, Mt. Hood, waterfalls or river rafting excursions and trips to the opera. Most students take the Goethe-Institut language proficiency exams that are offered at the end of the term and, given their intense engagement in the activities described above, approximately 90% of them pass. After such a demanding and rigorously academic immersive experience, everyone is simultaneously exhausted and exhilarated and their German is greatly improved.

The effectiveness of the *Deutsche Sommerschule am Pazifik* is largely dependent on its thorough incorporation of the aforementioned community building strategies that have been embedded in its structure and insisted and improved upon by previous directors H. F. Peters and Steven N. Fuller.[3] The schedule described above is enhanced by other programs that run concurrently. Each year, we organize a lecture series (*Grundkurs*) featuring 15 visiting professors who give talks or performances on the summer's theme and lead a discussion. Three times a week, all students at the school attend these lectures, engage in the discussion and eat lunch with the guest. During the final week of the school, the teacher-training seminar (*Lehrerfortbildungsseminar*) begins – a school within a school. Between ten and 15 teachers of

German attend a workshop led by a pedagogy specialist and collaborate with the regular attendees of the school at mealtimes and at various events and excursions. The established traditions mentioned above lead to remarkable language acquisition, help students progress towards their degree and create an unforgettable bonding experience.

Language acquisition

One of the most compelling reasons to send students to an immersion school concerns the remarkable strides in language acquisition that they make over a short amount of time. The most important factor that contributes to language acquisition at the *Deutsche Sommerschule am Pazifik* is a highly cultivated and structured environment that accommodates various learning styles and enables students to thrive. The time in the classroom (guided learning hours) is what one counts when estimating proficiency expectations. Generally speaking, it takes approximately 200 guided learning hours for a language learner to advance from one of the six CEFR (Common European Framework Reference) levels to the next. In traditional institutions of higher education, this is equal to approximately one year of language instruction. A typical class at a university or college might offer German four hours a week over 10 or 16 weeks (depending on whether they are on the quarter or semester system), which equals 40 or 64 hours of guided instruction per term or semester. After an academic year, the student will have had 120 to 128 hours of language instruction. Therefore, it is generally expected that the student will advance one CEFR level each academic year. After the first year, they will have likely reached A1 proficiency, after the second year, A2, after the third B1, and so on (although we all know from experience how conditional that can be).

Since the immersion environment at the *Deutsche Sommerschule am Pazifik* demands total participation and creates an intense and luxurious academic atmosphere with little room for distraction, students make rapid progress due to the high number of guided learning hours in a condensed amount of time. Over the course of their five-week stay, students are in language classes six hours a day for 25 of the 35 days, which equals 144 hours (they actually take exams after only 20 days – 120 hours). However, their learning is enforced in all areas of their time outside the classroom as well. Given the parameters of this full-bodied immersion, students are actively engaged with the language for 35 days, which is equal to 595 hours (averaging in seven hours of sleep a night). The Goethe-Institut states that B1 proficiency equals approximately 252 to 687 hours. With these numbers, it is no wonder that most of our students advance between one and two CEFR levels during their time at the *Deutsche Sommerschule am Pazifik*.

In addition, students' test scores demonstrate the effectiveness of our learning outcomes, together with the confidence students gain through successful language acquisition. Most of our students have a minimum of one to two years of college-level German or its equivalent when they arrive, and take the Goethe-Institut B1 language proficiency exam at the end of our program. In summer 2019, 17 of the 21 people who took the B1 exam arrived at the beginning of the school with approximately one year (120 to 150 hours) of German. Of these 17 students, all of them passed speaking and writing, 88% passed listening and 83% passed reading with 60 or above (Goethe-Institut standards). The other three (with more than one year of German) passed all four modules. In 2018, the results were even better. The same strides can be seen at the B2 and C1 levels although significantly fewer students take these exams (usually between two and five each summer). Students generally feel so good about themselves that they want to continue with their German. Upon graduation with a B.A. in German, one student wrote: "Without the *Sommerschule*, I would not have been able to get my C1. It made my education so much more well-rounded and gave me and others the opportunity to learn from a wider range of professors, historians, and other speakers." The test results demonstrate the efficacy of the aforementioned contact hours during the immersion school: in five weeks they advance to a level it normally takes one year to achieve. This rapid progress then encourages them to continue learning German.

The *Deutsche Sommerschule am Pazifik* is, furthermore, an essential tool in helping us at Portland State University to bridge the gap between second- and third-year German, and thus we heavily promote the school among our student body. Many students stop taking German once they have completed their two-year requirement, and the students who do go on often struggle with third-year content courses in German, which dissuade them from continuing. We address this in two ways: first, we incentivize the third-year program by offering the Goethe-Institut B1 language proficiency exam at the end (we give it as a final in spring); second, as stated above, we encourage our second-year students to attend the *Deutsche Sommerschule am Pazifik*. Students are often enticed by the idea of learning one year of German in five weeks, skipping the third-year sequence and moving directly into the fourth-year sequence. Students who attend the summer program are more likely to continue with German because they can fit a German minor or major into their four-year plan. After five weeks of German immersion, students are confident in their ability to tackle long texts and lectures, which changes the dynamic of many upper-division classes. They understand the rigor of an all-German classroom, and their speaking and writing skills are greatly improved. Our best performing students in our upper-division classes are the ones who attended the summer program and they often reach C1 proficiency by the time they get their degree. Students from other institutions return confident and prepared enough to enroll in upper-division courses at their home institutions, which are often the most under-enrolled courses in small German programs.

The academic environment at the *Deutsche Sommerschule am Pazifik* and the so-called "German Studies" concept with its focus on language, literature and culture (Pabisch 2020, 59) is truly exemplary and provides students with numerous opportunities to think about the field and imagine their role in it. But it is not only the hours spent in the language classroom that makes the program an ideal place to learn German quickly: students are treated as adults and respected as intelligent and capable thinkers whose opinions matter, even when they are in the process of figuring out ways to more elegantly configure their thoughts. The next section addresses the classes, the faculty, and the extracurricular opportunities that enable students to complement and contribute to their language acquisition and how this makes the *Deutsche Sommerschule am Pazifik* such a unique model for a small German program.

Academic environment

The classes offered at the *Deutsche Sommerschule am Pazifik* are representative of the most comprehensive German programs in the United States and include a nearly complete language program, differentiated and articulated upper-division courses on literature and film and a theater workshop. Our lecture series includes 15 academic lectures by guest professors, and we also take our students to various cultural events and concerts in addition to our regular extra-curricular excursions. For example, in 2019 we were able to see a Schubert *Liederabend* as well as Mozart's *Die Zauberflöte*. The lecture series, extra-curricular events and curriculum create a rigorous academic environment in which the students can thrive alongside the guidance they receive from their engaged professors.

Most of our faculty are German professors at universities across the country or have nearly completed their Ph.D., and all are native or near-native speakers of the language. They are some of the most dedicated, talented and patient teacher-scholars in the country who devote an extraordinary amount of time to the students and their academic needs. The culture of the school relies heavily on their camaraderie and expertise and they are essential to the formation of the academic community and student success. As soon as students arrive, they understand that they are on board for an intense academic journey and are simultaneously surprised, honored and grateful to work so closely with professors who take them so seriously. In many instances, faculty members have recruited students into graduate programs, mentored their research, helped them with applications and letters of recommendations and invited them to academic conferences. Two of the faculty members are so-called *Hauseltern*, whom the students can approach with any day-to-day needs. With between 40 and 50 students and seven full-time faculty members, the low student to faculty ratio eases students' anxiety and reminds them that they will be both challenged and supported.

The rigorous daily schedule is organized on various levels between undergraduate, graduate and professional development. On the first evening, students get to know each other at a mixer (*Schnupperparty*) and sign an oath to speak German only. The next morning, they take a placement exam and are interviewed by our faculty. Based on their scores, they are put in the language class that best serves their need (A2, B1, B2 and C1). That same afternoon, they visit the classes they intend to take during the Monday, Tuesday, Thursday, Friday and Saturday schedule. Students take their language classes every morning from 8:30–10:30 a.m. and then break for either an academic lecture or for office hours, followed by lunch together in the cafeteria. In the afternoons, students take two of the five upper-division core classes; the class times are generally two-hour blocks on the same or alternating days (depending on what the student chooses). Although the topics of the courses change from year to year, the levels remain the same: a 300-level and a 4/500-level literature course, a film seminar and a *Theaterworkshop*. Our fifth course (a recent addition) is a B1 preparation course that is meant to ready our students who are in need of B1 to advance to the next level in their programs and future internships. In addition to the undergraduate program and language classes, the *Deutsche Sommerschule am Pazifik* also offers graduate-level courses. Graduate students enroll in the upper-division content courses and work with faculty to adjust the syllabus to include more readings, presentations and a research paper. Like the undergraduate students, they also stay for the five-week program. All of our courses are organized around a universal theme (love, happiness, solidarity, etc.) and allow for, and encourage, diverse approaches and materials.

German plays have been a staple of many German programs for years (Cafferty 1982) and our *Theaterworkshop* is one of the most profound courses we offer whereby students perform an entire play in German near the end of the *Deutsche Sommerschule am Pazifik*. They are taught contextual information about the playwright, theater theory and the play and are expected to perform the play, which they always remarkably manage to do despite their fears. Some of the plays staged in the past include Bertolt Brecht's *Mutter Courage und Ihre Kinder, Furcht und Elend des dritten Reiches* as well as adaptations of fairy tales, novellas and cabaret. The course builds confidence alongside proficiency and connects the program to the community by drawing a large audience every year from the German community in Portland and surrounding areas. The German play is a perfect example of an intersection where language acquisition, academic rigor and intense bonding take place and represents an analogy and microcosm for the way the *Deutsche Sommerschule am Pazifik* works in general.

Bonding and community

Bonding is at the heart of any group experience, from summer camps to film productions, theater performances to cultural and group formation, and is essential to the identity, quality and longevity of the *Deutsche Sommerschule am Pazifik* and other surviving summer German programs as well. This experience is nicely exemplified in the "Notes on Camp" edition of the National Public Radio show *This American Life*, where host Ira Glass (1998) interviews a number of people – mostly kids – who attend different summer camps together. The people interviewed can hardly articulate full sentences because they are caught up laughing at internal jokes, singing songs and swearing their loyalty to each other and the camp in ways that are incomprehensible to those who did not live through the experience. The same summer camp "magic" is a hallmark of the experience at the *Deutsche Sommerschule am Pazifik*. It is demonstrated by the hugs, laughter and tears at our closing ceremonies, by the smiling faces in the photographs and albums that circulate and by the wistful thank-you notes we receive. The demanding and intense environment threatens students with the potential of their failure but simultaneously demands and ensures their success. The hands-on attention, mentorship, encouragement and freedom that the students receive throughout the challenging and rigorous academic environment helps them succeed on individual and collective levels. In the process, they strengthen their connection to themselves and each other and develop friendships that often last a lifetime.

The *Lehrerfortbildungsseminar* is another essential component of the *Deutsche Sommerschule am Pazifik* where community is cultivated. This one-week seminar takes place during the last week of the five-week program. It is taught by teaching scholars and aims to train and share the most relevant and up-to-date teaching techniques in the field with high-school German teachers, and undergraduate and graduate students who are interested in teaching. Both theoretical and practical training in the field is offered, and all participants are given the opportunity to develop materials relevant to their program and share their experiences with others. In addition, the *Lehrerfortbildungsseminar* is an immersion experience that allows teachers to rekindle their German and get to know other dedicated teachers across the country. The content and networking potential of this seminar is essential to our vision of creating a community of German learners and teachers in the United States.

As stated above, community is essential to our school and something we actively cultivate during our excursions, afternoons, in study rooms, at film screenings and at various parties and celebrations together. Despite the insistence that a strong pedagogical foundation, a rigorous academic environment and a low student to teacher ratio ensure student success, students often attribute the best learning moments of their experience to the extra-curricular activities (Godfrey 2013, 1034). Our extra-curricular activities take place on Wednesday and Sunday and generally include hiking trips to local natural attractions like Silver Falls State Park, where students can explore trails together that lead behind and underneath stunning waterfalls. Each year, at the midpoint of the school, we have a *Bergfest* – a variety show where classes present skits they created, and students demonstrate their talents. The next morning, we charter a bus and spend the day at the breath-taking coast of the Pacific Ocean playing beach volleyball, looking at tide pools and splashing in the waves. The excursions, and especially the *Bergfest* and ensuing trip to the coast, are essential to the program in that they provide emotional and physical release for the students who are otherwise engaged in the rigor of their classes. The songs, conversations and reading groups in the van, the shared picnic lunches, the hikes themselves, the games they play and the performances create spaces where students have more time to get to know each other and, together, form lifelong memories that transcend the expectations of their coursework.

The community and bonding that students experience at the *Sommerschule* also lead to life-long connections with the *Sommerschule* itself. Student and faculty alumni frequently recount their fond memories of the school and their experiences there, and many of the students we have were referred by professors who also attended when they were students, which attests to the formative role the school played in their academic trajectory. The large audience at the German play consists not just of community members interested in German, but of former attendees who are still connected to the school, want to support it, revisit their memories or see the friends they made. And recently, an alumnus from the 1960s gave $10,000 to start a scholarship fund. The significance of community was recently demonstrated by the attendance at our first online lecture in the *Grundkurs*, a format we had to adapt to given the Covid-19 pandemic. The Zoom meeting was attended by 40 people and was broadcasted live to an audience of 162 people. Many of the people in the YouTube audience were alumni and wrote emails expressing their gratitude. One alumnus wrote, "Thank you so much for this beautiful gift to the world, and, of course, to German Studies in the U.S.! ... The summer school always provides students the much-needed opportunity to develop their ideas in consortium with international scholars and artists in a warm and safe, encouraging space, and I feel very strongly that they need this more than ever, right now!"[4] Most students, teachers and even the faculty members maintain an almost reverent relationship to the school and their shared experiences during their time there. This terrific bonding in conjunction with the rapid and significant language acquisition and rigorous academic environment convinces students that studying German is a worthwhile endeavor and boosts their confidence. They return to the fall term at their respective institutions with a renewed interest and much-improved proficiency in German, ready to enroll in upper-division classes and claim minors and majors in German.

Conclusion

Steadily declining enrollments, shifting budget priorities, political border changes and ensuing national interests, ease of international travel facilitating study abroad and faculty retirements have all contributed to the decline from what was at least eight immersion schools in all regions of the United States in 1979 (Heckmann-French and Bond 1979) to three. One thing is certain: the decline in summer immersion programs is in no way due to any fault with the immersion method. The *Deutsche Sommerschule am Pazifik*, the *Deutsche Sommerschule von New Mexico* and the Middlebury German Language

School all offer engaged and effective models for students to learn German. While most people recognize the benefits of immersion, they hesitate when faced with common but ultimately misguided questions such as: 1) why would a student study German at an immersion school in the United States when they could go abroad or 2) getting upper-division credits at an immersion school will take away from the student credit hours at their home institution and decrease enrollment.

To address the first question of why a student would study German at an immersion school in the United States when they could go abroad, we must first understand its roots in language acquisition, global learning outcomes and financial concerns. First, students learn language better and faster at immersion schools than when they go abroad. In many study abroad programs, students are put together with other language learners, often have little contact with native speakers and spend much of their time in social situations speaking languages other than the target language (Godfrey 2013; Wang 2010). Often, students return from their study abroad trips with remarkable cultural experiences but without much linguistic improvement. The cultural and linguistic training at the *Deutsche Sommerschule am Pazifik* equips students with the confidence and skills they need to be successful at the next stage of their studies. Domestic immersion programs can better prepare students culturally and linguistically for upper-division classes or for more advanced programs abroad (Godfrey 2013).

Financial concerns can dictate an either/or approach to German education: *either* the student goes abroad *or* they do the immersion program when ideally, they do both. Retention and the bridge between second-year language classes and third-year language and content classes are some of our greatest challenges. If students attend the *Deutsche Sommerschule am Pazifik* after their second year, their remarkable progress often motivates them to continue with German and their increased proficiency makes third-year content courses more accessible. Considering the high number of students who drop their foreign language courses after the second year, a summer immersion program would help increase enrollment in third-year German. This success can be seen in the robust upper-division enrollments in programs at institutions like California State University, Long Beach and the University of Alabama who strongly encourage their students to attend immersion schools, return to their home institutions and take courses and also continue their studies abroad. Once they have been through the rigor of immersion, students are often ready (and even eager) to participate in and seek out more immersive situations while abroad.

The second question regards the misconception that attendance at an immersion school will decrease enrollment in upper-division classes during the academic year. Although it seems counterintuitive, sending students to a summer immersion program actually increases upper-division enrollment during the academic year. In the first place, students who attend a summer immersion program might not have enrolled in third-year courses otherwise.

Second, they return as role-models and are often admired by their peers because of their language abilities. Third, they strive to re-create the community they experienced through immersion in the classroom, which is inspiring to others. In addition to increasing third-year enrollments, the *Deutsche Sommerschule am Pazifik* also helps students claim minors and majors by earning between 4 and 12 credits in the summer. At Portland State University, a German minor is 24 upper-division credits and a German major 52. Students can earn a minor by participating in the *Deutsche Sommerschule am Pazifik* two years in a row or by taking one German class each term (Fall, Winter, Spring) and then finishing up during the summer. Participation in our summer program enables students to fit in minors and majors (and gives them the confidence and enthusiasm to do so) when they might otherwise drop out at these crucial moments. Encouraging your student to attend a summer immersion program would most likely keep that student in your program longer and at a higher level. The student credit hours lost in the transfer would not outweigh the student credit hours the student would enroll in, inspired by their positive experience at the immersion school. Taking classes at a summer immersion program can also be a more economical option for the student. At the *Deutsche Sommerschule am Pazifik*, students do not pay out-of-state tuition rates for their courses, which cost approximately $170 per credit (around $2,000 for 12 credits). The biggest cost determent is room and board, which is currently $3,127, bringing the total to $5,200.[5]

The programs at Portland State University and the *Deutsche Sommerschule am Pazifik* are the result of time, perseverance, resourcefulness, luck and love for the profession by so many people over more than 60 years. It is essential to acknowledge the work that has been put into established programs that have contributed so profoundly to German Studies in the United States, serve as a model, enrich the field and our livelihood and endeavor to share their resources with other programs to grow together in the spirit of the magic that goes hand-in-hand with language acquisition. Since 1958, the *Deutsche Sommerschule am Pazifik* has been a hallmark of German Studies in the United States and has played a formative role in cultivating students and connecting them to the field. As an outstanding program that offers many "choices and ways for students to be successful in learning German" (Davidheiser 1999, 60), the *Deutsche Sommerschule am Pazifik* is one of the most efficient and effective ways for student to gain proficiency, build confidence and experience the joy that comes with learning a language. As such, it can be understood as both a model and asset to small German programs.

Notes

[1] PSU cut funding for Graduate Teaching Assistantships in 2019, which will have a negative impact on the number of graduate degrees. In spring 2019, five students graduated with an M.A. in German. In spring 2020, there was one. The number of adjunct instructors is dependent on the number of courses each individual is willing

and contractually able to teach. PSU part-time faculty, adjuncts and lecturers are represented by the Portland State University Faculty Association, which is affiliated with the AFT, the AFL-CIO and AFT Oregon. Graduate Teaching Associates are represented by the Graduate Employees Union, which is affiliated with the AFT and AAUP.
2 "In addition to Middlebury's sixty-four-year-old program, other programs include Die Deutsche Sommerschule am Pazifik at Portland State University, *Die Deutsche Sommerschule von New Mexico* in Taos bei Santa Fe, sponsored by the University of New Mexico in coordination with the University of Texas at Austin, the Summer Language Institute at the University of California at Santa Cruz, *the Deutsche Sommerschule am Atlantik* at the University of New Hampshire, a German Summer Graduate School and Workshop at Millersville State College in Pennsylvania, and the *Deutsche Wellen am Keuka* See at Keuka College in New York" (87).
3 It would be remiss not to acknowledge the work of the Assistant and Interim Directors over the years: Anne Bender, Franz Langhammer, Timm Menke, Monika Fischer, Steve Harmon, Matthias Vogel and Kathleen Godfrey.
4 The 2020 online program featured five lectures that have been viewed over 800 times on YouTube.
5 The biggest cost determent is the room and board, which is currently $3,127, bringing the total to $5,200. For some context, the cost of the *Deutsche Sommerschule am Pazifik* is roughly the same as the *Deutsche Sommerschule von New Mexico* (currently approximately $4,800 for tuition, room and board) and much less than the German School at the Middlebury Language Schools which is currently around $10,000 for nine credits over seven weeks.

Bibliography

Cafferty, Helen. "German-Language Play Production as Cultural Mediation." *Die Unterrichtspraxis*, vol. 15, no. 2, 1982, pp. 240–243.
Davidheiser, James C. "Attracting and Retaining Students in Small Undergraduate German Programs." *Die Unterrichtspraxis*, vol. 32, no. 1, 1999, pp. 60–65.
Glass, Ira. "Notes on Camp." *This American Life*, NPR, 28 August 1998.
Freeman, Stephen A. *The Middlebury College Foreign Language Schools (1915–1970): The Story of a Unique Idea*. Middlebury College Press, 1975.
Godfrey, Kathleen Ann. *Global Learning Outcomes of a Domestic Foreign Language Immersion Program*. PhD Dissertation. Portland State University, 2013.
Heckmann-French, Hannelore, and Donna Diekman Bond. "German Summer Schools in the U.S." *Die Unterrichtspraxis*, vol. 12, no. 1, 1979, pp. 87–91.
Jaschik, Scott. "Foreign Language Enrollments Drop Sharply," *Inside Higher Ed*, 7 March 2018, www.insidehighered.com/news/2018/03/07/study-finds-sharp-decline-foreign-language-enrollments#:~:text=Foreign%20language%20enrollments%20dropped%209.2,from%20the%20Modern%20Language%20Association.&text=Decades%20of%20increases%20ended%20after,off%20more%20than%202015%20percent. Accessed 27 June 2020.
Larson, Victoria. "Another Magic Mountain: A Revolutionary Language School in Vermont Turns 100!" *German World*. Winter, 2012, pp. 20–25.
Looney, Dennis, and Natalia Lusin, "Enrollments in Languages Other Than English in United States Institutions of Higher Education, Summer 2016 and Fall 2016: Final Report." MLA, 2019, www.mla.org/content/download/110154/2406932/2016-Enrollments-Final-Report.pdf. Accessed 27 June 2020.

Pabisch, Peter. "45 Sessions: German Summer School of New Mexico 1975/6 to 2019/20." *German Life*, June/July 2020, pp. 57–60.
Pabisch, Peter, and Georg Peters. "Das deutsche Wochenende in New Mexico: Culture Through Experience." *Die Unterrichtspraxis*, vol. 9, no. 2, 1976, pp. 107–112.
Peters, H. F. *Deutsche Sommerschule am Pazifik: Thirty Years.*
Wang, Chillin. "Toward a Second Language Socialization Perspective: Issues in Study Abroad Research." *Foreign Language Annals*, vol. 43, no. 1, 2010, pp. 50–63.
"Which Colleges Grant the Most Bachelor's Degrees in Foreign Languages?" *Chronicle of Higher Education*, 29 Jan. 2019, www.chronicle.com/article/Which-Colleges-Grant-the-Most/245567. Accessed 27 June 2020.

Conclusion

The future is now: Saving German studies in a brave new world

Mirko M. Hall

Since the Great Recession of 2007–2009, the continued viability and vitality of small undergraduate German programs has appeared to look even more bleak than before. The recession's financial after-tremors – exacerbated by the unrelenting corporatization of higher education, the pervasive rhetoric of vocationalism and an all-too-familiar strain of American anti-intellectualism – have prompted many liberal arts colleges and research universities to eliminate or radically reduce their offerings in German language, literature and culture. To make matters worse, the economic fallout of the coronavirus pandemic of 2020 has now forced many post-secondary institutions to begin strict cost-cutting measures that could very well haunt higher education for years to come. The closure of 651 language programs, as the 2019 final report by the Modern Language Association (MLA) revealed (Looney and Lusin 2016), has not only had a detrimental effect on the wide-ranging humanities education of students, but also the careers of faculty members, who have dedicated their professional lives to prepare newer generations to successfully navigate today's complex world. As many of these programs have faded away, so too, it seems, have the memories of their pedagogical successes — sadly, often not with a bang, but a whimper.

While these facts and figures might be a cause for increased anxiety about the plight of German in North America, Germanist Carol Anne Costabile-Heming (2011) (the former president of the American Association of Teachers of German) reminds us that the publicly available data on this situation is "indeed contradictory" (404). Why? Because there are also many (unreported) stories of dedicated teacher-scholars, who are closely working with sympathetic administrators and motivated students, to keep German alive within our new normal in higher education. (Likewise, one should not forget the equally tireless work of those teaching in primary and secondary schools to rescue their own curricula from oblivion!) While the preceding chapters do offer a sobering assessment of the challenges that lie ahead, they also show how the deliberate use of best practices and new strategies – across undergraduate programs with varying institutional profiles and resources – can reenvision German as an important and valuable course of study. In this short reflection, I would like to highlight these key lessons surrounding program planning, building and management, and offer a few modest observations on how German might help our post-millennial students to lead interesting and meaningful lives. Like all of my colleagues in this project, I write from the trenches of a small undergraduate curriculum: as the sole professor of a vibrant German Studies program and the chair of a Department of Languages, Cultures and Literatures that has recently undertaken a number of similar curricular revisions. Lastly, I am inspired by Germanists William Collins Donahue and Martin Kagel's call in 2012 to not merely "talk to ourselves about the future of German studies," but rather act with all due haste, since the "future is now."

Best practices and new strategies

In this anthology, a talented pool of teacher-scholars from across North America have shared their successful experiences in leveraging teaching, curricular development, advisement and outreach to revitalize their German programs. These best practices and new strategies were developed through constant refinement and improvement and also involved some calculated risk-taking. The first half of the text explored how curricular revisions and cutting-edge pedagogy enhanced student learning, while the second half focused on how extracurricular and outreach activities encouraged more critical engagement with course materials. Besides advancing a program's explicit pedagogical goals, these experiences also enriched the overall student learning experience with new perspectives, thus attracting and retaining learners, and boosted the visibility of German instruction on and off campus. Essential lessons include the promotion of:

- Communicative, proficiency oriented language learning with cultural content at all levels of the curriculum (e.g. integrated, multiliteracies-based curricula)
- Student-centered instruction that engages authentic, real-world tasks
- Collaboration, communication and creativity in classroom activities (e.g., interactive technology, peer teaching, roleplaying)
- Strategically placed courses in English to attract students without any prior language instruction
- Active student involvement from traditionally underserved and under-represented populations (e.g., minoritized students)
- Intensive-immersion language programs and study-abroad opportunities
- Interdisciplinary and cross-collaborative connections with other academic fields (e.g. global studies, business, STEM)
- Extracurricular activities (e.g., cultural symposia, film series, karaoke nights, *Stammtische*)
- Outreach with influential community stakeholders (e.g., German businesses, heritage organizations)
- Professional preparation and development (e.g., career advice, networking and self-marketing, service learning)

- Robust social media presence to increase program visibility and recruit students.

For me, a key takeaway from these lessons is that a truly innovative undergraduate curriculum should not only strive to develop a student's linguistic and cultural proficiency in the language, but also channel their creative imagination and intellectual curiosity into life-long learning and self-reflection. To accomplish this goal, we must make the study of German "relevant, fun, attractive and useful without compromising pedagogical integrity or diluting linguistic [and cultural] content" (Meyertholen 156). Furthermore, in keeping with today's fierce urgency for better equity and inclusion in society, we must also reach out beyond the "typical" German heritage student and actively recruit those from historically disadvantaged backgrounds and marginalized communities.

Translingual and transcultural competence

For those of us that began teaching at the turn of the millennium, the above practices and strategies are logical outcomes of the paradigm shift from a traditional model of *Germanistik* (with its philological emphasis on language and literature) to the newer model of German Studies (with its interdisciplinary emphasis on culture). An important reason for this reorientation was the need to develop a comprehensive program of study that would address – by way of intercultural awareness and competence – the fundamental interrelationship between language and phenomena such as art, culture, history and politics in a globalized world. The MLA's Ad Hoc Committee on Foreign Languages affirmed this position in 2007 by famously advocating for a "broader and more coherent curriculum [for language departments] in which language, culture, and literature are taught as a continuous whole, supported by alliances with other departments and expressed through interdisciplinary courses." This approach is committed to expanding the core curriculum of national literatures and cultures into the peripheries, while engaging German-related interdisciplinary and cross-collaborative projects in the arts, humanities and sciences. It must be stressed, however, that the MLA did not in any way suggest the demise of communicative, proficiency oriented language instruction. As Donahue and Kagel (2012) rightly argue: "Before emerging into that intoxicating realm of interdisciplinarity, students need to gain proficiency in German to make sense of an explosively productive and ever-changing German culture." This interdisciplinary model of German Studies also highlights the increasingly multicultural and multinational aspects, and even hidden foundations, of German-speaking culture. Efforts to diversify and decolonize second language programs are now on full display and inspired by the latest research in critical disability, gender, race and sexuality studies (Criser and Malakaj 2020). Here, particular attention has been drawn to the lived experiences and unique cultural contributions of

German-speakers with African, Asian and Middle Eastern ancestry, who have often been glossed over in the curriculum by ethno-nationalist concepts of German identity.

German for commerce

The invested interest of German Studies in fostering cross-cultural knowledge and collaboration – as embodied by the phrase "translingual and transcultural competence" (MLA Ad Hoc Committee 2007) – is directly challenged by the incessant "get a (real) job!" rhetoric of some students, parents and pundits, who are skeptical of the outcomes of a liberal arts education. Even in several of our chapters, there occasionally arises a productive tension between the vocational utility and the humanistic value of studying German. On the one hand, there is a clear need to prepare our students for the demands and contingencies of the 21st-century workplace. And, on the other, there is also the academy's time-honored calling to prepare them for a future life of happiness in a just world. As I hope to argue in the following pages, I do not believe that these two positions are mutually exclusive — and, to be perfectly clear, neither do my colleagues. The ability to effectively work across multilingual and multicultural realities is a skill set that can be harnessed to place "commerce [into dialogue with] humanity" (to riff on High et al. 127). The study of languages, literatures and cultures – by teaching how meaning is produced and negotiated in different symbolic texts and social contexts – provides learners with opportunities to grow as creative and critical thinkers, empathetic communicators and resourceful problem-solvers. These qualities, which are all hallmarks of a liberal arts degree, are highly transferable to the workplace. When I am asked by students and parents about the career prospects of a German Studies degree, I like to share with them the many online interviews with CEOs of Fortune 500 companies (many of whom were liberal arts majors themselves) in which they praise these very qualities. I also direct them to the results of two sweeping productivity studies by Google in the 2010s, which determined that the tech giant's most innovative ideas did not emerge from STEM-related technical expertise, but rather a skill set that closely resembles that of a second language major. Largely centered around emotional intelligence, Google's successes were attributed to open-minded employees, who solved complex problems with creativity, communicated with empathy and confidence and valued collaborative work. These abilities are "not just workforce ready but *world* ready" (Strauss 2017).

German for humanity

The above workforce skills are also part of an invaluable intellectual and emotional toolkit that allows students to rationally negotiate a world in which a "new wave of political isolationism and tribalism" (Jensen et al. 45) threatens human freedom. Second language education participates in this critical project by allowing learners to cultivate a deeper understanding of human diversity while recognizing the common humanity of all, and to clarify their own values while developing a deeper appreciation for those of others. The need to promote such self-reflection was the forceful conclusion of a special report by the American Academy of Arts and Sciences in 2013. The report's authors (which included noted Germanist and current President of Amherst College, Biddy Martin) stated that the U.S., and by extension the world, requires an enlightened citizenry: "equipped with … cultural understanding, knowledge of social dynamics, and language proficiency" in order to actively participate in its own democratic governance and foster global peace (Commission). As I write this conclusion in 2020, America finds itself in a volatile political moment that is working through a dangerous convergence of Ayn Rand individualism, post-truth politics and white nationalism. How might the study of German help us to understand and resist such illiberal machinations?

It goes without saying that German-speaking culture and civilization has made impressive contributions to the history of human consciousness by producing many ground-breaking artists, musicians, philosophers, scientists and writers. This "tremendous wealth of great literature and culture" is not only "likely to attract students and command intellectual respect" (421) as Germanist Mark Roche (2011) suggests, but can also serve as a powerful hermeneutic framework to explore and gain new insights into the human condition. For example, the atrocities of 20th-century German history – including the genocide of the Herero and Nama by the German Empire in South-West Africa and, of course, the unspeakable horrors of the Holocaust by the Nazi regime, can help us understand how discourses of national identity can be hijacked by racial prejudice and populist authoritarianism. Yet, at the same time, the German classical cultural heritage – with its emphasis on the "individual pursuit of happiness in service of the happiness of the whole" (High et al. 131) – can still show us how we might educate our students to become caring individuals, who work for the greater good without conflict. Post-unification Germany's status as a beacon of democracy within and beyond the European Union is an undeniable return to this cherished tradition. In discussing German Studies' relevance for cultural analysis and critique, we should also highlight how Germany has become the artistic, economic, political and technological powerhouse of Europe and how this reality can make the knowledge of its language and culture a complementary course of study.

Teaching and program building for success

A final takeaway from this anthology is that the success of small undergraduate German programs ultimately depends on dedicated and passionate teacher-scholars, who often work long hours with limited resources to develop creative, outcome-based curricula. They provide students with close individual attention and guidance throughout their studies and regularly serve as compassionate advisors on all issues of school and life. These actions generate a great amount of goodwill, and form lasting bonds between students and teachers. Yet trying to simultaneously manage career demands with the expectations associated with program building can be painfully difficult. (For the sake of sanity, I will avoid unpacking the brutal regime of administrative minutiae that requires us to continuously justify the existence of our programs.) I know too many colleagues, who, despite their best intentions, are always intellectually and emotionally exhausted at the end of the academic year. To alleviate this condition, faculty members need to be ambitious, but also practical in their program building (and remember that all curricular development is local); seek out a network of trusted mentors and colleagues, who can help and advise them; and – most importantly – practice self-care.

I am reminded here of my distinguished predecessor at Converse College. As the learning of German was being decimated across the country by the ethnic prejudices unleashed during WW1, and despite being the nation's second most commonly spoken language, my (then) small liberal arts college for women made an unusual commitment to preserving the study of German by hiring Bessie Howard Summerell in 1916. She quickly became a full professor and faculty star for the next three decades: an innovative teacher of a rigorous *Germanistik* program that modeled itself after Columbia University; an influential leader in the college's efforts to achieve accreditation and academic excellence; and a close confidante and counselor to students and colleagues alike. But yet, upon her retirement, Summerell was clearly *kaputt* by her many years of demanding teaching and service responsibilities. She is, nevertheless, a remarkable testament to what a single teacher-scholar can accomplish through sheer will and when given the chance and support by their institution!

So what is to be done if you are seeking to revise, revitalize or save your German program? After finishing this anthology, you should follow the advice of Germanist Charlotte Melin (2010) and develop a strategic plan that is "at once boldly aspirational and pragmatically data-driven" (2). You should, then, begin the admittedly hard, but very rewarding work of transforming your curriculum with the generous help of allies, colleagues and other stakeholders. The transformative learning of your students; the calling of your pedagogical acumen and expertise; the continuing new normal in higher education; and a brave new world's cry for keeping human happiness at the fore make it all the more imperative. The future is, indeed, now!

Bibliography

Commission on the Humanities and Social Sciences. "The Heart of the Matter: The Humanities and Social Sciences for a Vibrant, Competitive, and Secure Nation." *American Academy of Arts and Sciences*, 2013, www.aau.edu/sites/default/files/AAU%

20Files/Key%20Issues/Humanities/Heart-of-the-Matter-The-Humanities-and-Social-Sciences-for-a-Vibrant-Competitive-and-Secure-Nation.pdf. Accessed 10 June 2020.

Costabile-Heming, Carol Anne. "Responding to the MLA Report: Re-Contextualizing the Study of German for the 21st Century." *The German Quarterly*, vol. 84, no. 4, 2011, pp. 403–413.

Criser, Regine, and Ervin Malakaj, editors. *Diversity and Decolonization in German Studies*. Palgrave, 2020.

Donahue, William Collins, and Martin Kagel. "Saving German Studies, via Europe." *The Chronicle of Higher Education*, 1 January 2012, www.chronicle.com/article/Saving-German-Studies-via/130154. Accessed 10 June 2020.

Looney, Dennis, and Natalia Lusin. "Enrollments in Languages Other Than English in United States Institutions of Higher Education, Summer 2016 and Fall 2016: Final Report." Modern Language Association, June 2019, files.eric.ed.gov/fulltext/ED599007.pdf. Accessed 10 June 2020.

Melin, Charlotte. "Notes from the Field: Toward a Model for Saving German Studies." *Neues Curriculum: Journal for Best Practices in Higher Education German Studies*, vol. 2, Spring 2010 2010, www.neues-curriculum.org/papers/melin_2010.pdf. Accessed 1 April 2012.

MLA Ad Hoc Committee on Foreign Languages. "Foreign Languages and Higher Education: New Structures for a Changed World." *Profession*, 2007, pp. 234–245.

Roche, Mark W. "Ensuring a Flourishing (German) Department: A Dean's Perspective." *The German Quarterly*, vol. 84, no. 4, 2011, pp. 414–422.

Strauss, Valerie. "The Surprising Thing Google Learned about Its Employees – and What It Means for Today's Students." *The Washington Post*, 20 December 2017, www.washingtonpost.com/news/answer-sheet/wp/2017/12/20/the-surprising-thing-google-learned-about-its-employees-and-what-it-means-for-todays-students/. Accessed 10 June 2020.

Index

Locators in *italics* refer to figures.

18th-century German texts 7, 118–119; Lessing's *Nathan der Weise* 119–123; literature 127–132; plays 123–127
3D modelling project *see* digital Vienna 1900

academic professional development 196–197; *see also* foreign language departments
adjective endings 166
age, generational attitudes 26–27, 43–44
American Association of Teachers of German (AATG) 65, 173
American Council for the Teaching of Foreign Languages (ACTFL): Can-Do Statements 54, 181, 184; "Community C" 23; German program building 2; life-long language learners 43; performance-based tasks 174
American Council of Trustees and Alumni (ACTA) 1–2
American Council on Germany (ACG) 40
American culture *see* cultural understanding; German-American culture
Aschenbrodel 162, 166, 167
Aschenputtel 162, 167; *see also* Cinderella
attendance *see* enrollment trends
autonomous cultural production 48–50
autonomous learning 90–91, 94–95, 98

Bergfest 198–199
best practices 205–206
biogas experiment 183–184
blogging, digital Vienna 1900 145
Bloom's taxonomy *180*, 180, 182
business, German for 207

Butler University case study 178–182

California State University, Long Beach (CSULB) 119, 127–132
campus outreach 59
Can-Do Statements 54, 181, 184
career readiness 5; autonomous cultural production 48–50; flipped learning 53–57; generational attitudes 26–27; graduate skills 45, *46*; innovative outreach 57–60; professional training vs. broad education 127–128; student professionalism 51–53; transferable skills 45–48
Carnegie Mellon University (CMU): institutional context 136; technology-enhanced learning 135–136
Chatham University language lab 91–99
Cinderella (fairy tale) 162, 167; *see also* Aschenputtel
Claremont Colleges 119
class setting: decline in classes 1–2; in-class community events 28–30; STEM-based lesson plans 182–185; undergraduate German program case study 4–5
collaboration: digital Vienna 1900 137–138, 141; flipped learning 56–57; Southern Illinois University Carbondale 83–84
commerce, German for 207
communication skills: curricular integration 12–14; drama-based teaching techniques 164–165; flipped learning 56–57; interpersonal and presentational speaking 18–19; performative teaching approach 120–121;

professionalism 51–53; undergraduate German program case study 18–19
communicative teaching approach: compared to literacies-based approach 12; drama-based teaching techniques 158, 165; interpersonal and presentational speaking 18–19; task-based approaches 174
"Community C" 23
community engagement: ACTFL's "Community C" 23; community connections in the greater region 40; Concordia University case study 111; connecting to local organizations 34–40; connecting to the global community 41–43; departmental and university-level 30–34; *Deutsche Sommerschule am Pazifik* 191, 197–199; global and local 23–24; in-class events 28–30; Marian University case study 5, 28–44; promoting student professionalism 51–53
competencies, transferable skills 45–48
Concordia German Language Student Association (CGLSA) 111, 112, 114
Concordia University: community building 111; curriculum (re)design 104–108; extracurricular activities in Montreal 110–111, 115; multidisciplinary minor in German 108–109; program description 103–104; social media 113–114; *Stammtisch* 111, 112–113
cough remedy experiment 184
creativity 46
critical framing 16
cross-cultural critical thinking (CCCT) 53–57
cultural competence 89–91, 97–99, 157, 174; *see also* intercultural communicative competence; transcultural competence
cultural production 48–50
cultural understanding 6; American Council on Germany 40; diversity programming 64–73; flipped learning 53–57; foreign language learning 157–158; Indiana German Heritage Society 35–39; innovative outreach 57–60; language lab case study 88–99
current affairs: case studies as a window to the world 80–82; independent work 95, 98; innovative outreach 58–60
curricular integration 12–14; *see also* interdisciplinarity

curriculum development: Concordia University redesign case study 6–7, 104–108; language lab case study 88–99; technology-enhanced learning 7–8

demographics: diversity programming 64–73; generational attitudes 26–27, 43–44
Deutsche Sommerschule am Pazifik 8, 189–192, 199–201; academic environment 196–197; bonding and community 197–199; foundation and history 192–193; language acquisition 191, 194–196, 197, 199–200; structure 193–194
Deutsche Welle 95
Dietrich College 136–137
digital Vienna 1900: course structure and materials 146–148; limitations and future directions 150–153; reconceptualising Vienna 137–138; student evaluations 148–150; students' learning process 144–146; theoretical foundations and course design 138–144
direct speech 166
Diversity, Decolonization, and the German Curriculum (DDGC) 65
diversity programming 5–6, 64–73
diversity work 65–67
drama-based teaching techniques 161–169
drama pedagogy 8, 120–123, 158–159

East Carolina University (ECU): autonomous cultural production 48–50; courses 47–48; flipped learning 53–57; innovative outreach 57–60; student professionalism 51–53
East Germany 160–169
Eberly Center 145–146
economic recession (2007–2009) 204
engaged pedagogy 68–69
engineering *see* STEM-based lesson plans
enrollment trends: decline in classes 1–2; Franklin & Marshall College 19–20; funding pressures 156; program closures 135, 204; small German programs 189; Southern Illinois University Carbondale 75–76; student motivation 26–27; summer schools 199, 200–201; universities and colleges 11
environmental protection 178, 181–182

Index   213

evaluation *see* feedback to students; student evaluations
experiments (science) in the classroom 182–185
extracurricular activities 110–111, 112, 115

face-to-face social interactions 96–97
feedback to students 97–98
field trips: digital Vienna 1900 147–148; Marian University case study 29–30, 40, *41–42*; museums 40, 90; *see also Deutsche Sommerschule am Pazifik*; studying abroad
film project, East Carolina University 49–50
films, watching for cultural understanding 162, 167–168
flipped learning 53–57, *57*, 168
foreign language departments: academic professional development 196–197; Carnegie Mellon University 136; Concordia University 103–104; departmental and university-level community engagement 30–34; funding pressures 156; Marian University 24–25; reasons to study languages 1–2; Southern Illinois University Carbondale 77–78, 83–84
foreign language learning: common humanity 207–208; cultural understanding 157–158; decline in classes 1–2; drama pedagogy 158–159; funding pressures 156; transcultural competence 206–207
foreign language literacy 13
foreign travel, studying abroad 25, 30, 41–43, 92
formative assessment 181
Franklin & Marshall College, undergraduate German program case study 4–5, 11–12; curricular integration through a literacies-based approach 12–14; designing materials 14–15; interpersonal and presentational speaking 18–19; reading 15–17; reinvigorating the German program 19–20; writing 17–18
French language studies 28
funding: the humanities 102; pressures on FL programs 156; summer schools 200; universities 75
future of German studies 8–9, 204–205; best practices and new strategies 205–206; German for commerce 207; German for humanity 207–208; teaching and program building for success 208–209; translingual and transcultural competence 206–207; *see also* enrollment trends

generational attitudes 26–27, 43–44
genre-focus 17–18
geography of Germany 19
German 319 land of science and innovation course 179–182
German-American culture: American Council on Germany 40; diversity programming 68; Indiana German Heritage Society 35–39
German Democratic Republic (GDR) 160–161
German for commerce 207
German for humanity 207–208
German geography 19
German holidays 34
German immersion school *see Deutsche Sommerschule am Pazifik*
German language program building 2–4, 208–209
German language studies literature review 3–4
German Studies 108–109, 195–196, 206–207
Germanistik 3, 120, 206, 209
'global citizens' 11, 67
global community: cultural competence 89–91, 97–99, 157, 174; innovative outreach 58–59; intercultural communicative competence 184, 185; Marian University case study 41–43; transcultural competence 206–207; *see also* cultural understanding
global issues, international studies program 80–82
Goethe-Institut 109
Goethe, Johann Wolfgang von 118, 123–124
graduate skills 45, *46*; *see also* career readiness
Grand Challenge Seminars 136–137
Great Recession (2007–2009) 204
Grimm fairy tales 162, 167

Handbuch Sprachförderung im Fach (Leisen) 176–177
happiness of humanity 128–129

high intermediate German II course 160–161
higher education *see* universities
historical German texts 7, 118–119; Lessing's *Nathan der Weise* 119–123; literature of 18th-century Germany 127–132; plays, 18th-century German 123–127
historical Germany 37–38, 160–169, 209
holidays, teaching about Germany 34
the humanities: technology-enhanced learning 135–136; value of 102–103, 189–190
humanity, promoting understanding of 207–208

iGen'ers 27, 43
immersion 199–200; *see also Deutsche Sommerschule am Pazifik*
independent work 90–91, 94–95, 98
Indiana German Heritage Society (IGHS) 35–39
indirect speech 166
innovative outreach 57–60
inquiry-based learning approach (IBL) 139–140, 144
institutional context 91–92
intercultural communicative competence 184, 185
interdisciplinarity 108–111, 137, 151–152, 206–207
international studies programs: Chatham University language lab 91–99; global issues 80–82; Southern Illinois University Carbondale 77–84
internationalization 11
interpersonal speaking: undergraduate German program case study 18–19
intrinsic motivation 179–182, 184–185

jobs *see* career readiness

Kansas University 156–158; drama-based teaching techniques 161–169; drama pedagogy 158–159; high intermediate German II course 160–161
knowledge economy 47

language acquisition: applying skills 27–28; cultural understanding 94; *Deutsche Sommerschule am Pazifik* 191, 194–196, 197, 199–200; STEM-based lesson plans 175–176, 179
language lab case study 6, 88–99

language learning *see* foreign language learning
learner autonomy 90–91, 94–95, 98
'learning society' 47
Lehrerfortbildungsseminar 198
Lessing's *Nathan der Weise* 118, 119–123
life-long language learners 43, 179, 206
Limited Term Appointments (LTAs) 103–104, 108, 111, 113
literacies-based approach 12–14
literature of 18th-century Germany 7, 118–119, 127–132
local organizations 34–40

Märchenfilme 162
Marian University: ACTFL's "Community C" 23; community connections in the greater region 40; community engagement 28, 43–44; connecting to local organizations 34–40; connecting to the global community 41–43; departmental and university-level community engagement 30–34; in-class events 28–30; institutional and departmental profile 24–25; structural challenges and opportunities 25–28
maths *see* STEM-based lesson plans
McGill University 110
model-based, process-oriented, genre-focused (MPG) approach 17–18
Modern Language Association (MLA): cultural competence 93, 157; curriculum design 11–12, 104; enrollment trends 172, 204; face-to-face social interactions 96; foreign language learning 88; transcultural competence 206–207
Montreal, German community 110–111, 115
motivation *see* student motivation
multidisciplinary German programs 108–111
museum trips 40, 90
music 163

Nathan der Weise (Lessing) 118, 119–123

online social interactions 95–96
oral skills *see* communication skills; speaking
outreach: diversity programming 64–73; innovative outreach for promoting German culture 57–60; language lab case study 93, 96–97

pedagogical practices 118–119
performance-based tasks 122, 174
performative teaching approach 7, 120–123
Peters, H. F. 192–193
plays, 18th-century Germany 123–127
pleasure and learning 90
politics of visibility 69–73
pop culture 162–163
Portland State University 190, 201; *see also Deutsche Sommerschule am Pazifik*
presentational speaking: digital Vienna 1900 144–145; undergraduate German program case study 18–19
Prinz 167
process orientation 17–18
professional achievement 51
professional development 196–197
professional success 51–52; *see also* career readiness
professionalism of students 51–53
program building 2–4, 208–209
project-based learning (PBL) 139–141, 144
public engagement *see* community engagement
public spending: the humanities 102; pressures on FL programs 156; summer schools 200; universities 75

QR codes 113–114
queer students 71–72

race, diversity programming 66–67, 72–73
reading journal workbooks 15–17
reading skills 15–17
recession (2007–2009) 204
refugee crisis, Germany 58–59
regional outreach 59–60; *see also* community engagement
Rhizomatic Response Projects (RRPs) 106–107

Sam Houston State University (SHSU) case study 69–73
scaffolding 142–144, 168–169
science *see* STEM-based lesson plans
self-assessment 152
self-directed learning 90–91, 94–95, 98, 148–149
service learning 52–53
situated practice 16

skills *see* career readiness; communication skills; transferable skills
social interaction, language lab case study 95–97
social justice 72–73
social media 113–114
socialism, German Democratic Republic (GDR) 160–169
Southern Illinois University Carbondale (SIUC) 75–76; case studies as a window to the world 80–82; challenges and collaboration 83–84; description 77; international studies introductory course 79–80, 84; international studies program 77–84
Spanish language studies 28
speaking: drama-based teaching techniques 164–165; flipped learning 56–57; literacies-based approach 12–14; undergraduate German program case study 18–19
Special Interest Group (SIG) 2
Stammtisch 111, 112–113
STEM-based lesson plans 8; Butler University and the course 178–179; concerns and drawbacks 185–186; experiments in the classroom 182–185; German 319 179–182; incorporating STEM in German 174–178; pedagogical benefits for STEM-integration 173–174; rising interest in STEM in the German curriculum 172–173; transcultural competence 207
Stiefmutter 167
student bonding 197–199
student diversity 64–73
student evaluations, digital Vienna 1900 145–146, 148–150
student feedback 97–98
student motivation 26–27, 98–99, 179–182, 184–185
student professionalism 51–53; *see also* career readiness
studying abroad 25, 30, 41–43, 92
summative assessment 181
summer school *see Deutsche Sommerschule am Pazifik*

task-based approaches 174
teaching for success 208–209
technology-enhanced learning 7–8, 135–137; course structure and materials 146–148; digital Vienna 1900 137–153;

students' learning process 144–146; *see also* STEM-based lesson plans
textbooks 14, 104–106, 175–178
theater traditions 120, 123–127
transcultural competence 11–12, 206–207
transferable skills 45–48
translingual competence 206–207

undergraduate German *see* Franklin & Marshall College, undergraduate German program case study; universities
universities: best practices and new strategies 205–206; career readiness 5; departmental and university-level community engagement 30–34; professional training vs. broad education 127–128; public spending 75; reasons to study languages 1–2; *see also individually named institutions*
University of Toronto 107–108

value of learning 26–27
vertical integration 15
visibility, politics of 69–73

whiteness 66–67; *see also* diversity programming
wood experiment 183
World Poetry Day 31
World War 1 38, 209
World War II 37
writing: drama-based teaching techniques 164, 166–169; foreign language literacy 13; undergraduate German program case study 17–18

For Product Safety Concerns and Information please contact our EU
representative GPSR@taylorandfrancis.com
Taylor & Francis Verlag GmbH, Kaufingerstraße 24, 80331 München, Germany